Netbooks
The Missing Manual®

Netbooks: The Missing Manual

BY J. D. BIERSDORFER

Published by O'Reilly Media, Inc., 1005 Gravenstein Highway North, Sebastopol, CA 95472.

O'Reilly books may be purchased for educational, business, or sales promotional use. Online editions are also available for most titles (*safari.oreilly.com*). For more information, contact our corporate/institutional sales department: 800.998.9938 or corporate@*oreilly.com*.

Editor: Nan Barber

Production Editor: Nellie McKesson

Copy Editor: Carla Spoon

Indexer: Bob Pfahler

Cover Designer: Karen Montgomery

Interior Designer: Ron Bilodeau

Print History:

August 2009:   First Edition.

 This book uses RepKover™, a durable and flexible lay-flat binding.

ISBN: 978-0-596-80223-3

[M]

Contents

The Missing Credits vii
Introduction 1

Part 1: Meet Your Netbook

Chapter 1
Buying and Setting Up Your Netbook. 7

What to Look for When Buying a Netbook. 8
Customizing and Buying Your Netbook 14
Setting Up Your Netbook 16
Transferring Files to Your Netbook 19
Netbook Battery Options 25
A Note About Netbook Keyboards. 26

Chapter 2
Getting to Know Your Windows Netbook 29

Which Windows? 30
Seven Things You Should Know About Windows 7 32
Setting Up a Windows XP Netbook 33
The Start Menu: Where It All Begins 35
Windows Desktop Basics 37
Taking Control with Control Panel 42
A Tour of the Windows Programs Menu 43
Adding More Programs 46
Removing Programs 48
Organizing and Finding Files. 49
Checking Hard Drive Space 53
Backing Up Your Windows Netbook. 54
Closing Down Your Netbook. 56

Chapter 3

Getting to Know Your Linux Netbook **59**

Which Type of Linux? 60

Setting Up a Linux Netbook 61

Exploring the Linux Desktop 63

Applications Menu: All Your Programs 69

Places Menu: Organizing and Finding Files 73

System Menu: Preferences and More 76

Seeing How Much Hard Drive Space Is Left 82

Backing Up Your Linux Netbook 84

Closing Down Your Linux Netbook 85

Chapter 4

Connecting Devices to Your Netbook **87**

Mice, Trackballs, and Tablets 88

Connecting an External Monitor or TV 94

Setting Up a Printer 96

Storing Data on External Drives 103

Capturing Images: Connecting Scanners and Webcams 105

Listening to Music: MP3 Players and External Speakers 109

On the Road: Cases and Cables 112

Part 2: Taking Your Netbook Online

Chapter 5

Getting Online **115**

Ways to Connect to the Internet 116

What You Need to Connect 117

Getting an Internet Service Provider 118

Setting Up a Wired Network 118

Setting Up a Wireless Network 123

Connecting to a Wireless Network 124

Common Wireless Network Problems 126

Using Public Wireless Networks 127

Getting Online with a Wireless Broadband Card 128

Using Your Mobile Phone as a Modem 129

Using a Dial-Up Connection with Your Netbook 130

Chapter 6
Email and Web Browsing **133**
    Setting Up an Email Program 134
    Email Basics 143
    Using a Web Browser 151
    Transfering Bookmarks from Another Computer 157
    Adding Tools to Your Web Browser 159

Part 3: Working on Your Netbook

Chapter 7
Business Basics: Word Processing and More **163**
    Microsoft Office for Windows Netbooks 164
    Microsoft Office Live Workspace 169
    OpenOffice.org: Free Word Processing, Spreadsheets, and More 171
    Google Docs: An Online Alternative 175
    Working with Contacts 178
    Staying on Track with Calendars 186
    Online Calendars 189
    Viewing PDFs with Adobe Reader 191
    Working with Graphics 193
    Welcome to the Free World: Software 195

Chapter 8
Collaborating with Others **197**
    What You Can Do Online 198
    Setting Up Instant Message Software 199
    Voice Chat by Instant Messenger 203
    Video Chat by Instant Messenger 205
    File Transfer by Instant Messenger 207
    Making Phone Calls with Skype 208
    Working Together with Google Docs 211
    Online Collaboration Sites 212
    Social Networking Sites 215

Chapter 9
Multimedia Fun: Photos, Music, and Video **219**
    Importing Digital Photos 220
    Organizing Your Photos 223
    Editing Photos 225
    Sharing Photos Online 230

Photo Sharing Websites   232
Popular MP3 Jukebox Programs   236
Playing Digital Music on the Netbook   239
Recording and Editing Sound   244
Watching TV and Video Online   246

Chapter 10
Playing Games **251**
Games That Come with Your Netbook   252
Gaming Websites   254
Downloading Games   257
Serious Gaming on a Netbook   258

Part 4: Taking Care of Your Netbook

Chapter 11
Protecting You and Your Netbook **261**
Ten Online Safety Tips for Netbooks   262
Keeping Viruses at Bay   264
Putting Up a Firewall   268
Other Security Software for Netbooks   271
Public Wireless Network Security   275
Protecting Yourself: Ergonomic Tips   276

Chapter 12
Troubleshooting Your Netbook. **279**
Troubleshooting Common Problems   280
Built-In Windows Help Files.   282
Tuning Up with Windows System Tools.   283
Using Remote Assistance   287
Reinstalling Windows   289
Built-in Linux Help Files   290
Maintaining a Linux Netbook   291
Ubuntu Remote Desktop   293
Installing (or Reinstalling) Ubuntu   295
Finding Help and Information Online   299

Index. **301**

The Missing Credits

About the Author

J.D. Biersdorfer is the author of *iPod: The Missing Manual* and *The iPod Shuffle Fan Book*, and is co-author of *iPhoto '09: The Missing Manual*, *The Internet: The Missing Manual* and the second edition of *Google: The Missing Manual*. She has been the computer Q&A columnist for *The New York Times* since 1998 and occasionally writes about books and art for the newspaper. She studied theater at Indiana University and likes to play the banjo or watch the BBC news when not on deadline. Email: *jd.biersdorfer@gmail.com*.

About the Creative Team

Nan Barber (editor) has worked with the Missing Manual series since the previous millennium. She lives in Massachusetts with her husband and G4 Macintosh. Email: *nanbarber@oreilly.com*.

Nellie McKesson (production editor) lives in Brighton, Mass., where she spends her free time playing in her band Dr. & Mrs. Van der Trampp (*http://myspace.com/drmrsvandertrampp*) and making t-shirts for her friends (*http://mattsaundersbynellie.etsy.com*). Email: *nellie@oreilly.com*.

Carla Spoon (copy editor) is a freelance writer and copy editor. She works and feeds her tech gadget addiction from her home office in the shadow of Mount Rainier. Email: *carla_spoon@comcast.net*.

Bob Pfahler (indexer) is new to the O'Reilly creative team. After working in an Information Technology department managing a business support team for many years, he started his own document indexing business. When not working, he likes to take bike rides on the Denver foothills' many trails. Bob also likes reading, writing, and has the Sudoku bug. Email: *bobpfahler@hotmail.com*.

Adam Flaherty (technical reviewer) is from Northern California. He recently edited O'Reilly's iPhone Hacks and has tech reviewed other O'Reilly books including Linux Unwired. He also blogs for Makezine.com.

James Turner (technical reviewer) is a freelance journalist who has written for publications as diverse as the *Christian Science Monitor, Processor, Linuxworld Magazine, Developer.com,* and *Wired* Magazine. He has also written two books on Java web development: *MySQL & JSP Web Applications* and *Struts: Kick Start*. He has spent more than 25 years as a software engineer and system administrator, and currently works as a senior software engineer for a company in the Boston area. He lives in a 200-year-old colonial farmhouse in Derry, N.H. along with his wife and son.

Acknowledgements

No matter whose name is on the cover, books are always a group effort. This one wouldn't have been possible without the efforts of many talented individuals: editor Nan Barber, technical reviewers Adam Flaherty and James Turner, copy editor Carla Spoon, and indexer Bob Pfahler. Big thanks as well to Nellie McKesson, Ron Bilodeau, and Karen Montgomery for making the book look good. I'd also like to thank Pete Meyers and Dawn Frausto of O'Reilly for getting this project rolling in the first place. On the home front, I am deeply indebted to my friends and family (especially Betsy Book) for putting up with me during those long days of writing and muttering about teeny tiny computers for six months in a row.

—*J.D. Biersdorfer*

The Missing Manual Series

Missing Manuals are witty, superbly written guides to computer products that don't come with printed manuals (which is just about all of them). Each book features a handcrafted index; cross-references to specific pages (not just chapters); and RepKover, a detached-spine binding that lets the book lie perfectly flat without the assistance of weights or cinder blocks.

Recent and upcoming titles include:

Access 2007: The Missing Manual by Matthew MacDonald

AppleScript: The Missing Manual by Adam Goldstein

AppleWorks 6: The Missing Manual by Jim Elferdink and David Reynolds

CSS: The Missing Manual, Second Edition by David Sawyer McFarland

Creating a Web Site: The Missing Manual by Matthew MacDonald

David Pogue's Digital Photography: The Missing Manual by David Pogue

Dreamweaver 8: The Missing Manual by David Sawyer McFarland

Dreamweaver CS3: The Missing Manual by David Sawyer McFarland

Dreamweaver CS4: The Missing Manual by David Sawyer McFarland

eBay: The Missing Manual by Nancy Conner

Excel 2003: The Missing Manual by Matthew MacDonald

Excel 2007: The Missing Manual by Matthew MacDonald

Facebook: The Missing Manual by E.A. Vander Veer

Google SketchUp: The Missing Manual by Chris Grover

FileMaker Pro 9: The Missing Manual by Geoff Coffey and Susan Prosser

FileMaker Pro 10: The Missing Manual by Susan Prosser and Geoff Coffey

Flash 8: The Missing Manual by E.A. Vander Veer

Flash CS3: The Missing Manual by E.A. Vander Veer and Chris Grover

Flash CS4: The Missing Manual by Chris Grover with E.A. Vander Veer

FrontPage 2003: The Missing Manual by Jessica Mantaro

Google Apps: The Missing Manual by Nancy Conner

The Internet: The Missing Manual by David Pogue and J.D. Biersdorfer

iMovie 6 & iDVD: The Missing Manual by David Pogue

iMovie '08 & iDVD: The Missing Manual by David Pogue

iMovie '09 & iDVD: The Missing Manual by David Pogue and Aaron Miller

iPhone: The Missing Manual, Second Edition by David Pogue

iPhoto '08: The Missing Manual by David Pogue

iPhoto '09: The Missing Manual by David Pogue and J.D. Biersdorfer

iPod: The Missing Manual, Seventh Edition by J.D. Biersdorfer and David Pogue

JavaScript: The Missing Manual by David Sawyer McFarland

Living Green: The Missing Manual by Nancy Conner

Mac OS X: The Missing Manual, Tiger Edition by David Pogue

Mac OS X: The Missing Manual, Leopard Edition by David Pogue

Microsoft Project 2007: The Missing Manual by Bonnie Biafore

Office 2004 for Macintosh: The Missing Manual by Mark H. Walker and Franklin Tessler

Office 2007: The Missing Manual by Chris Grover, Matthew MacDonald, and E.A. Vander Veer

Office 2008 for Macintosh: The Missing Manual by Jim Elferdink

Palm Pre: The Missing Manual by Ed Baig

PCs: The Missing Manual by Andy Rathbone

Photoshop Elements 7: The Missing Manual by Barbara Brundage

Photoshop Elements 6 for Mac: The Missing Manual by Barbara Brundage

PowerPoint 2007: The Missing Manual by E.A. Vander Veer

QuickBase: The Missing Manual by Nancy Conner

QuickBooks 2009: The Missing Manual by Bonnie Biafore

QuickBooks 2010: The Missing Manual by Bonnie Biafore

Quicken 2008: The Missing Manual by Bonnie Biafore

Quicken 2009: The Missing Manual by Bonnie Biafore

Switching to the Mac: The Missing Manual, Tiger Edition by David Pogue and Adam Goldstein

Switching to the Mac: The Missing Manual, Leopard Edition by David Pogue

Wikipedia: The Missing Manual by John Broughton

Windows XP Home Edition: The Missing Manual, Second Edition by David Pogue

Windows XP Pro: The Missing Manual, Second Edition by David Pogue, Craig Zacker, and Linda Zacker

Windows Vista: The Missing Manual by David Pogue

Windows Vista for Starters: The Missing Manual by David Pogue

Word 2007: The Missing Manual by Chris Grover

Your Body: The Missing Manual by Matthew MacDonald

Your Brain: The Missing Manual by Matthew MacDonald

Introduction

Modern personal computing is all about having the largest screen, the most muscular processor, and the biggest hard drive, right? Not when all you want is an ultraportable way to read your favorite blog or shoot off an email from your local café. And without breaking the bank after all you spent on that widescreen display and dual-core tower for your desktop. Enter the Netbook. Don't think cheap, tiny, and underpowered—think economical, lightweight, and peppy.

With their smallest screens measuring around 7 inches diagonally, the tiniest netbook is a good 10 inches smaller than desktop-replacement laptops with their 17-inch screens and processors that can heat up the whole basement after a few hours of gaming. Booting one of these up just to check email is like driving an armored tank down to the corner store for a gallon of milk.

If you just need a small machine to check your email, browse the Web, see what people are talking about on Twitter, or feed that Peggle addiction, a netbook is more than big enough. Better still, it probably costs at least a thousand dollars less than that big bruiser of a laptop. Instead of *more* firepower than you need, a netbook gives you *just* what you need.

Perhaps you're considering a netbook because you want an inexpensive traveling companion that's bigger than a smartphone but smaller than your 15-inch regular laptop. Or maybe you're considering getting a netbook for the kids to keep them off your work laptop. Or maybe cost is a consideration and you need the computer equivalent of a subcompact car to get you out on the road and on your way.

Whatever your reason, you're not alone—industry analysts predict netbook sales will reach 22 million in 2009. Welcome to the club. Let *Netbooks: The Missing Manual* be your membership guide.

Why Netbooks Are Not Notebooks

But what specifically makes a laptop a netbook? It's really a number of factors, including:

- **Size.** Netbook screen sizes range from 7 inches to around 12 inches in diagonal width, making them smaller than the smallest typical notebook computer, which usually has a screen size of at least 13 inches. With the smaller screen size, the keyboard dimensions and the overall weight of the netbook are much less than those of regular notebook computers. Netbooks tend to weigh around three or four pounds, making them much less of a hassle to lug around.

- **Processor.** Netbooks use efficient processors that focus on *saving* power rather than *having* a lot of power. You don't exactly need a super-computer to do the most basic computing chores like web browsing to begin with, but the average netbook processor can go far beyond that. You won't be breaking any speed records, but you can use office applications, organize your digital audio and video, and even play games on most netbooks.

- **Cost.** Sporting no-frills hardware (and less of it), netbooks keep their price—as well as their weight—down. On most models, there's no DVD drive, no backlit keyboard, no video-friendly widescreen. And the majority of netbooks still run inexpensive operating systems like the open-source Linux or the outdated Windows XP. (This situation will change as Windows 7 and other new systems make a run at the netbook market.) All these cost-savings mean you can buy a netbook for anywhere from $250 to $600.

 By the way, the cost factor is what disqualifies Apple's MacBook Air from being a netbook. Starting at $1500, it's a notebook. A thin, wispy notebook. But Apple enthusiasts haven't let lack of official Mac hardware stop them from installing their favorite operating system on popular netbook models like the Dell Mini 9 or MSI Wind. If this sort of thing appeals to you, the Hackintosh site has tutorials (*www.hackintosh.com*).

For these reasons and more, netbooks are *not* notebooks. In June 2009, the market-research firm NPD Group released the results of a survey that found that 60 percent of the people they talked to thought that netbooks and notebooks could do all the same things. Many of these people were disappointed when they found out that this was not the case.

Notebooks are bigger, stronger, faster—and most of them can entertain you with DVD movies on an airplane. True, notebooks are generally heavier and more expensive than netbooks, but they can do more. You need a notebook, not a netbook, if you want to comfortably edit home video, see an entire row of your monster spreadsheet, or make a photo collage.

The Evolving World of Netbooks

The decision to buy a netbook means you have to make a few other choices as well, like *what kind* of netbook. The playing field here is changing rapidly as Mini-Me PCs become more popular.

A simple decision like which operating system to get isn't so simple on a netbook. You can go with good old Windows XP or cutting-edge Linux. Complicating things further, Microsoft is gearing up for netbook-compatible editions of its new Windows 7 operating system, due out in October 2009.

And there are even newer operating systems on the horizon, designed just for netbooks and mobile devices like smartphones. For example, Intel (maker of the Atom chip that currently powers a huge percentage of netbooks) is helping to develop the Moblin operating system, a Linux variation designed just for the particular space and processing needs of tiny computers. And Google (developer of the world's most popular search-engine) is set to unleash its open-source Android operating system (yep, the same one used on mobile phones) on netbooks very soon, too. Both Moblin and Android are expected to be available by late 2009 or early 2010.

In July 2009, Google announced it was also working on an operating system aimed squarely at netbooks. If everything goes according to plan, the Chrome OS—a shiny user interface running on top of a humming Linux engine—should show up on netbooks by the end of 2010.

About This Book

You may also be asking yourself, "What exactly can I do on a netbook once I pick one out?" And that's where *Netbooks: The Missing Manual* comes in. This book is not a guide to a specific model of netbook or a single operating system. Instead, it's a guide to the hardware realities, the software possibilities, and the *potential* of your netbook to be something more than the 21st century version of a Smith Corona portable typewriter.

But if you want to make it a typewriter, there's nothing stopping you. After all, it's your netbook. You can use it for composing poetry in the park—or writing a book about netbooks.

About the Outline

This book is divided into four parts that each focus on a particular aspect of netbook living.

- **Part 1: Meet Your Netbook.** Maybe you've been researching your potential netbook purchase for months to make sure you got just the right model for your needs and are *this close* to getting out the credit card. Or maybe you just bought one on a whim at Best Buy because it just looked so darn cute. No matter where you are in the netbook-purchasing timeline, this section of the book is devoted to helping you find and buy the right model for your mobile-computing needs. It also shows you how to get your new purchase up and running as smoothly as possible. You'll get a quick tour of the Windows and Linux operating systems, as well as instructions on how to get that netbook working with a printer, scanner, mouse, and other external hardware.

- **Part 2: Taking Your Netbook Online.** The *net* in netbook is the Internet. This section of the book explains how to get that computer online in a number of ways, from the airy freedom of a WiFi network to the old-school dial-up connection. And once you get your netbook linked to the Internet, you'll probably want to do the top two things most people do on computers of any size: web browsing and email. Chapter 6 tells you how to get your netbook doing both—and even how to bring your bookmarks from another browser to the new machine so it feels more like home.

- **Part 3: Working on Your Netbook.** Contrary to what you may have heard, you can do a whole lot more with a netbook than just send email or browse blogs. This section shows you how you can work (on documents, spreadsheets, and presentations) or play (Minesweeper, Peggle, or Civilization, anyone?) on your netbook—whether you have an Internet connection or not. Games aren't the only entertainment netbooks offer either: The mini-laptop can also double as an MP3 jukebox, online radio receiver, photo album, and video player. You'll also see how easy it is to set up video and audio chats with friends online.

- **Part 4: Taking Care of Your Netbook.** This final section of the book shows you how to keep your netbook running smoothly, what to do if something does go wrong, and how to help protect yourself from the malicious and destructive software lurching all over the Internet.

Along the way in each chapter, you'll find tips, tricks, and links to deeper resources for many aspects of netbook computing. Finding the proper netbook and getting it set up according to what you want to use it for is key. And once you get all that squared away, you may find yourself spending more time discovering the things you can *do* with a netbook, rather than lamenting the things that you *can't*.

About→These→Arrows

Throughout this book, and throughout the Missing Manual series, you'll find sentences like this one: "Open the My Documents→Renovation Project→Contractor Estimates folder." That's shorthand for a much longer instruction that directs you to open three nested folders in sequence, like this: "On your hard drive, you'll find a folder called My Documents. Open that. Inside the My Documents window is a folder called Renovation Project; double-click it to open it. Inside that folder is yet another one called Contractor Estimates. Double-click to open it, too."

Similarly, this kind of arrow shorthand helps to simplify the business of choosing commands in menus.

About the Missing CD

It's a multimedia world these days, so you'll find more to **Netbooks: The Missing Manual** than just the book you're holding in your hands. As you wander through the chapters, you'll notice links to additional documentation, commercial software, inexpensive shareware, open-source programs, how-to videos, and even entire sites devoted to the growing world of netbooks. And since typing in URLs from a book is just *so* 20th century, you can find all these links rounded up and waiting for you online at *www. missingmanuals.com/cds*.

Once you land on the Missing CDs page, scroll down the page to **Netbooks: The Missing Manual** and click Missing CD-ROM link. Here, you'll find all the links mentioned in the book, nicely organized by chapter and ready for clicking.

You can also find updates to this book on the Missing CD page by clicking the "View Errata for this book" link at the top of the page.

You're invited and encouraged to submit corrections and updates for this book, too, by clicking the "Submit your own Errata" link on the Missing CD page. To keep the book as up-to-date and accurate as possible, each time we print more copies, we'll include any confirmed corrections you've suggested. We'll also note all the changes to the book on the Missing CD page, so you can mark important corrections in your own copy of the book, if you like.

About Missing Manuals.com

To see the latest Missing Manuals videos, tips, tricks, and articles by Missing Manuals authors (including the author of this book!), the most recent community tweets about Missing Manuals, and special offers on Missing Manuals, go to the Missing Manuals home page (*www.missingmanuals.com*).

We'd love to hear your suggestions for new books in the Missing Manual line. There's a place for that on the website, too.

And while you're online, you can register this book at *www.oreilly.com* (you can go directly to the registration page at *http://tinyurl.com/yo82k3*). Registering means we can send you updates about this book, and you'll be eligible for special offers, like discounts on future editions of *Netbooks: The Missing Manual.*

You might also want to visit O'Reilly's feedback page (*http://missingmanuals. com/feedback.html*), where you can get expert answers to questions that come to you while reading this book. You can also write a book review on this page, as well as find groups for folks who share your interest in *Netbooks: The Missing Manual.*

Safari® Books Online

 When you see a Safari® Books Online icon on the cover of your favorite technology book, it means the book is available online through the O'Reilly Network Safari Bookshelf.

Safari offers a solution that's better than e-Books. It's a virtual library that lets you easily search thousands of top tech books, cut and paste code samples, download chapters, and find quick answers when you need the most accurate, current information. Try it free at *http://my.safaribooksinline.com*.

1 Buying and Setting Up Your Netbook

With an average price around $400, a netbook may sound like a one-size-fits-all deal—limited selection, low-cost components, and few custom options. It's like buying a stripped-down economy car with a price so low that you basically get four wheels and an AM/FM radio, right?

Wrong.

True, netbook hardware is leaner and less powerful than some of the big honking laptops meant to serve as both road machines and desktop computer replacements. But that doesn't mean you don't have choices to make: Which operating system? Regular hard drive or solid-state drive? How big a screen? How small is too small for a keyboard?

This chapter gives you an orientation tour of Netbook Land. Once you see what's out there, you'll have the information you need to pick the system that's best for you. But buying the netbook is just the beginning. You'll also get the scoop on what comes after you pull that pee-wee PC out of the box: setting it up, getting your stuff on it, and getting ready to take it out on the road, the Internet—or both.

What to Look for When Buying a Netbook

With every computer and gadget company coming out with its own take on the netbook, you can get overwhelmed by all the models. Size is the first factor to consider. The smaller the netbook, the less it weighs. But make sure you factor usability into the mix so you don't end up with cramped hands and a permanent James Dean squint from staring at a tiny screen.

A good netbook is the sum of its parts, and here are the major parts to consider:

- **Screen.** While the first netbooks sported 7-inch screens too small for even a guinea pig to use comfortably, current models have expanded their screen dimensions. Common netbook screen sizes are a diagonal 8.9 inches (like HP's smallest HP Mini 1000 Mi) and 10.2 inches (like Lenovo's IdeaPad S10). At 12.1 inches, Dell's Inspiron Mini 12 pushes the screen size almost into notebook screen territory. A smaller screen means a smaller, lighter netbook and less LCD real estate for the battery to power—but imagine trying to work on a complicated spreadsheet on a screen that can hide behind a piece of copier paper.

- **Keyboard.** Sure, a nine-inch netbook fits well in a purse or manbag, but can you type comfortably on a keyboard that's 85 percent the size of a normal laptop's? If the computer is for a child or a petite-fingered person, keyboard size may not matter as much. If you have large hands or a heavy typing workload, you may want to consider a netbook with a more normal-sized keyboard or also purchasing a folding, full-sized USB keyboard.

- **Processor.** Low-power, low-cost processors are the heart of a netbook's motherboard. Intel's Atom and VIA's Nano are the two most common, with other chip shops like AMD developing versions as well. While these processors are generally not robust enough for high-def video-editing or graphic-heavy games, they're just fine for tasks like surfing the Web, watching YouTube videos, emailing, and word-processing.

- **Battery.** With their energy-minded processors, lack of disc drives, and smaller screens, netbooks generally consume less power than their larger laptop cousins. But because the computer itself is shrunken, the battery is smaller, too. A smaller battery equals a shorter time between charges. Depending on the netbook model, battery life can range from under two hours to over seven hours. If you expect to be traveling a lot and don't want to fight other passengers for airport recharging stations or the spare wall outlet at the gate, pay attention to battery life. Batteries are often described by the number of *cells* they contain. A 3-cell battery provides around 1.5 to 2 hours of power, a 6-cell battery can go up to 4 hours between charges, and some 9-cell batteries can last 7 hours or more. And guess what? A bigger battery adds more weight to the netbook.

- **Operating System.** Most netbooks come in either Windows or Linux flavors. (See the next section for the pros and cons of both.)

- **Hard drive.** Regular motorized, spinning hard drive or state-of-the-art solid-state drive? Go to page 12 to see which is best for you.

 Note Although lesser-known Taiwanese companies made the first netbooks, most major manufacturers—Dell, Hewlett-Packard, and Lenovo—have jumped aboard the netbook train. If you have a computer from one of these big players and you're happy with it, you may feel more confident buying a netbook from the same company. But don't overlook the smaller manufacturers like ASUS, Acer, and MSI. They may be smaller and lesser known, but they often offer friendlier price tags.

The Operating System: Windows vs. Linux

Along with size, a netbook's operating system has a big impact on your productivity and pleasure. When it comes to netbooks and their low-powered processors, you have two choices: Windows XP Home Edition or Linux. Linux is a free, alternative operating system that, on the surface anyway, looks an awful lot like Windows or Mac. You can use Linux by pointing and clicking or by typing old-school commands like a real-live programmer.

Linux has been in continual development since 1991, when a young Finnish programmer named Linus Torvalds first shared his hobby with other computer enthusiasts. It's grown into a serious operating system that now runs websites, corporate servers, and university networks all over the world. (Linux is also at the heart of Moblin and Android, two up-and-coming netbook operating systems.)

Both systems have their strong points, but most people will automatically choose Windows XP for one main reason: They're used to it. Still, Linux has its advantages (especially for people who *loathe* Microsoft) and, despite its übergeek command-line roots, Linux now comes in easy-to-use versions designed especially for netbooks. Here's a quick look at what you get with each system.

Windows XP

Introduced in the fall of 2001, Windows XP went on to become the Operating System That Refused to Go Away. In the summer of 2008 when Microsoft forcibly retired XP by refusing to offer it for new desktop and laptop computers, netbook manufacturers brought Windows XP back as a preinstalled option. The rationale was that netbooks were too underpowered to run XP's burly, power-hungry successor, Windows Vista, but people needed an alternative besides Linux.

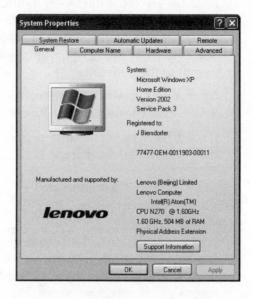

Running Windows XP on a netbook has many advantages:

- **Hardware compatibility.** Peripherals like printers and external CD drives work predictably on Windows XP, thanks to years of companies designing products just for XP.

- **Software compatibility.** Need to run Microsoft Word or Picasa on your netbook? No problem for Windows XP. The programs may just run a bit slower than on a powerful desktop machine.

- **Human compatibility.** Most people, except for die-hard Mac fans (and you know about *them*), have used Windows XP at some point—in an office, school, or Internet café. Many folks find Windows XP easier to learn than Linux. For Vista refugees, coming home to XP is like slipping on a comfy pair of slippers (that don't demand your password every time you want to adjust their settings).

But on the flip side:

- **Cost.** Linux, an open-source system developed over the years by thousands of volunteers, is free. This means manufacturers don't pay for the software as they do with Windows XP—and can pass the savings along to you.

- **Size.** Windows XP is user-friendly, but it's large and hogs more processor power than many versions of Linux. As a result, an XP netbook may seem a bit poky compared to a Linux system that's been fine-tuned for running on a netbook.

- **Security.** More than a million viruses and other pieces of malicious software prowl around the Internet, waiting to infest unprotected machines. Almost all of them are designed to attack Windows computers, so you'll need to spend time and money implementing security software.

Linux

Linux excels in the very places Windows XP falters—cost, system size, and general security. Compared to Windows, Linux generally saps less of your netbook's power, starts up quicker, and takes up less hard drive space.

However, Linux isn't for everybody. Most Windows software can't run on it without some techie wrangling, certain hardware peripherals lack Linux compatibility, and the system can be harder for new users to troubleshoot than good ol' XP.

If you're looking for the cheapest netbook possible and plan to do most of your netbooking, well, *on the Net*, Linux might be a good choice for you. Web-based applications like Google Docs & Spreadsheets, Facebook, and Flickr work just fine on the Linux edition of the Firefox Web browser. (Firefox is actually included with many versions of Linux.)

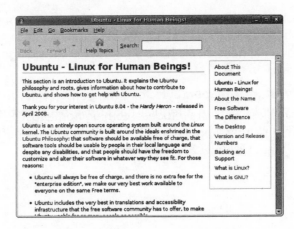

The various flavors of Linux are called *distributions* in geekspeak. Ubuntu, for example, a popular user-friendly distribution that's free to download at *www.ubuntu.com,* is available preinstalled on Dell's netbooks. Ubuntu includes OpenOffice.org, a business software suite that rivals Microsoft Office, plus email and instant-messaging programs, photo editing and organizing software, Firefox, and several games.

Choosing a Netbook Internal Drive

In addition to your choice of operating system, most netbook manufacturers let you choose between different types of internal drives for storing your programs and files. Your usual options are a regular disk-based *hard drive* or a *solid-state drive*, but a combo of the two called a *hybrid drive* is emerging as well.

When deciding what kind of drive to get, take into account where you plan to use your netbook. For example, if you want to carry tons of files with you, go for a regular hard drive. Or are you on the go with more opportunities for the netbook to get banged around? Perhaps a durable solid-state drive would be a better choice. Can't decide? Get a hybrid.

Hard drive

Ah, the humble hard drive. Your netbook can rely on the same motorized device that's been storing stuff on regular desktop and laptop systems for decades. Traditional hard drives have a number of advantages over their solid-state rivals:

- **Hard drives are cheaper.** Byte for byte, you can get more storage bang for your buck with a regular hard drive because the technology has been around for a long time and manufacturers know how to make them for less money.

- **Hard drives copy big files faster.** When it comes to copying big chunks of data on and off the netbook, the hard drive can do it quicker than most solid-state drives can (due to the way hard drives write data).

- **Hard drives hold more stuff.** Solid-state drives are getting bigger, hitting 64 GB and beyond, but a 160 GB hard drive, common in netbooks, is more economical.

But on the downside, traditional hard drives—made of a motor, spinning magnetic platters, and read/write heads—are more fragile than solid-state drives. First, the drive's motor and ball bearings eventually wear out. As the old saying goes, "It's not *if* your hard drive dies, it's *when*." Second, one unfortunate long fall onto a hard surface can kill that poor hard drive for good—and take all your files with it. And finally, a constantly spinning hard drive drinks a fair amount of battery juice.

Solid-state drive

A solid-state drive is a cousin to those ubiquitous flash-memory drives that dangle from key chains. Although it's tucked inside the machine instead of plugged into the USB port, a solid-state drive works on the same principle. Your files are electrically stored in memory cells without the need for spinning platters, magnetic heads, and other moving parts. And unlike memory chips that need electricity to retain information (like the RAM in your computer) flash memory is *non-volatile*, which means it doesn't need a steady supply of power to remember stored data. (That's why pocket flash drives don't have power cords.)

The advantages of a solid-state drive include:

- **Solid-state drives are more energy efficient.** Since it doesn't need all the motorized spinning, a solid-state hard drive consumes much less of your netbook's battery power, giving you more time between charges.

- **Solid-state drives are more durable.** With no moving parts, a solid-state drive is less vulnerable to breaking or crashing if the netbook is dropped, banged, or bumped.

- **Solid-state drives start up faster.** Since it doesn't have to sit around and wait for its motor to start spinning up the disk platters, a solid-state system wakes up much more readily.

The two main disadvantages of solid-state drives are high price and low capacity—just the opposite of a conventional hard drive.

Hybrid drive

Like automakers, computer manufacturers are experimenting with hybrid drives that combine the best features of hard drives and solid-state drives. MSI's Wind U115 netbook was one of the first to come with a hybrid drive. The Wind's hybrid drive mainly runs on its 8 GB solid-state side to save battery power, but its 160 GB hard drive side offers plenty of room to store files.

 Tip Even if you choose a system with a small internal drive—8 GB, 16 GB, whatever—you can always add several more gigabytes of storage space with external USB memory sticks, Secure Digital cards, or even external USB hard drives.

Customizing and Buying Your Netbook

Many netbooks are sold over the Internet, either on manufacturers' sites or through online stores like Amazon.com or BestBuy.com. If you want to examine your possible purchase before you buy it, visit your local computer store and look at some samples. Live and in person is the best way to get a realistic grasp on screen and keyboard size.

You may also be able to find netbooks on display in stores like Best Buy, Costco, Staples, and Target. Buying a netbook off the shelf provides instant gratification and a distinct lack of shipping fees, but you may find yourself stuck with whatever configuration the store has in stock.

The HP Mini 2140

If you want to build your own machine, visit your selected netbook maker's website. Here's a sampling of popular manufacturers to help you get started:

- **ASUS** started the current netbook stampede in 2007 with the original Eee PC and has since added a variety of models to the line. (*www.asus.com*)

- **Acer** has Aspire netbooks in three different screen sizes and a handful of colors. (*www.acer.com*)

- **Dell** originally offered Inspiron Mini netbooks in three different screen sizes, from a small 8.9 inches to an almost-normal 12.1 inches. The 10- and 12-inch models are currently available. (*www.dell.com*)

- **Hewlett-Packard** was one of the first major American companies to jump into the netbook market and now has several HP Mini models to choose from. (*www.hp.com*)

- **Lenovo**, which bought IBM's ThinkPad line several years ago, has expanded the laptop line with its IdeaPad S series of netbooks in a rainbow of sprightly colors. (*www.lenovo.com*)

- **Micro-Star International**, also known as MSI, makes the Wind line of netbooks and was one of the first companies to offer a hybrid hard drive/solid-state drive as an option. (*www.msi.com*)

- **Samsung** has added netbooks (which it calls "mini-notebooks") to its consumer electronics lineup. (*www.samsung.com*)

- **Sony.** Arriving fashionably late to the netbook party in July 2009 was Sony's 10.1-inch Vaio W. The Vaio W has a higher-resolution screen than most other netbooks, along with a higher price tag of $500. Initially available in white, pink, or brown, Vaio W's page on Sony's site may make you suddenly crave Neapolitan ice cream. (*www.sonystyle.com*)

- **Sylvania** sells several sizes of netbooks in playful colors that include pink and yellow as well as more somber hues. (*www.sylvaniacomputers.com*)

Most manufacturer sites walk you through the customization process. You select your model, choice of color, screen size, operating system, internal drive type, and other important elements. Depending on the manufacturer, you may also be able to add other enhancements to your new netbook like more memory, a webcam, or additional software.

 Many netbooks come with 512 MB of memory. That's typically enough to run Linux and get on the Web (a netbook's core mission, after all). If you're getting a Windows XP netbook, adding memory to get the total up to a gigabyte or more will make that machine a lot zippier, especially if you plan to run several programs at once. If you don't have the option to add more memory when buying your netbook, check its specifications to make sure the motherboard has room to add more memory. Then go to a RAM site like Crucial (*www.crucial.com*) or Kingston (*www.kingston.com*). Here, you can look up your netbook model, see how much memory it can handle, and buy the right chip to install yourself.

Because of their lightweight, no-frills design, netbooks almost never include a CD/DVD drive. If you run Linux, which can install new programs from online repositories, you can get by without one. If you're a Windows XP user, you'll need to get an external CD/DVD drive to install your favorite copy-protected programs from discs.

Some manufacturers like Dell and Hewlett-Packard let you add on a compatible USB-based external disc drive when you buy the netbook. You'll have to pay an extra $80 to $100 up front, but having a disc drive not only makes software installation easier, it's also invaluable in a crisis if your netbook suffers a meltdown and you have to reinstall the operating system from the computer's recovery discs. Chapter 4 has more on adding disc drives and other hardware to your netbook.

Setting Up Your Netbook

When your new netbook arrives—whether from a clerk fetching it from the stockroom or a delivery person dropping it off—the portable fun begins. First of all, admire the tiny size of the box—hardback books come in bigger cardboard containers!

Next, open the box and unpack the netbook and its accessories. In most cases, there are three or four things besides your netbook:

- The netbook's battery
- Software discs (or a pamphlet on how to use the netbook's recovery system)
- Quick-start sheet
- An AC power cord

Keep the discs and manuals handy for now, but first snap the battery into its slot on the back or bottom of the netbook. Then take the AC power cord and plug the matching end into the netbook's power jack. Plug the other end with the prongs into an electrical outlet to start juicing up your netbook's battery.

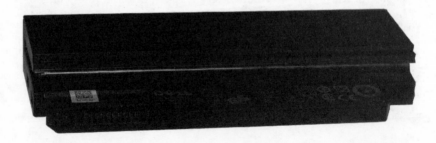

Getting Up, Running, and Online

While the computer is getting AC power from the wall, press its power button and let it start up. As with many new computers, the first time you start it up, it asks you to create a user account. These steps vary depending on operating system; if you need help, Chapter 2 has instructions for setting up a user account in Windows XP, while Chapter 3 has the same information for Linux. (Some netbooks running custom versions of Linux may skip the entire user account thing and take you straight to the desktop.)

Now it's time to put the *Net* in netbook—not only to get online for photos of cranky cats saying wacky things, but also to update your system software, register your purchase, and take care of similar setup chores. Chapter 5 has the details for getting your netbook on the Internet, either through an Ethernet cable or, more likely, through the wonderful world of wireless.

 Tip Some netbooks have a button on the keyboard that toggles its WiFi and Bluetooth radios on and off. If you're trying to get on your home wireless network and nothing's happening, check the manual to find where the button is. You may have bumped it when you were taking the netbook out of the box and need to toggle it back on.

If you've set up a laptop or three, setting up the software side of netbook for the first time will seem pretty straightforward, especially if you're a Windows person and you went with Windows XP. But if you're less familiar with a netbook's compact form, now's a good time for a tour.

Ports of Call: Your Netbook's Jacks

As the name implies, a netbook's main job is to be your super-cheap, super-portable transportation to the World Wide Web. That's why you won't find heavier or nonessential components like disc drives, large battery compartments, or fancy high-definition video ports.

That slimmed-down netbook style doesn't mean you're toting around just a screen, keyboard, and wireless chip, though. The average netbook still has plenty of ports for plugging in external devices like USB flash drives and printers, connecting the netbook to a larger screen, or even hooking up audio equipment. Here's a quick roundup of the data jacks you'll find on most netbooks:

1. **USB.** The humble little Universal Serial Bus is the go-to connector for any type of external hardware except monitors. Most netbooks have at least two USB ports. (If you run out, you can easily add more with a USB hub that makes four ports out of one; page 113 has details.)

2. **Microphone/Audio In.** Many netbooks have built-in cameras and microphones for online video chatting. Many also include the standard round 3.5 mm port to plug in an external microphone (if you're recording a podcast, say, and want better-sounding audio without all the background noise).

3. **Headphones/External speakers.** Even though it may not matter as much with YouTube clips and other Web video, odds are your netbook doesn't have the ultimate in high-fidelity speakers. But you can take matters into your own ears with the netbook's 3.5 mm jack for connecting earbuds, headphones, or external speakers.

4. **VGA Connector.** See that trapezoidal-shaped port with 15 little pinholes on the surface? That's for plugging in an external monitor or projector to display the netbook's stuff on the big screen.

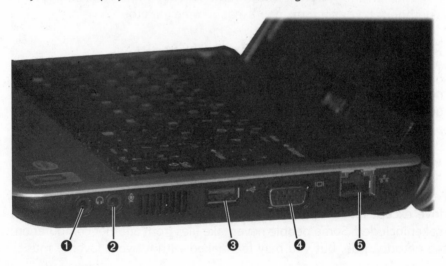

5. **Ethernet/Network.** Also known as an RJ-45 jack, this rectangular port awaits when there's no wireless signal. It looks like a wider version of the RJ-11 jack on telephone cords and old dial-up modems, but the Ethernet jack is wider and—compared to the misery of dial-up connections—much, much faster.

6. **Media card reader.** Some netbook models come with slots on the side for plugging in a memory cards from a digital camera, MP3 player, or personal organizer. Secure Digital, MultiMedia Cards, and Memory Sticks are the common types of cards accepted. Once you plug in the card, you can copy photos, songs, and files to and from the netbook.

7. **Kensington slot** or **security slot.** Some netbooks may also include this place for attaching a cable to the computer so that it doesn't, ahem, walk off by itself. If your netbook has a security slot, check its manual to see what types of locks and cables fit.

If you bought your netbook purely for use with Web-based applications and online activity, you may not even bother with any of its ports (except for the AC power jack). If you do want to hook up printers, external drives, mice, trackballs, or other hardware items, take a stroll to Chapter 4.

Transferring Files to Your Netbook

Fresh out of the box, that shiny new netbook doesn't have much on its drive except for its operating system and whatever extra programs its maker included. Some people never take files from another computer on the netbook ride, but you may feel naked without your favorite music, photos, novel-in-progress, and so on.

Depending on your netbook's model and configuration, its internal drive may be a lot smaller than the one in your desktop or laptop—especially if you opted for a solid-state drive. Keep size in mind when rounding up files you want to copy over to the netbook.

 Thankfully, netbooks have so far managed to avoid the avalanche of sample programs and trial software (dubbed *craplets* by a Wall Street Journal columnist) that manufacturers traditionally dump onto desktops and laptops. But you may find a few of these demo apps along for the ride, especially if you go the Windows XP route. Chapters 2 and 3 have instructions for uninstalling the junk you don't want on your netbook.

Moving a Small Batch of Files

If you just need to copy a small number of files to your netbook, moving them over on a USB pocket flash drive is probably the easiest way. Here's one way to do it:

1. Plug a USB thumb drive into the old computer.

   Make sure the drive is big enough to move all your stuff, unless you want to do it in separate batches.

2. Visit the folders containing the files you want to copy to the netbook.

   For example, Documents, Pictures, Music, or whatever.

3. Ctrl-click the icons of the files you want to copy until you've selected all the ones you want from that particular folder. Then right-click one of the bunch and choose Send To→[Name of USB Drive] from the shortcut menu.

   The computer sends copies of the selected files to the USB drive.

4. When you've gone through and dumped copies of all files you want to take on the USB drive, eject it from the old computer, plug it into the netbook, and drag the files to wherever you want them on the netbook's drive.

   Depending on the files, you may want to store them in Documents, Pictures, or Music folders, for example.

Moving a Big Batch of Files

If you have a bigger bundle of your favorite files that you'd like to put on your netbook, you have various ways to get them from Point A to Point B. Some of them include:

- **By hard drive.** Use a USB external hard drive instead of a USB pocket flash drive and follow steps 1 to 3 in the previous section to move files or whole folders from Old Computer to New Netbook.

- **By disc.** If you bought an external disc drive to use with your new netbook, connect it. Burn the desired files onto a CD or DVD on the old computer and then pop the disc into the drive connected to the netbook. Drag files from disc to netbook. (This method has the bonus feature of making a backup disc of your favorite files, so you can keep it around after you transfer the goods.)

- **By network connection.** Once you get your netbook online (Chapter 5), you can copy files to it over a network, from an online storage site, or by emailing them to yourself. See page 22 for information about transferring and sharing files between computers.

Remember, though, that you're moving files and folders here, not the actual programs that can open them. To use the files on your netbook, your netbook must have the software to open them. The netbook has basic system software to open common file formats like JPEG photos, MP3 audio files, documents in Rich Text Format (.rtf), or plain text. But if you're copying files created in a specific program (like, say, Microsoft PowerPoint), you need to have either PowerPoint or an application that can open the files — like OpenOffice.org or Google Docs (Chapter 7)—installed on the netbook.

Tip Got hundreds of Internet favorites bookmarked on another computer that you'd like to transplant right into your netbook's browser? Page 157 has instructions.

Using the Windows XP Files and Settings Transfer Wizard

If you're trying to turn your Windows XP netbook into a miniature version of your older Windows XP machine, you can use the built-in Files and Settings Transfer Wizard to copy over everything from documents to desktop backgrounds. (You can use the wizard with a removable drive like a USB flash drive or external hard drive, as well as over a network or cable connection.)

Start by connecting a USB flash or hard drive to your old computer. When that's done, your next steps are:

1. On your old XP machine, summon the wizard by choosing Start→All Programs→Accessories→System Tools.

   The Wizard box pops up and asks if this is your old computer or the new one. Click the button next to Old Computer and then click Next. If the panicky Windows Firewall tries to stop you, click Unblock.

2. On the next screen, pick the transfer method.

   You can choose direct cable connections, network connections, removable drives, or network drives. If you don't want to deal with cables and haven't set up your netbook's network access, choose either "removable media" for smaller USB flash drives or "removable drives" for external hard drives. Click the button for the option you want and make sure the external drive's name appears in the box. Click Next.

3. On the left side of the box, select what you want to transfer—files, settings, or both files and settings.

   Now, go through the list on the right side of the box and select all the items you want to transfer, including Internet Explorer settings, desktop settings, and documents—everything you want (or can fit) on the netbook. Click Next when you're done, and Windows XP gathers it all up.

4. When Windows is done, click Finish. Eject the external drive and connect it to the netbook.

5. On the netbook, repeat the wizard-summoning by choosing Start→All Programs→Accessories→System Tools.

   Click Next and tell the wizard that this is your new computer by clicking the button next to New Computer. Click Next again.

6. A box pops up asking if you have a Windows XP CD.

   Ignore everything except for the last item, which you should select: "I don't need the Wizard disk. I have already collected my files and settings from my old computer." Click Next.

7. When Windows asks where to find the files and settings, point it in the direction of your removable drive.

   Once you select your removable drive and click Next, Windows grabs all your saved files and settings and puts them on your new netbook.

Restart the netbook to see all of your old files and settings in place on the new machine.

The Wizard doesn't transfer programs, though, so you have to install those from the Web, installer files on an external drive, or discs on an optional external disc drive.

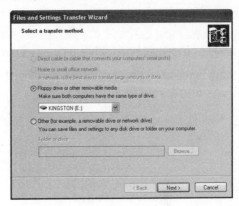

Customizing Your Desktop

The next couple of chapters explain how to get your Windows XP or Linux netbook organized and tricked out to your satisfaction. But you can do something right now to make your new netbook feel like home: Choose your own desktop background.

Windows XP

Windows comes with a bunch of stock photos and other soothing images you can use as desktop wallpaper. If you've just copied photos over to the netbook, you can also use one of your own pictures for that truly personal touch.

1. Choose Start→Control Panel→Display.

   Click the Desktop tab. If your computer is set to see the Control Panels by Category view, click Appearances and Themes and then "Change the desktop background."

2. In the Background area, select one of the image options and click Apply to see a sample.

3. If you want to use one of your own pictures, click Browse, locate the photo on the netbook's drive, and click Apply to add it to the Background list.

   If your picture is smaller than the desktop, use the Position pop-up menu to stretch, center, or display the picture as a series of tiles. (You can also choose to use just a solid color instead of a picture.)

4. Click OK when you have the wallpaper of your choice in place.

Your netbook has just gotten a dose of your personality.

 Tip As a shortcut to the Display settings, right-click anywhere on the desktop background, choose Properties from the shortcut menu, and then click the Desktop tab in the box to get to the background settings.

Linux (Standard Ubuntu)

One of the things you should know about Linux is that there's not just one Linux. There are dozens of flavors, but Ubuntu is the one that pops up most on netbooks these days, and it's the one you'll mostly see in this book.

 Note Some netbook makers install their own modified versions of Ubuntu, so the steps described here may not work due to the custom variations.

Here's the wallpaper customization drill for the standard distribution of Ubuntu:

1. In the menu bar at the top, choose System→Preferences→Appearance.

   The Appearance Preferences box opens.

2. Click the Background tab and then choose a different wallpaper pattern from the samples displayed in the box (or use the pop-up menu to select a solid color).

3. If you want to use one of your own photos, click Add. Locate the photo you'd like and then click Open.

   In the Style pop-up menu, you can adjust the way the photo looks on-screen by centering it, zooming in, scaling it, or tiling it.

Click Close when you've made your selection. Your new desktop background now fills the netbook's screen.

Netbook Battery Options

A netbook's battery can last anywhere from two to nine hours between charges, depending on the manufacturer, the battery's size, and what you're doing. Watching hours of streaming video over a WiFi connection runs through a power charge faster than, say, typing your memoirs in a coffee shop with the netbook's wireless radios turned off.

If you expect to travel a lot and need to keep that netbook up and running for as long as possible throughout the day, consider buying either a second battery or an *extended* battery. An extended battery does just that—extends the amount of time you can go between charges. But in order to fit all that extra power in there, an extended battery adds to your netbook's weight and may make it look like it's wearing a 19th-century lady's bustle.

Still, if you need power, you need power.

To make sure you're getting exactly the right battery for your netbook model, buy it from the company that sold you the netbook. See the list of major netbook manufacturers on page 14 for website addresses.

If your netbook's own maker doesn't sell extra or extended batteries for your model—or wants to charge you an arm and a leg for one—you have other options. For example:

- **Amazon.com.** The online superstore sells netbooks, netbook batteries, and extended netbook batteries, especially for ASUS and Acer computers.

- **Batteries.com.** You can find power cells for all kinds of netbooks and notebooks here.

- **Calcellular.com.** This site specializes in batteries for small things like cellphones and calculators (hence the name), but you can find netbook batteries too, including those for Dell's Inspiron Mini 9 and HP's Mini Note netbooks.

Prices vary depending on the battery's capacity and computer model, but expect to pay somewhere between $60 and $100 for an extra battery.

A Note About Netbook Keyboards

The biggest adjustment many new netbook owners have to make is getting used to the keyboard. As part of the small-size compromise for some of the 9- and 10-inch models, the netbook's QWERTY keyboard looks like it shrunk in the dryer.

If you bought the netbook mainly to surf the Web, the point-click action and occasional URL typing is perfectly fine on the smaller keyboard. If you bought the netbook to surf the Web *and* get some work done on the road, the keyboard may take some getting used to.

To help with typing comfort, most models try to keep the letter keys close to the standard size found on desktop and laptop keyboards. For touch typists, the F and J keys have little raised bumps to help you feel home row.

The keyboard compromises usually target everything else that's *not* a letter key:

- Number keys along the top row may be smaller, as are formatting keys like Tab, Shift, and Caps Lock.

- Your netbook may not include a separate row of Function keys along the top. The Function keys (F1, F2, and so on) are instead remapped to other keys. On the Dell Inspiron Mini 9, for example, F1 through F10 piggyback on the A through semicolon keys in the middle of the keyboard. You summon the F keys by pressing the Fn key in the bottom row, so pressing Fn+A = F1.

- Punctuation keys may be a third smaller and located in weird spots. You may find the apostrophe hiding down by the space bar, for example.

While children and petite-fingered folk won't care as much about keyboard size, people with larger hands will be the most affected by a shrunken keyboard design. If you have big paws, pay close attention to the keyboard layout when doing your netbook shopping research.

If you've already bought the netbook and feel like you're typing on a Texas Instruments graphing calculator, take some time and get to know your netbook's specific keyboard layout. Type stuff on it. It may still feel a little small and cramped once you leave the alphabet keys, but learning where everything is helps your fingers get used to it.

And just keep telling yourself: *this netbook weighs three pounds.* What your fingers may complain about at first, your back and shoulder will love.

2 Getting to Know Your Windows Netbook

Although the early netbooks that appeared before 2008 ran on modified versions of Linux or their own operating systems, it didn't take long for Microsoft to get in on the action. By spring of 2009, about 90 percent of netbooks sold were running Windows.

The vast majority of these netbooks aren't running the latest version, Windows Vista, either. Thanks to Vista's greedy hardware requirements and somewhat intrusive approach to security, many people don't even want it on their desktop computers, let alone their netbooks. Instead, Windows XP Home Edition—which Microsoft attempted to retire during the summer of 2008—made a comeback as the netbook operating system of choice.

If you're a die-hard Mac fan with no Windows experience, this chapter will give you a basic guide to the system. Even for those rare times when you're not tapped into a wireless connection, Windows XP Home has enough built-in features to keep you busy and productive when your head's not in the Cloud. Or if it's been awhile since you've used good ol' Windows XP Home, you can use this chapter as a refresher course.

Which Windows?

When it comes to Windows on a netbook, Windows XP Home Edition is the most widely available choice. For now, anyway. Thanks to the "low-power, low-weight, low-cost" mantra of the netbook makers, installing Windows Vista on one of your average netbook models is like trying to stuff an elephant into a Honda Civic. In October 2009, Microsoft is planning to release netbook-friendly versions of its new system, Windows 7.

 Microsoft's stripped-down versions of Windows, like Windows CE and Windows Mobile, have been largely confined to devices even tinier than netbooks, like personal organizers and smartphones.

Windows XP

When Windows XP was released in 2001, it came in two flavors: Windows XP Home Edition and Windows XP Professional. The Pro edition adds business-oriented features like Multi-Lingual User Interface, Scheduled Tasks Console, and more advanced security and networking features, but if you just want to use your netbook for email, web surfing, and updating your Facebook page, Windows XP Home is perfectly fine.

For people nervous about netbooks' ability to be ***real*** computers, Windows XP Home can be a comforting presence. It sports pretty much all the features of Windows XP Professional, but on sized-down hardware.

Windows 7

Windows XP may not last long at the top of the netbook heap, though. Microsoft has said that its post-Vista system, Windows 7, will have versions that work on netbooks.

Windows 7 brings better built-in security and a slick new interface to the PC experience. Among the improvements are:

- **Jump Lists.** These are sort of like the XP Start menu's Recently Used list, but divided up by programs. For example, to see your most recent Excel documents, right-click the Excel icon to see the jump list for spreadsheets. And, as with the Start menu, you can permanently anchor specific programs within easy reach with the ability to "pin" frequently-used documents or files to a jump list.

- **Enhanced taskbar.** Bigger, bolder, and more translucent than the taskbar in previous editions of the system, the Windows 7 taskbar can also show full-screen previews of open (but hidden) windows.

- **Improved hardware management.** Big clear icons show all your connected devices, from printers to smartphones.

- **Windows Live Essentials.** This free set of programs you can download in one fell swoop includes instant-messaging, email, and blogging programs. You also get photo- and video-editing tools that let you easily share your creations online.

Windows 7 is expected to arrive in October 2009 and may be the system that finally retires Windows XP once and for all. The one major disadvantage that might crash the netbook party? The new state-of-the-art operating system is probably going to show up in the price tag, making that netbook a "low-power, low-weight, not-quite-as-low-cost-as-it-used-to-be" PC.

Seven Things You Should Know About Windows 7

On the fence about getting a Windows 7 netbook or upgrading your current Windows XP model to the newer system? Here are some points to ponder:

1. **Windows 7 is more advanced than Windows XP.** Windows XP, as beloved as it is, has been around since 2001 and has been showing its age for years. In addition to the glossy Aero look (which debuted on Windows Vista), Windows 7 brings with it overhauled versions of Paint and WordPad, zippier performance, and much tighter system security.

2. **Windows 7 takes up more hard-drive space than Windows XP.** Plan to give up about 16 gigabytes of netbook drive space for the Windows 7 operating system. That's not too much of a pain for netbooks with roomy hard drives, but it can be a tight squeeze for those with solid-state drives.

3. **Windows 7 needs at least a gigabyte of memory to run.** If a netbook has Windows 7 preinstalled, you can assume it has enough memory. But if you want to upgrade an older Windows XP netbook to upgrade to Windows 7, make sure it has at least a gig. For even better performance, add as much memory as you can. Windows 7 is, after all, Windows.

4. **Windows 7 comes in many different editions.** Microsoft says netbooks can run any version of Windows 7. Two main editions of the new operating system will be the most popular—Windows 7 Home Premium (aimed at the consumer home crowd) and Windows 7 Professional (aimed at businessfolk). Even more advanced (and costlier) editions, known as Windows 7 Enterprise and Windows 7 Ultimate, are also available at the higher end of the pricing scale. There's also a low-end edition called Windows 7 Starter.

5. **Windows 7 Starter = Windows 7 Stripped Down.** Even though it may come preinstalled on some new netbooks, Windows 7 Starter's limitations may have you pondering an upgrade to Windows 7 Home Premium right out of the box. For example, Starter doesn't include the glossy Aero interface, DVD playback ability, multiple monitor support, or even the ability to change your desktop background and system sounds. If you just want to surf the Web, you may not care about these features, but if you're a long-time Windows maven, you'll itch for more control.

6. **There's no easy way to upgrade directly from Windows XP.** If you decide to put Microsoft's newest baby on your XP netbook, block out a whole afternoon to do it. You'll have to do a *clean installation*, which means copying your netbook's current files to an external drive, erasing everything on the netbook, and then installing Windows 7. Then you have to put all your files and programs back on the netbook. You'll also need an external DVD drive to run the Windows 7 installation DVD—unless you can download the system from Microsoft's website or install it from a USB drive.

7. **Windows 7 may not be able to run older Windows XP programs.** And you may not find out until you try to run an old favorite program on the new system. Fortunately, though, Windows 7 includes a Compatibility Mode that can sometimes tricks programs into thinking they're running on an older operating system. The Professional and Ultimate editions of Windows 7 include an optional virtual Windows XP Mode that can handle XP software, but your netbook's modest processor may not be able to handle this mode.

> **Tip** Still not sure if your netbook can run *any* edition of Windows 7? Download Microsoft's free Windows 7 Upgrade Advisor program, which scans your current hardware and gives you an onscreen report on the netbook's ability to run Windows 7. Download it at *www.microsoft.com/windows/windows-7/get/upgrade-advisor.aspx*.

Setting Up a Windows XP Netbook

Pull your Windows netbook out of the box, snap the battery in, and plug the whole thing into the wall with the AC power adapter so it can get some juice (page 16). After you plug it in, press the Power button—usually in the top-left corner or centered above the keyboard—to start it up.

If it's your first time starting the netbook, you have to go through the initial Windows XP setup procedure. As you may recall if you've set up other Windows XP machines, this process is quick. You just answer questions on a few screens as tinny, techno-Muzak plays in the background. (The din may inspire you to find your netbook's mute button;

look for the key with a pictograph that looks like a speaker horn with an "X" or a slash on it.)

As you click the green Next button to advance through the setup screens, Windows asks basic questions, like:

1. What is your name and address?

   Microsoft uses this information to register this copy of Windows XP in your name. You have the choice to sign up for "free news and offers" from the company here as well.

2. What do you want to call the computer?

   Give the netbook a short name (MINI_ME is a popular choice). This name is what your netbook goes by when you connect it to a network. It's the name that appears to other connected people, security software, or the network administrator.

3. Do you want to protect the new computer by automatically turning on Microsoft's Windows Update feature?

   Turning on automatic updates is a good idea, mainly so you don't have to remember to check for them. These updates to the system software also often include the latest and greatest security patches.

4. What are the names of the users who need accounts on this computer?

   If it's going to be just you using the netbook, type your name or nickname in the first box. Congratulations, you are now the computer's Administrator, or boss account. If you plan to share the netbook with other family members, you can type their names in the boxes below to give them their own accounts.

If you have a spare Ethernet network cable connected to your home network's router, or by your desk at work, plugging it in before you start the setup process can speed things along. This quick Internet lifeline lets Windows send off your information and download updates instead of complaining that you don't have a network connection.

Later, once you get out of the setup screens and land on the Windows desktop, you can configure your netbook to use a wireless network; Chapter 5 explains how. If you don't have a wired Ethernet connection to temporarily use during the Windows setup process, fill in the screens anyway, and Windows will send it all off when you do get the netbook online.

Once you finish with the XP setup screens, the system deposits you on the Windows desktop, ready for action.

 Some netbook makers include a trial subscription of antivirus and other security software. You may be asked to set up this software right after you finish the basic setup screens for Windows XP. Chapter 11 covers security software and practices in detail. If you agree to use the preinstalled software now, that software runs through its own setup, downloading updates and scanning your system. If this trial software pesters you to sign up for an account that wants to do more than just download updates and you don't want to do it, try clicking the Next button three or four times without filling in the requested personal information until the box goes away.

The Start Menu: Where It All Begins

That big green Start button in the lower-left corner of the Windows XP screen is the first daily stop for many people. Unless you have a bunch of desktop shortcuts scattered around the screen (page 39), the Start menu is where you, well, *start*.

The concept is simple: Choose the Start menu, select what you want from its lists or submenus, and off you go. It's sort of like one-stop shopping for all the stuff on your PC.

So click the Start button and up pops your Windows world. The Start menu is divided into two columns, each with its own collection of things.

Left column, starting from the top:

- Your email and web browser programs of choice, all ready to launch when you select the appropriate icon.

- Programs you've recently used appear in the lower part of the Start menu. This list changes and shifts as you use different programs.

- The *All Programs* menu, easily recognizable by its big green triangle pointing the way to the rest of the applications installed on the netbook.

 Tip Want to make a frequently used program always appear in the Start menu, no matter what else you use? In the lower part of the Start menu, right-click the program's icon and choose "Pin to Start Menu" from the shortcut menu. This moves a permanent icon for the program up to the top half of the Start menu. If the program you want to pin isn't currently on the Start menu, choose Start→All Programs. Find the program's icon in the list, right-click it, and choose "Pin to Start Menu."

Right column, starting from the top:

- All "My" folders—the places Windows uses to store certain kinds of files. There's **My Documents**, **My Music**, and **My Pictures**, where Windows usually tries to save, respectively, your word processing documents, your MP3 and WMA music files, and your digital photos. After you've opened some documents, a **My Recent Documents** menu appears. You can also get to the hardware information listed in **My Computer** (page 53) from here.

- **Control Panel**, **Set Program Access and Defaults**, and **Connect To** are all jumping-off points for adjusting the settings for the way Windows XP looks and feels, and how it handles various bits of hardware and software.

- **Help and Support**, **Search**, and **Run** are three self-explanatory items. Select Help and Support to get to the electronic guidebook for Windows XP. (The Help and Support center can answer a lot of questions or show you how to accomplish certain tasks like connecting a digital camera.) Search is

a file finder that lets you hunt down just about anything, from documents stored on the netbook's hard drive to information on the Web. Run is the box for typing wonky commands to open files and programs. Type *telnet* in the Run box, for example, and the Windows XP telnet program opens, ready to connect you to a remote computer.

- Your netbook's manufacturer usually owns the last menu item in the right side. It may be a shortcut to the company's own help guide or the netbook's System Properties box, which displays information like the amount of memory and the type of processor inside the machine.

 Tip Want to change the size of the icons, the number of items, or what's shown on the Start menu? Right-click the green Start button and choose Properties from the shortcut menu. In the Properties box, click the "Start menu" button and then click Customize. The General tab lets you change the way the Start menu looks. The Advanced tab has the settings for how the Start menu behaves, like opening submenus or highlighting newly installed programs. Click OK after you've made your changes.

Windows Desktop Basics

Back in the early days of computers, you had to type all instructions to the machine in cryptic commands. Some systems—notably Unix—still work this way.

Things got better for people without computer-science PhDs in 1984, when Apple released its first Macintosh computer. Now, instead of typing instructions on a *command line*, you had a *graphical user interface*. On this type of system, you use a mouse to point and click to tell the computer what you want to do. Twenty-five years later, GUIs dominate the computer landscape, and Windows XP is no exception.

The basic motif of any GUI is the *desktop*. This screen is your most visible working surface on the computer. Keeping with the office theme, *files* are all the documents, spreadsheets, digital pictures, programs, audio tracks, and so on that make up the computer's contents. A *folder* is a graphical representation of a dedicated area of the computer to store files. Windows gives you several folders to start with, like My Documents.

The desktop can be as clean or as cluttered as you want it to be and can even serve as a launching pad for opening files. You can leave files out on it and double-click them to open them, instead of selecting them from the Start menu.

With the desktop in the background, these are the other parts of the Windows workspace.

1. **Taskbar.** Nestled between the Start button and the system tray, the taskbar displays the names of currently open windows and documents. Click the name to switch around between windows. Because netbooks have such small screens, you can set the taskbar to auto-hide so it only appears when you wave the mouse over the bottom edge of the screen. Right-click the Start button, choose Properties, and click the Taskbar tab. Turn on the checkbox next to "Auto-hide the taskbar" and click OK.

2. **System tray/Notification area.** Shortcut icons to common system settings like sound and the battery level sit on the right side of the taskbar. Small icons for frequently used programs can live here as well. When Windows XP wants to alert you to something minor (like unused icons on your desktop), a yellow *notification balloon* pops up from this area.

3. **Desktop icons.** Files, folders, and programs don't have to live only in the Start menu. The files themselves can hang out on the desktop, as can *shortcuts*. Shortcuts are special icons with a black arrow in the corner; they open up a program or folder without you having to find the actual program or folder.

4. **Windows.** Like their counterparts in the real world, windows let you look inside something. Except instead of a house, you're peeking into files, folders, and programs. To open a window, just double-click a file, folder, or program on the desktop—or choose it from the Start menu.

5. **Recycle Bin.** Don't worry—no separating paper from plastic here. The Recycle Bin is where you drag unwanted files or shortcuts to get rid of them. You can also click an icon to select it and then press Delete to send it to the Recycle Bin. Accidentally toss something? Double-click the Recycle Bin icon to open it, right-click the file you need to retrieve and choose Restore from the shortcut menu.

 Note Just because you've sent something to the Recycle Bin doesn't mean it's gone forever. If you accidentally toss out something you still need, you can get it out of the bin. This phenomenon can work against you if someone else using the computer finds something incriminating you thought you'd gotten rid of. To permanently flush the files out of the Recycle Bin, right-click its icon and choose Empty Recycle Bin. Once you're done, the only way to retrieve the contents is with special file-recovery software.

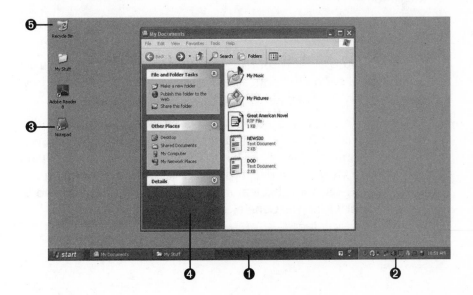

Managing Windows

Unlike windows in houses, desktop windows are easy to move. You can drag them around the desktop, resize them, and even reduce them to tiny labels on the taskbar. Doing all this on a netbook may feel a little cramped due to the small screen size, but your windows work the same way as on the past six versions of Windows.

Here are the basic parts of a Windows window:

- **Title bar.** The text in the blue strip at the top of the window is the name of the open folder or folder. You can rearrange small windows around the screen by dragging their title bars.

- **Buttons.** The three square buttons at top-right let you control the window's size—or close it all together. Click the minus (-) button to *minimize* the window; that is, shrink it down to just a title in the taskbar. Click its title in the taskbar to bring it back out on the desktop. Click the middle button to *maximize* the current window to full-screen size; or click it again to return it to the original size. Click the red X to close the window.

- **Menu bar.** The top of the window has menus and controls for navigating folder windows.

- **Scroll bar.** If the window contains too much to see all at once, you can use the scroll bar on the right side of the window. Click or hold down the mouse button to zip down deeper into the window.

- **Task pane.** The blue-shaded area on the left side of an open window suggests specific activities for the contents in the main part of the window. For example, "Play all" or "Shop for music online" are task pane items for the My Music folder. If you don't need Windows making suggestions, you can turn this feature off. Open any folder and choose Tools→Folder Options→General and click the button next to "Use Windows classic folders."

Changing Your Window Views

Windows XP gives you a lot of ways to look at the same stuff. If you like the linear precision of a list, you can look at your folders and files in long lists. If you prefer colorful, easy-to-spot icons, you can view them that way instead.

To change how a window displays its contents, choose a folder from the Start menu (My Documents is a good one). From the toolbar at the top of the folder's window, choose View and then select the option you want from the middle of the menu. Your choices are:

- **Thumbnails view** shows a miniature preview image of the file. This thumbnail reflects the file's contents—a small version of a photo or graphic file, say, or a tiny representation of the contents of a PDF file. If Thumbnails view can't come up with a preview, it just shows a generic icon.

- **Tiles view** has large icons that show you details like the file's date or size.

- **Icons view** displays a pictograph of the file or folder with its name listed underneath.

- **List view** shows very small icons in multiple rows across the screen, with each file's name listed next to the icon.

- **Details view** looks much like List view, except the small icons and names are arranged in a single vertical column along with file type, size, and date.

- **Filmstrip view** is available only for picture folders. It displays a large preview of the selected photo above a row of smaller previews of the other pictures in the folder. You can move through the pictures by tapping the netbook's left and right arrow keys or by clicking the onscreen arrows. The two other buttons underneath the big preview image let you rotate photos clockwise or counterclockwise so you can get your vertical shots oriented the right way.

 Tip Right-click inside any open folder window and choose View from the shortcut menu to get to these options quicker.

Taking Control with Control Panel

Anytime you need to adjust a setting or add hardware like a printer to your netbook, you inevitably end up in the Start menu's Control Panel area. For control freaks, this panel is a trip to Disneyworld.

To get there, choose Start→Control Panel. Now, depending on which view you've selected, the Control Panel looks very different:

- **Category View** groups all the Windows settings into themed categories, like "Printers and Other Hardware" or "Performance and Maintenance." This scheme makes for a very tidy screen, but you kind of have to know what you're looking for. For example, if you want to change the setting that automatically turns off the netbook's screen after a period of inactivity, you have to know that the Power Options control panel is grouped in the Performance and Maintenance category.

- **Classic View** shows all the control panels as separate icons in a window—with the effect of tons of little colorful objects scattered all over the screen. This view can cause sensory overload for some people. On the other hand, you don't have to guess at categories and can zero in on the one control panel you need, like Display or Fonts.

To switch back and forth between views, click an option in the Task pane at the left side of the Control Panel window.

A Tour of the Windows Programs Menu

Even before you add your own software, your netbook's All Programs menu has plenty of preinstalled applications programs to get you rolling. The programs in the list vary based on which netbook you have, as some companies may add things like antivirus software or the Microsoft Works suite of home-office applications. This section lists the programs that come standard with Windows XP.

Accessories

The folder in the All Programs menu reveals a nestled *subfolder* with all kinds of helpful little apps. These include:

- **Address book.** An electronic Rolodex for storing contact information.

- **Calculator.** On the surface, this program looks like a simple little adding machine for tallying up, say, a batch of checks for deposit. But choose View→Scientific, and the calculator transforms itself into a math nerd's best friend, capable of working in the Hex, Decimal, Octal, and Binary numeral systems.

- **Command Prompt.** If you miss typing DOS commands to find files and jump around the PC, relive the glory days here.

- **Notepad.** Need to jot down a quick bit of text like a shopping list? Notepad is just the thing. It lets you create plain-text files virtually any word processing program out there can open.

- **Paint.** It's no high-end Photoshop-type program, but humble little Paint can create hand-drawn graphics and do basic photo-editing tasks like cropping or resaving files in different image formats.

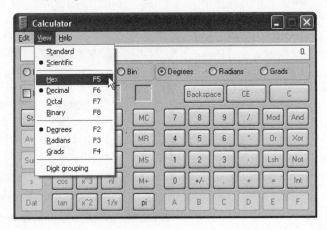

- **Windows Explorer.** More like a helicopter ride than a program, Windows Explorer (page 50) shows your netbook's contents as a vertical tree of folders and documents, making it easy to see how Windows itself is organized.

- **WordPad.** More technically sophisticated than Notepad, WordPad can handle basic text formatting and open documents created in older versions of Microsoft Word. Unlike Word, WordPad doesn't include a lot of editing features like a built-in spellchecker, thesaurus, and 37 different toolbars.

In addition to various *wizard* programs that walk you through chores like connecting a photo scanner, the Accessories folder contains its own subfolders. These store different applications like:

- **Accessibility.** Built-in tools for people with special visual and audio needs are grouped here, like a screen magnifier and a program that reads text on screen out loud.

- **Communications.** Software for setting up network connections.

- **Entertainment.** Here lives the Windows Media Player program for listening to digital music and watching video, plus the Sound Recorder app for doing your own recording.

- **System Tools.** Utility programs like Disk Defragmenter and Disk Cleanup—intended to help keep the computer running well—are stored here (and explained in greater detail in Chapter 12). This toolbox also contains the Character Map for finding special symbols on the keyboard, the Files and Settings Transfer Wizard (page 22), and the bacon-saving System Restore tool (page 286).

Games

It's not a personal computer unless it has a solitaire program, and Windows XP includes three: Solitaire, Spider Solitaire, and the free-form FreeCell (pictured). There's also Hearts, MineSweeper, and Pinball. Windows XP also includes five online games that let you pit your skills against other players over the Internet: Backgammon, Checkers, Hearts, Reversi, and Spades. Chapter 10 has more on netbook gaming.

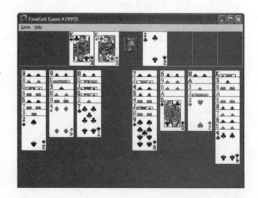

Startup

This folder shows you what programs automatically start up when you turn on the netbook. You can add or delete shortcuts in this folder (page 39), but remember: The more stuff you have starting up all at once, the longer it'll take Windows to lumber into action when you boot up the netbook.

 Tip Want a quick way to open a program, folder, or file without having to dig around in folders or the All Programs menu? Make a desktop shortcut of it. Right-click the item's icon and choose Send To→Desktop (create shortcut) from the menu. Just double-click the new shortcut on the desktop to open the item.

Other programs

Applications included with Windows XP, like Outlook Express for email and Internet Explorer (both in Chapter 5), are full-time residents on the main level of the All Programs menu. The Windows Messenger instant-messaging program (page 200) and the Windows Movie Maker video-editing software (page 249) are also neighbors on the All Programs list. Depending on which netbook you have, you may also find Internet security software (page 264), the Adobe Reader program for viewing PDF files (page 191), and other surprises from your netbook company as well.

And, of course, any new software you install yourself ends up in the All Programs menu as well.

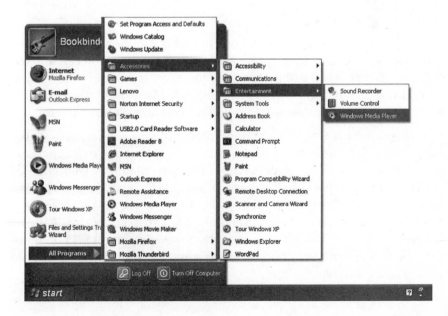

Tip As you add new applications to the netbook, the All Programs menu may get a little disorganized and your most frequently used items will get lost in the crowd. If you don't have room to pin them all in the Start menu (page 36), you can rearrange the menu to your liking instead of keeping it in the order of programs installed.
With the All Programs menu open, drag the applications you want to move to more convenient places on the list. If you'd rather use the organizational power of the alphabet, right-click any program title and choose "Sort by Name" from the shortcut menu. The programs regroup themselves in alphabetical order, so you just have to remember that Picasa comes after iTunes.

Adding More Programs

Windows XP comes with all the programs you need to browse the Web, write and send email, compose documents, and enjoy digital photos, audio, and video. But unless you plan to use online applications (page 175) for the stuff Windows lacks, odds are you'll install additional software on your netbook.

You can install software either from a CD or DVD (using an add-on disc drive), or from a Web download. Before you buy any new software, check the program's system requirements. Some programs may require a certain processor speed or take up a huge chunk of drive space, so make sure your netbook can handle it. You don't want to end up with a program that won't even launch and takes up a gigabyte of precious netbook real estate as it silently mocks you for not reading the system requirements page.

Installing programs from the Web

Downloading programs straight from the Web is currently the quickest and most popular way to get software for any computer. You can find everything from antivirus utilities to word processors to robust photo-editing programs ready to download to your netbook. Many of these are free, inexpensive, or cheaper than they would be if you bought them on disc.

Software company websites are good places to check for downloadable wares. Shareware archives are also great places to find free or inexpensive programs written by developers who don't have the financial oomph or marketing muscle to get their software boxed, shrink-wrapped, and placed on a store shelf. Sites like *www.download.com*, *www.versiontracker.com*, and *www.tucows.com* are bursting at the seams with software for Windows XP. And, unlike some less-than-reputable shareware sites out there, these three have scanned their goods to make sure the programs don't contain viruses and spyware.

Once you find a program you want and click the Download link on its web page, you may see a box asking if you want to *Run* the program installer you're downloading or *Save* it. Choose Run to immediately install the program on your netbook with minimal fuss.

Windows typically sticks the program's Installer files in its temporary files folder and flushes them when it empties the Temp folder (which you can schedule with the Disk Cleanup tool described on page 283).

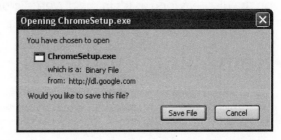

Choose Save if you don't want to install the program right away. The installer file lands on your Windows desktop (or whatever folder you directed it to). Once the file arrives, double-click its icon to start the installation process. The advantage to picking Save here means that you get to add the program when you feel like it and hang on to the installer file in case you need to reinstall later.

Installing software from a disc

With regular desktops and laptops, many larger programs like Microsoft Office come on install discs that you just pop into the CD/DVD drive. You can install software on your netbook this way, too, by hooking up an external USB-based disc drive. Dumping the built-in disc drive is one way netbook designers make their machines smaller, lighter, and more power-efficient. You'll only miss the drive on three occasions: backing up to disc, watching movies, and, well, installing software.

So if you sprung for a disc drive, connect it to the netbook's USB port, slide in the install disc, and follow the onscreen instructions to install the software on the netbook. See page 103 for more on connecting an external disc drive to your netbook.

Got another Windows computer with a working disc drive on your home network? With a little tinkering, you might be able to tap into it to get files off discs or run installer programs. Start by putting the disc you want to use into the other computer's disc drive. Open the My Computer icon and right-click the drive's icon. Choose Sharing and Security from the pop-up menu and turn on the checkbox to share the folder or drive on the network.

On the netbook, open Windows Explorer (page 50) and choose Tools→Map Network Drive. Click the Browse button and locate the disc drive from the other computer that you just shared. Click OK when you find it. Then click Finish in the Map Network Drive box. You should be able to get to any files on the disc—as long as it's in the drive. (Microsoft has more on all kinds of file sharing at *http://support.microsoft.com/kb/304040*.)

Removing Programs

If a program you've installed needs to come off the netbook because it's crashing, outdated, annoying, or taking up too much space on the drive, it's time to *uninstall* it.

You can remove programs in a couple of ways. Dragging the program's icon into the Recycle Bin or right-clicking its icon on the All Programs menu and choosing Delete may seem obvious, but they aren't the best or safest ways to dispense with a program. You may be leaving behind all the program's internal files on your drive or merely deleting the desktop shortcut (page 39) that points the way to the real program file.

Once you've decided which program or programs you want to remove from your netbook, try one of these removal methods instead:

- In the All Programs menu, find the program you want to remove and look in its folder for an uninstall option. If it has its own Uninstaller application, launch it and follow the onscreen steps.

- If the program doesn't have its own uninstaller application, go to Start→Control Panel→Add or Remove Programs. Wait for the "Add or Remove Programs" box to gather up a list of all the software you have on your netbook—and how much space each application is taking up on your drive. It may take a few seconds, but once the list appears, find the program you want to delete. Click its name in the list and then click the Remove or Change/Remove button. If a box pops up to ask if you're sure, say Yes and proceed with the uninstallation.

Organizing and Finding Files

Like brand-new houses, new computers start out relatively fresh and un-cluttered. But as you inhabit a computer, like a house it tends to accumulate various souvenirs of life—documents, music, video, photos, and so on. Depending on your personal level of organization, finding things may be easy or hard. But on the netbook you have some handy tools to track down what you're looking for—without turning the house upside down.

How to Organize Your Files

As mentioned earlier in this chapter, a folder is the basic organizational unit of Windows XP (and any other operating system where you work on a desktop). If you have a bunch of files scattered all over the desktop, here's one way to corral them:

1. Right-click the desktop and choose New→Folder.

   A new yellow folder called New Folder appears on the desktop. The words "New Folder" are highlighted in blue, meaning you can edit them.

2. Type to name the folder something more descriptive, like *Recipes*.

3. Drag all the loose documents cluttering up the desktop on top of the new folder to put them inside it.

With all the files now in the Recipes folder, you can move the whole thing at once off the desktop and put it in, say, the My Documents folder. For example, choose Start→My Documents to open the My Documents folder window on the desktop, and then drag the Recipes folder onto the open window.

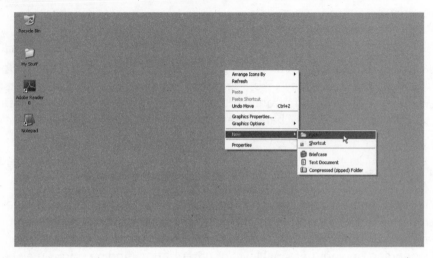

Tip Need to rename a file? Right-click its icon, choose Rename from the shortcut menu, and then type the new name.

You can have folders inside of folders like Russian nesting dolls. For example, within My Documents, you could have a folder called Taxes, and inside that, separate folders for 2008 Taxes, 2007 Taxes, and 2006 Taxes. Inside the 2008 Taxes folder, for example, you could have files called Deductions List and Form 1040. It's just a matter of how organized you want to be.

Finding Files with Windows Explorer

One way to get a good overall look at the contents of your netbook is to summon *Windows Explorer*. Not to be confused with Internet Explorer (Microsoft's web browser) or MSN Explorer (Microsoft's *other* web browser that integrates Windows Live Hotmail and other applications), Windows Explorer is your netbook's file-management program.

Windows Explorer lets you see all the files and folders on your netbook at a glance, including what files are inside which folders and where everything lives on your netbook's drive. In addition to seeing how all your stuff is organized, you can use Windows Explorer to copy, move, and rename files on the netbook.

Getting to Windows Explorer is easy:

- Right-click the green Start menu button and choose Explore from the shortcut menu.

- Choose Start→All Programs→Accessories→Windows Explorer.

Once you open Windows Explorer, it pops up and displays all the contents of your computer, neatly laid out in a vertical family tree. A plus sign (+) next to an icon or folder means there's more stuff inside. Click the plus button to see what's in there, and click the minus (–) button to close it back up again.

As you click file and folder names on the left pane of the Windows Explorer window, the right pane displays its contents. This arrangement makes it all very easy to see where everything lives on the netbook.

 If you have a folder window open, you can jump into Explorer mode by clicking the Folders button in the toolbar. The Windows Explorer tree appears in the window's left pane so you can see where the file is stored.

Searching for Files

When you *really* can't find what you're looking for, it's time to use Windows XP's Search function. Search can track down everything from a downloaded MP3 of "It's a Long Way to Tipperary" on your hard drive to the song's original lyrics on Google.

Choose Start→Search.

The Windows XP Search Companion pops up in the left pane of the window, complete with a list of search options and a small animated dog to keep you company. Next, click the green arrow next to the type of file you're looking for—like a music track or a word processing document. On the next screen, the Search Companion prompts you for more information about the file you seek. *What type of file is it? Do you have the name or part of the name?* Click the icon for advanced search options to get even more results-narrowing questions. When you have entered all the information you know, click the Search button.

The Search Companion scours the netbook's drive for any files that match your criteria and displays them on the right side of the window for your inspection.

Need to find information on the Web? Click the "Search the Internet" option, type your query, and click Search. Windows XP will probably display your results on an MSN page, but you can pick your favorite search engine like Google or Yahoo instead.

To change your default Search engine, click Change Preferences on the main Search Companion screen. On the next screen, click "Change Internet search behavior." On the resulting screen, you can choose how you want to search—with the Search Companion's suggestions, or with a regular search engine page. At the bottom of the pane, you can pick your preferred search engine from the list. Click OK when you've made your choice.

Tip Your faithful little Search Companion comes running when you click the Search button at the top of any open folder window.

Checking Hard Drive Space

If you plan to store a lot of files on your ultraportable PC, you'll have to keep an eye on your internal drive space. Netbooks don't have the biggest drives to begin with, especially if you opted for a solid-state drive. And it's amazing how quickly space disappears once you start installing programs or adding digital photos, video, and music.

To take a quick peek at how much drive real estate you have left, choose Start→My Computer. When the My Computer window opens, right-click your netbook's C: drive icon and choose Properties from the shortcut menu.

Note Some netbooks have a D: partition. The manufacturer set up this special area of the hard drive as a system recovery rescue plan.

On the General tab in the box that pops up, you see the amount of space you've used and the amount of space you have left on your netbook's drive. You also see a blue and magenta pie chart visually depicting the same information.

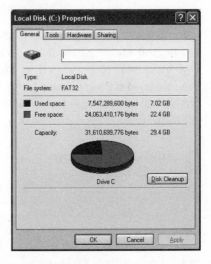

You don't have to worry about hard drive space until you have less than 20 percent of your drive is free. Once the hard drive gets too full, you may start to notice sluggish performance or have insufficient space to install any more programs.

If you find your netbook doesn't have enough room to maneuver, page 283 explains how you can take back some turf on your drive.

Backing Up Your Windows Netbook

Of all the things you can do on a computer, backing it up is one of the most important—but overlooked—tasks. Some netbook owners may not have much of anything on their drives. These are the folks that prefer to just keep the operating system and a couple of programs on there, while storing their email, text files, and photos *online*, for example, in the repositories of Gmail, Google Docs & Spreadsheets, and Picasa web albums.

But then there are others who like to have all their stuff with them. And if you have your life on the netbook's drive, backing it up can be a real life-saver. There are several ways to back up your netbook:

Built-in backup

Depending on your make and model, your netbook may come with all the backup you need right on the drive in an extra *partition*, or separate section, reserved for making backups of your netbook's data. Lenovo, for example, includes its OneKey Rescue System on its IdeaPad netbooks; Samsung includes a similar utility. The downside: If your netbook gets stolen or your hard drive fails, your backup disappears, too.

USB flash drive

Say you just have a handful of files you need to back up each night—for example, the folder you're using to store your current project spreadsheets. One quick way to back up the folder is to plug a USB flash drive, right-click the folder, and then choose Send To→[Name of USB Drive] from the shortcut menu. Large capacity USB flash drives come in sizes like 16, 32, and 64 GB these days, so you can back up a lot of data on one stick.

External drive backup

If you want to back up the whole netbook at once, connecting an external USB hard drive and using dedicated backup software is a time-honored tradition. You can set the software to back up part or all of the netbook's drive daily, weekly, or whenever you want.

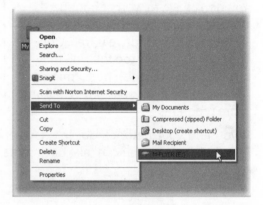

Most external drives include their own backup software, but you can also buy your own preferred program to use with the drive. Western Digital (*www.wdc.com*), Iomega (http://*go.iomega.com*), and Maxtor (*www.maxtor. com*) all sell backup drives. Just make sure to buy one large enough to hold all the stuff on your netbook. As for software, Genie Backup manager ($50 at *www.genie-soft.com*) and NTI Backup Now ($30 to download at *www. ntius.com*) are among the many programs out there.

Online backup

Netbooks—small, light, and built to be online—can store their files on-line, too. This method has its advantages, mainly in that your files are safely backed up on servers, no matter where you or the netbook happen to be. On the downside, copying files over the Internet can be slow, especially the first time you back up your entire drive at once. (Later backups, which just copy over new or modified files, take much less time.) Several companies offer online backup services. Mozy (www.*mozy.com*), for example, offers 2 GB of online server space free, and unlimited amounts of backup space for $5 a month. SOS Online Backup (*www.sosonlinebackup.com*) charges $20 a year to back up 2 GB of data and goes up to $50 a year to back up 15 GB.

 Note Windows XP Home Edition has its own Backup program, but you must manually install it from the Windows disc that came with the computer. Your netbook may have not come with a disc drive, and you may not even have a Windows disc if its maker decided to put backup and recovery utilities on a hard drive partition instead. Still, if you have the Windows disc, a disc drive, and the desire to use Microsoft's backup software, connect the drive, pop in the disc, and look in the ValueAdd folder for the Ntbackup.msi file. Microsoft has its own page of instructions at *http://support.microsoft.com/kb/302894*.

Closing Down Your Netbook

When it's time to quit for the day, Windows XP gives you several options for closing down your netbook. Each way saves power by turning off the screen and hard disk; the differences are in how long it takes to start back up again.

Choose Start→Turn Off Computer. The box that pops up gives you three (or four) options: *Stand By* (or, if you hold down the Shift key, *Hibernate*), *Turn Off*, or *Restart*.

 Note Choosing Restart shuts down all your programs before turning the netbook off and on again, and it's a great way to reset a cranky machine. The other three choices are the ones that actually power down the netbook in some form.

- **Stand By.** Choosing Stand By keeps your currently open programs open, but settles the netbook into a low-power mode where it consumes much less energy. In this state, the netbook can wake up again pretty quickly. The hard drive, fans, and screen are turned off, but the computer still uses a bit of power to store your current work in its memory. (If you have a power blip or failure, though, all the information stored in the net-book's memory is flushed out.) When it's time to get back to work, tap the netbook's Power button to instantly bring it out of Stand By mode.

- **Hibernate.** This mode is similar to Stand By, but the computer saves all the information from open files and programs currently in its memory to the hard drive. This way, it can completely power off and save more battery life. Since it has to pull everything out of the hard drive's temporary storage, waking up from Hibernate takes a little longer than from Stand By mode.

Two other considerations: You need to have enough drive space left to store the hibernated system, and you may have to turn on the Hibernate feature before you can use it. To do so, choose Start→Control Panel→Power Options→Hibernate and turn on the "Enable hibernation" checkbox. (Choose Start→Control Panel→ Performance and Maintenance→Power Options→Hibernate if you're using the Category view instead of the Classic view of the Control Panel.) Then, when you're ready to Hibernate, choose Start→Turn Off Computer and press Shift to turn the yellow Stand By button into a yellow Hibernate button. Press the netbook's Power button to pop it out of Rip Van Winkle land.

- **Turn Off.** Choosing the red button in the middle shuts down the computer entirely. This choice is appropriate if you plan to be away for a while or just want to make sure the netbook is completely off. To start up the netbook again, press the Power button and wait for it to boot up.

Now that you know a bit about how Windows XP works on a netbook, it's time to get that netbook working for you. Skip over the next chapter (unless you really want to learn the basics for Linux on a netbook) and proceed to Chapter 4 to learn how to outfit your netbook with a mouse, printer, external drive, and more.

3 Getting to Know Your Linux Netbook

I f you're stopping by this chapter, you probably just bought a Linux-based netbook—or you're weighing the purchase of one against a Windows XP model. This chapter will give you an overview of Ubuntu Linux, an *open-source* operating system, which means that everyone is free to edit its code and potentially make it better. Linux was one of the first systems to join the netbook party.

Linux started out as one man's hobby and has grown into a robust modern operating system, complete with its own Windows-like interface. And it's an ideal system for a netbook. Thanks to the efforts of thousands of volunteers, corporate backing, and brilliant programmers writing (mostly free) software for it, Linux lets you do all the standard computing tasks: email, Web browsing, instant messaging, word processing, games, and so on.

Later, you'll learn about the software you can run on your Linux netbook. This chapter is a guided tour of the Linux system itself: how to get started with it and where to find stuff. So grab your netbook to see how Linux looks and works.

Which Type of Linux?

Unlike Windows and Mac OS X (which are created, updated, and sold exclusively by either Microsoft or Apple), Linux is available from many different sources. Linux is an open-source program—crafted, improved, and spun off in its early years by an army of volunteers in a software version of an Amish barn-raising. These days, big companies like Oracle and IBM are developing Linux for corporate and professional use.

Because of this freedom to create, many different flavors or **distributions** of Linux have popped up over the years. Linux distributions are often colorfully named: BlueCat Linux, Yellow Dog Linux, or Red Hat Linux. Then there's Mandriva Linux, Linpus Linux, Debian/GNU Linux, SuSE Linux, Slackware Linux, and the list goes on. (You can see the list yourself at *http://www.linux.org/dist/list.html*.)

An open source program's **source code** (or digital DNA, if you will) is open for anyone to look at and potentially tinker with. By contrast, **closed** or **proprietary** software prohibits modification and has strict licenses stating what you can do with the program. Windows falls into this camp.

But open source doesn't always mean **free**. Yes, open source programs can cost money. Richard Stallman, a software developer, writer, and activist has an essay on the difference between open source and free software at *http://www.gnu.org/philosophy/open-source-misses-the-point.html*.

The version of Linux you get on your netbook depends on whom you bought it from. This book focuses on Ubuntu Linux, specifically version 8.0.4.

Why Ubuntu? Mainly, it's one of the most popular distributions available. For example, Dell offers it as an option on its Inspiron Mini netbooks and HP has a variation of Ubuntu powering the Linux editions of its HP Mini netbooks. The Web is full of stories from people who've replaced whatever distribution of Linux came on their netbook with Ubuntu. The system even inspired a distribution called MinBuntu, crafted just for the HP 2133 Mini-Note. (If your netbook came with a different flavor of Linux and you want to try Ubuntu instead, see page 295.)

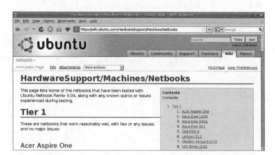

Tip Ubuntu isn't just for netbooks—the system works great on older PC hardware that's often considered too outdated to run the latest versions of Windows. Ubuntu's suggested system requirements—384 megabytes of memory, 8 giga-bytes of hard-drive space, and a 700-megahertz processor—are well within range of many older computers and can give them a new life. You can order a free CD or download a disk image from *www.ubuntu.com*, which also has instructions for installing the system.

Ubuntu is free to anybody who downloads it. Even though your netbook maker may have paid a little bit for it, you paid less for your netbook than your Windows XP buddy did. And it's updated regularly. Ubuntu includes all the software you need to get started, including the Firefox browser, an email program, the OpenOffice.org business software suite, and more.

 Note And it has a totally cool and inspiring name. According to its official website (*www.ubuntu.com*), the word *ubuntu* is an African word that means "humanity towards others" or "I am what I am because of who we all are."

Setting Up a Linux Netbook

The exact steps for getting your Linux netbook up and running depends on which netbook you bought and which version of Linux the manufac-turer decided to use on it. But all models have certain things in common.

First, take the battery out of the box and snap it into the netbook. Next, fish out the AC power adapter, plug the matching end into the power jack on the back or side of the netbook, and plug the other end into a wall outlet so the new battery can start to get juiced. Press the Power button to fire it up.

If you have a wired network cable from, say, your home network or an ex-tra Ethernet connection at work, plug it into the netbook before you turn it on. This way, you can get on the Internet immediately for registering the computer and downloading updates.

If you don't have a wired network connection available, don't worry—you can get your netbook on your wireless network almost as quickly; Chapter 5 has the details. Just be sure to turn on the netbook's wireless radio but-ton (it's usually the one with a radio tower or radio-wave symbol).

Before you start using the netbook, Linux will likely ask you to set up a user name and password. This step is important because:

- To install new software or make certain changes to the way the system works, you have to type your password. Password-protection makes it harder for malicious software to install itself on the computer.

- If more than one person uses the netbook, all of them can have their own user accounts on it. This arrangement keeps their system settings separate, so not everyone has to look at the desktop wallpaper of frolicking golden hamsters that you so enjoy. And user accounts help keep the system safer—unless you're logged on (or know the password) for the all-powerful administrator account, you can't make major changes to the system. This super user account is also known as the *root* account.

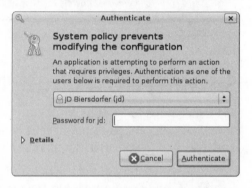

During the setup process, Linux asks other questions, like what language you'd like to use, what type of keyboard you have, and where you're located so the system can set its date and time.

Once you've completed the basic netbook setup process, you can start exploring the Linux desktop. If you've used Windows or the Mac OS before, much of it will feel familiar.

Exploring the Linux Desktop

Before netbooks hit the scene, some people had no idea what a Linux was—a European luxury car? A rare African antelope? The Windows and Mac faithful considered it a hobbyist computer system requiring tricky typed commands. But the small population of Linux junkies knew it was an open-source, grassroots operating system that was becoming more flexible and friendly with each passing day.

Linux has come a long way, baby.

Sure, it started out as a typed-command kind of system, like DOS—or any pre-1984 computer. But over the years, Linux has acquired a *graphical user interface* of its own, much like Windows. Now you can travel around Linux's menus and windows with point-and-click convenience.

The basic motif of the interface is the *desktop environment*. Linux, having come up as a community project, has several desktop environments to choose from, with names like KDE and Gnome. Ubuntu uses the Gnome desktop, which you'll learn more about on page 64.

Which Netbook Desktop?

In an attempt to make Linux seem more attractive and accessible, some netbook makers put their own simplified interfaces over the standard desktop. For example, your netbook may have a glossy translucent toolbar or screen that puts icons for all your favorite programs and websites right up front.

Dell adds its Dell Desktop Launcher to its Ubuntu-based netbooks. The Launcher features five buttons along the top of the screen, grouping the netbook's programs into categories like Web, Communication, Entertainment, Productivity, and Games.

If you want to do something productive, say, like writing a novel, just click the Productivity icon to open a window revealing all the programs in the Productivity category. Click the Document icon there to start the Open-Office.org word processor.

 Tip Click the big + button on the right side of the Dell Launcher to add your own categories or shortcuts to the window. Click the + at the top of the screen to add a Category (Shooting Games or Music, say), or click the + in the lower-right corner to add a shortcut like a bookmarked website to the category you're in.

But Ubuntu has its own perfectly nice desktop, too. It's not as simple or as slick as the one the manufacturer may have slapped on top, but it keeps icons to all the netbook's programs, folders, and settings under smaller, more discreet icons. In fact, it looks quite a bit like the Windows Start menu, with access to your programs, settings, and files all tucked neatly away on the edge of the screen.

To get to the real Ubuntu desktop, look for an icon in the top menu bar that lets you switch desktop modes. On the Dell Inspiron Mini 9, for instance, click the small black triangle under the house icon in the top-left corner of the menu bar and choose Switch Desktop Mode; the next box lets you pick Classic Desktop, which is Dellish for "the standard Ubuntu/Gnome desktop." You can also stay in the standard desktop and pop into the Ubuntu menus by clicking the small orange-and-red Ubuntu icon in the top panel.

Gnome Desktop

The desktop is Linux's main workspace. Keeping with the office metaphor, *files* are all the documents, spreadsheets, digital pictures, programs, audio tracks, and so on that make up the computer's contents. A *folder* is a graphical representation of a *directory*—a dedicated area of the computer for storing files. Ubuntu gives you several folders to start out with under the Places menu—like Documents, Music, Pictures, and Videos.

Your desktop can be as tidy or as messy as you want. You can make it a serene vista to meditate upon or use it as a launching pad for opening files and programs. You can leave files out on the desktop and double-click them to open them, instead of selecting them from the Applications or Places menu.

With the desktop in the background, these are the other parts of the Ubuntu's Gnome desktop workspace:

1. **The top panel.** This gray strip running along the top of the screen contains a number of menus (Applications, Places, Systems) and some program shortcuts, along with other information like the netbook's current battery strength and sound level. There's more on the top bar on page 67.

2. **Desktop icons.** Files, folders, and programs can move beyond the Places menu. The files themselves can hang out on the desktop.

3. **Windows.** Like their counterparts in the real world, windows give you a glimpse inside. Except instead of a house, you're peeking into files, folders, and programs. To open a window, just double-click a file, folder, or program on the desktop or choose it from the Start menu.

4. **The bottom panel.** The tiny icon at lower-left that looks like a TV screen is the Show Desktop button. Click it to hide all open windows and get back to your desktop. The middle section of the gray bar running along the bottom of the main window shows open programs and hidden windows. The second icon from the right is the Desktop Switcher: If you have multiple desktop windows open, you can click here to switch between them. The icon on the far right corner is the Trash can, which serves as a virtual container for files you want to delete. To actually remove the files from your netbook, right-click the Trash can icon and choose Empty Trash from the shortcut menu.

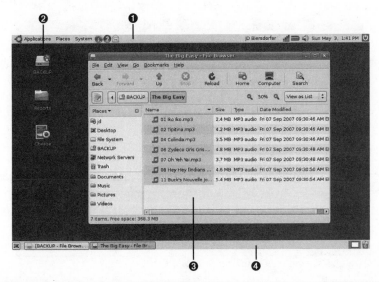

Tip You can toss a file by right-clicking it and choosing "Move to Trash" from the short-cut menu.

Managing Windows

Windows on Linux work much like windows on, er, Windows. You can drag them around, shrink them into tabs on the bottom bar, and resize them in a number of ways.

Here are the basic parts of a window:

1. **Title bar.** The text in the strip at the top of the window is the name of the open folder or folder. You can rearrange small windows around the screen by dragging them by their title bars.

2. **Buttons.** The three square buttons at top-right control the window's size—or close it completely. Click the minus (–) button to minimize the window—that is, shrink it down into just a title in the bottom bar. Click its title in the bottom bar to maximize it on the desktop. Click the middle button to expand the current window to the full screen, or click it again to return to the original size. Click the X button to close the window.

3. **Menu bar.** The top of the window has its own menus and controls, depending on what type of window it is.

4. **Scroll bar.** If the window contains more than you can see at one time, a scroll bar appears on the right side. Click or hold down the mouse button on the scroll bar to zip down deeper into the window.

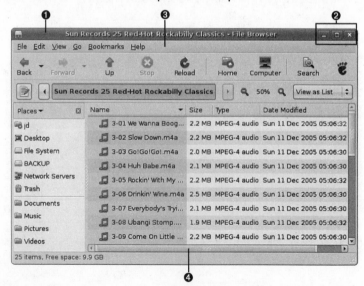

Tip Unless it's already full-screen width, you can also resize a window by dragging the bottom-right corner, which has a small triangular pattern of dots that simulate a textured gripper strip.

Top Panel Menus

When you get right down to it, many versions of Linux sort of look like recent versions of Windows: a desktop with a few icons and a collection of menus. In Ubuntu Linux, these all live at the top of the screen, whereas the Windows Start menu and taskbar are found on the bottom. But they all work the same way: You click a menu to see what's in it and then pick what you want.

The bar at the top of the Ubuntu desktop has three menus:

- **Applications.** All of the netbook's programs are listed here, grouped into categories like Graphics or Internet. Ubuntu gives you a lot: a photo-editing program called the GIMP (page 229), a Microsoft Office-like collection of business programs called OpenOffice.org (page 171), plus plenty of Web and multimedia programs. To launch a program, just choose it from the Applications menu.

- **Places.** This menu offers elements similar to Windows' Explorer, Start menu, and My Computer. Here, you can quickly jump to built-in folders called Documents, Music, Pictures, and Videos that store specific types of files. You can also browse files on a connected USB drive, connect to a network server, or search for files on the netbook.

- **System.** All the netbook's settings and administrative tools live in this menu, which roughly corresponds to the Windows Control Panel or the Mac OS X System Preferences. Here, you can pick a default printer, change the time and date settings, fiddle with the netbook's screen saver preferences, and so on.

Next to the three menus are three icons of a globe, an envelope, and a question mark. These are shortcuts to the Firefox Web browser, Ubuntu's built-in Help, and the Evolution email program, respectively.

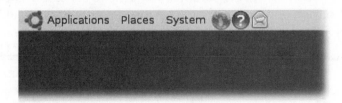

Tip You can easily add or remove panel icons—right-click a program icon to *remove* it from the panel. If you're in the Applications menu, right-click and choose the option to *add* it to the panel.

On the right side of the screen, Ubuntu's menu bar displays the name of who's logged onto the netbook (that would probably be you), plus a few icons for:

- **Network.** If you're on a wireless network, the current signal strength is displayed in cellphone-like bars. A small icon of two computers means you have a wired connection.

- **Battery.** Click the battery icon to see the amount of time left on your current charge. There's also a menu option for Suspend, which puts the netbook to sleep. (Press the Power button to wake it up again.)

- **Sound.** Volume controls and a Mute option are under this speaker-shaped icon.

- **Date and Time.** The netbook's calendar day and clock are clearly visible in the menu bar. Click the date to get a mini-calendar of the whole month, a graphic showing which areas of the world are currently in day-light or darkness, and a chance to edit your clock preferences. Right-click the Date and Time menu to copy the current date or time (to paste into a docu-ment), adjust the preferences, or stop displaying the date and time.

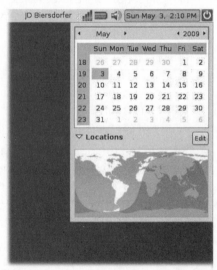

- **Shut Down.** Click the Shut Down icon in the top-right corner of the menu bar to turn the net-book off, log out, change users, lock the screen, restart the netbook, or put it to sleep. See page 85 for more on this particular menu.

If your netbook is automatically set to check for software updates, an addi-tional icon may appear in the menu bar just to the left of your name. When it's time to check for updates, you usually see an exclamation point inside a yellow alert triangle. Right-click it to see your update options. Chapter 12 has more on updating and maintaining your Linux netbook.

Applications Menu: All Your Programs

One of the reasons the Ubuntu version of Linux is so popular is because you not only get a fast, flexible operating system, you get a ton of useful programs with it. Having a spreadsheet program, an image-editing application, and a handy electronic dictionary right there is a comforting sight indeed. Sure, you get a lot of that stuff—or trial versions of it, anyway—when you buy a new Mac or Windows machine, but with Ubuntu, you get it all for *free*.

As one would expect, all of these programs are kept under the Applications menu in the upper-left corner. The menu contains several categories of programs:

- **Accessories.** Here you have lots of helpful little programs for those moments when you need to do math or find an umlaut on the keyboard. Some of the applications here include Calculator, Character Map, Dictionary, Disk Usage Analyzer, and Text Editor, all of which are self-explanatory. Wonkier applications include Manage Print Jobs, Password and Encryption Keys, Take Screenshot, and Terminal. (Don't worry, Terminal here isn't referring to the health of your netbook—it's just the name of the command-line program that comes with Linux.)

- **Education.** Ubuntu has whole editions designed for schools, and the Education menu has several learning programs on board. Some of these include Kanagram (an anagram game), programs for learning math and vocabulary, and the stunning Stellarim, a full-screen astronomy application for viewing the night skies.

- **Games.** No computer system is complete without a collection of video games. Ubuntu includes golf, marbles, and a penguin racing game.

- **Graphics.** Programs devoted to managing your digital photos, image editing, and creating your own graphics are found here. The F-Spot Photo Manager and the GIMP Image Editor (both discussed in Chapter 9) let you organize and fine-tune pictures, while the XSane Image Scanner can import new images from a connected scanner. OpenOffice.org's drawing program is also here for anyone wanting to whip up come computer-generated artwork.

- **Internet.** Online apps abound on this menu. You'll find the usual suspects—web browsing, email, and instant-messaging—in Mozilla's Firefox browser (page 151), the Evolution Mail program (page 139), and Pidgin Internet Messenger (page 201). Other programs that let you reach out and communicate include the Ekiga Softphone Internet telephone and videoconferencing program, and the Remote Desktop Viewer for connecting to other Ubuntu machines.

- **Office.** When it's time to stop playing games and goofing off on the Internet, the more business-like programs live under this menu. The word processing, spreadsheet, and presentation programs in the OpenOffice.org suite (page 171) live here, as does the Adobe Reader software for reading PDF files, and the calendar component of the Evolution Mail program.

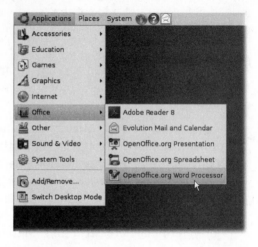

- **Sound & Video.** Ubuntu includes programs for converting audio tracks and burning CDs, which may not be useful if your netbook doesn't have an external disc drive. However, you can watch and play video and audio files downloaded from the Internet with the Movie Player and Rhythmbox Music Player. The Sound Recorder program lets you import or record your own audio.

- **System Tools.** Depending on which version of Ubuntu you have and how you have it configured, this menu may be empty or full. If it's empty, you can add programs like the Configuration Editor by choosing System→Main Menu→System Tools and turning on the checkboxes for the system utility programs you want to see.

At the bottom of the Applications menu are two options for customizing the menu. The first is Add/Remove, which lets you download and install new games and programs from online software archives; the next section has the details. The last item on the menu is Switch Desktop Mode, explained back on page 63.

> **Tip** Hate having to go up to the menu to get the programs you use all the time? You can drag icons (which Ubuntu calls *launchers*) from the menus and drop them on the Linux desktop to create clickable shortcuts. You can also right-click a program icon in the menu and choose either "Add this launcher to panel" to stick a shortcut icon in the menu-bar panel at the top of the screen or "Add this launcher to desktop" to make a desktop icon.

Adding and Removing Programs

As you can see, Ubuntu Linux comes with preinstalled programs for everything you need to browse the Web, send and receive email messages, write documents, create spreadsheets, view pictures, and play digital audio and video. But there's a whole universe of software out there and you may want *more*.

Installing software for Linux can be tricky for beginners. This section shows you the easy way to install software on your Ubuntu netbook by tapping into program collections that live on the Internet. Make sure you have an Internet connection, and then:

1. Choose Applications→Add/Remove.

   A progress bar pops up to scan for software in the online Ubuntu repositories, and then the Add/Remove Applications window appears.

2. On the left side, choose a program category, like Games or Sound & Video.

   A list of available programs in that category pops up in the top part of the window. Use the Show pop-up menu to see a list of all available applications, or winnow the list down to all open-source applications, all supported applications, or all third-party applications. You can also see a list of what applications are already installed.

3. Turn on the checkboxes next to the programs you want to install.

   Each program entry has a brief description of what it does and a star rating showing its popularity among Ubuntu fans.

4. Click the Apply Changes button.

   A box asks if you're sure.

5. Type your administrator password.

   Type the password you picked when you were setting up the netbook for the first time.

6. Wait as Linux installs the software.

   Linux downloads the software and installs it on your netbook. A final box asks if you want to add or remove more applications or close the box.

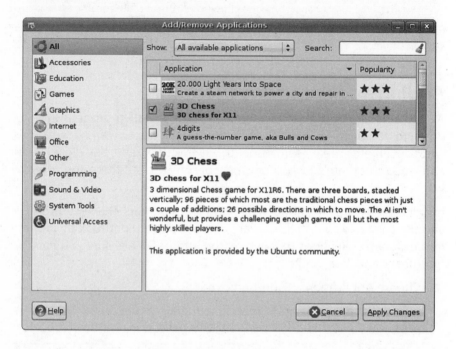

Repeat steps 2–6 to add more programs. If you choose Close, the Add/Remove Applications window goes away and you can go find your new program under the Applications menu in the same category you found it online (Games, Sound & Vision, or whatever).

There are a few other ways to install software, and some of them are rather complicated, involving **package manager** programs (to corral all the little pieces of an application), typed commands, and other things that contribute to Linux's lingering geeky reputation. Ubuntu also includes the Synaptic Package Manager (page 82), another program for installing programs that works much the same as the Add/Remove Applications option. Synaptic is a little more versatile and is often better for clearing old programs off your drive (page 292).

Removing software

If you want to clean up your Applications menu and get some space back on your netbook's drive, you can remove programs in almost the same way you install programs. Just choose Applications→Add/Remove. In the Add/Remove Applications box's Show pop-up menu, choose "Installed applications only." Turn off the checkboxes next to the programs you don't want anymore before clicking the Apply Changes button. You must confirm your decision and type your administrator password again, but then the unwanted apps are safely removed from your system.

Installing software from a disc

You'll find most Ubuntu-friendly programs come from either the Web or an online repository, but it's possible to install additional programs from a disc, like an Ubuntu installation CD, if you have a CD drive connected to the netbook. Pop in the disc, and then choose System→Administration→Software Sources. Click the Third-Party Software tab. At the bottom of the window, click Add CD-ROM so the system can see which programs from the disc you want to install.

Places Menu: Organizing and Finding Files

If you're looking for a file, the Places menu is a good place to start looking. Here, you have a tidy list of folders and other locations on your netbook (including the Desktop). You can peek into a place just by selecting one of them from the menu. Need a text file? Try choosing Places→Documents.

Your Home folder, the place where all the files associated with your user account live on the netbook, is another good place to look, although it can be rather large depending on what you have on there. To go Home, just choose Places→Home folder.

External drives, USB keychain drives, and connected file servers also show up in the Places menu.

But when you open one of these places, you get a special type of window: the Nautilus File Browser, which helps navigate your way around Ubuntu. The file browser, sort of a cross between a web browser window and Windows Explorer, has its own distinct parts.

1. **Menu Bar.** Six options are listed here:

   — **File** lets you open and close new windows, create new folders or documents in the current window, empty the Trash, or view a file's properties.

   — **Edit** offers cut, copy, and paste functions. It also lets you select some or all files on view, duplicate files, and control the look and feel of the file browser (under Preferences).

   — **View** contains all the controls for adding or removing elements on the file browser, the main toolbar, or side pane. You can also zoom in or out, or choose to see files as icons or in list form.

   — **Go** is a set of navigational options that let you step back through previous open folder windows or jump to specific locations like your Home user folder or recently used folders. Choose "Search for Files" if you're on the hunt for a certain file.

   — **Bookmarks** is a nifty menu with a command to add a bookmark for a specific folder to the file browser—making it easy to jump back there quickly instead of burrowing down through layers of folders. Saved bookmarked locations live here, too.

   — **Help** contains the Nautilus user guide.

2. **Toolbar.** Much like the buttons on a web browser (page 152), the Back and Forward buttons on this toolbar let you retreat or advance through folders you've visited, or use the Up button to pop back to the previous folder level. Stop halts the window's contents from loading and Reload refreshes the view. The Home, Computer, and Search buttons are shortcuts to those screens.

3. **Location Bar.** The Location bar is just below the main toolbar, and it shows you where you are in the file system. You can choose to see these coordinates represented as a traditional computer file path or as a series of icons that you can click to change your current location. Controls for increasing or decreasing the size of the icons in the window—and a pop-up menu where you can choose between looking at icons or looking at a list of files in the main window—are on the right.

4. **Side Pane.** The panel on the left side of the window lets you see your netbook's contents in a number of ways, including a vertical tree view that shows which folders are inside other folders. Or you can view files by place (page 73). You can also see a history of your recent travels through folders or get information about selected ones, like the number of items in that folder and when it was last modified.

5. **Main Window.** This big central part of the file browser window displays the contents of a selected folder.

6. **Status Bar.** The strip at the bottom of the Nautilus window shows the number of items in the selected place or folder, and also displays the amount of space left on the netbook's drive.

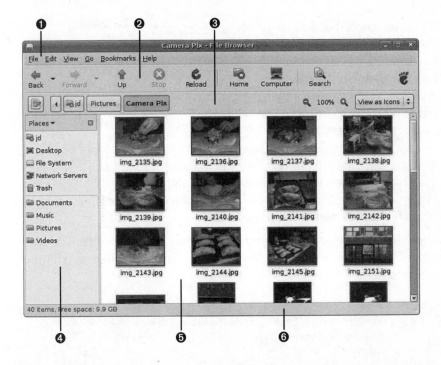

Tip The Places menu also lets you see what's on the netbook (page xx). Need to connect to a file server on a home or office network? Chose Places→Connect to Server.

Searching for Files

If you've browsed files until you're cross-eyed with Nautilus and still can't find what you're looking for, it's time to call in the expert: Ubuntu's Search feature. You can get to it a couple of different ways:

- Choose Places→Search for Files.

- To look inside a huge folder of files, like Pictures, click the Search button at the top of the Nautilus browser window.

Either way, you'll see a search box where you can type the name of the file you're looking for.

If you are using the "Search for Files" menu command, you have more options for narrowing down the quest. In addition to the name (or part of the file's name), you can instruct the system to look in a certain folder. Click the flippy triangle next to "Select more options," and you can type a bit of text that the document might contain. Other searchable options include the date you think the file might have been last modified and the size of the file—helpful if you've misplaced a giant video file somewhere on your netbook.

Click the Find button when you're done filling in fields. The Search program hunts through the system and brings back any files matching your search criteria.

 Tip If you can't find the file you were just using the other day, try looking in Places→Recent Documents to see a list of items that were open in the not-too-distant past.

System Menu: Preferences and More

The System menu in the top panel contains two major submenus and links to more information about the system software installed on the netbook, namely the Gnome desktop and Ubuntu itself. If you're interested in the free software movement, checking out these menu items is definitely worth a look.

But Preferences and Administration are the two items that you'll use most of the time. The exact items in each menu depend on the netbook model and what's installed on it, but this section will give you a rough idea of what to expect.

Preferences

The items in this menu are a bit like Windows' Control Panel or Mac OS X's System Preferences. You go here when you want to do things like adjust the netbook's trackpad for a left-handed user or change the color scheme of Ubuntu's windows.

- **About Me.** This section contains a virtual address card where you type your personal contact info. There's also a button to click if you want to change your password.

- **Airplane Mode.** As the name implies, go here when the cabin crew tells you to turn off your electronic devices. Just type your password to turn off the Bluetooth and WiFi radios.

- **Appearance.** Personalize your netbook's look by changing the Theme, Background, Fonts, and Interface settings. These settings are also helpful if you need to make the system type bigger or choose window colors that are easier on the eyes.

- **Assistive Technologies.** These settings help you make your netbook easier to use if you're visually or hearing impaired. You can, for example, create your own keyboard shortcuts and choose preferred applications for certain tasks. If you have a repetitive-motion injury like carpal tunnel syndrome, click the Keyboard Accessibility button and turn on the Typing Break tab to set up a locked screen timeout that enforces rest periods.

- **Bluetooth.** You'll find settings for wireless Bluetooth file transfers and other hardware connections like Bluetooth mice and headsets here.

- **Default Printer.** Lets you choose a primary printer on the network (or one that's directly connected to the computer) to handle your hard-copy needs.

- **Encryption and Keyrings.** If you scramble files with PGP (Pretty Good Privacy), the settings and password keyrings live here.

- **Keyboard.** Contains tabs where you can select a specific keyboard layout, adjust the sensitivity of the keys, or even allow cursor control from the keyboard.

- **Keyboard Shortcuts.** Lets you see (and learn!) your netbook's keyboard shortcuts. For example, you can close an open window by pressing Alt+F4 or hide all open windows and hop to the desktop with Ctrl+Alt+D. You can also assign clickable tasks to keystrokes of your choice.

- **Main Menu.** Change the programs you see listed in your netbook's menus—or make new menus of your own—in this box.

- **Mouse.** Adjust the mouse orientation for southpaws or right-handers, change the double-click speed, and see your touchpad settings here.

- **Network Proxy.** If you have to use a special configuration to get on the network, you can add or edit the settings for it here.

- **Palm OS Devices.** If you want to sync data from a Palm-based digital organizer or smartphone, you can configure them in this box.

- **Power Management.** Here's where you'll find the netbook's settings for how it behaves when running on electrical power or the battery. To save juice, for example, you can have the computer turn off the screen after 30 minutes of inactivity or put the machine to sleep if the battery power gets dangerously low.

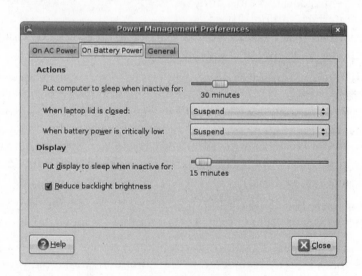

- **Preferred Applications.** Lets you pick which programs you want to handle different types of files. Want to use Mozilla Thunderbird instead of Evolution Mail as your email program? Choose it here.

- **Remote Desktop.** In this section, you can choose to let someone else on Ubuntu see what's on your netbook's desktop—or go see what's on theirs. Remote desktop is the way to go if you have another Ubuntu computer at home that you want to tap into from your netbook. Tech-support people may also ask you to let them work on your machine via remote desktop. See page 293 for more information.

- **Removable Drives and Media.** Here's where you control how the netbook behaves when you plug something into it, like a USB flash drive, portable music player, a digital camera, a printer, or just about any other piece of hardware. For example, if you don't want the Nautilus file browser to pop up when you plug in a USB drive (page 103), you can turn off that behavior.

- **SCIM Input Method.** The Smart Common Input Method preference lets you use non-Western characters from languages like Chinese, Japanese, and Korean.

- **Screen Resolution.** Lets you choose specific screen settings that some programs require.

- **Screensaver.** Although they once served to stop images on the desktop from burning permanently into the computer's screen, animated screen saver programs are now mainly just for fun and privacy. (There's a version of the old favorite Flying Toasters, for example.) You can also set the amount of time it takes until the screen saver kicks in.

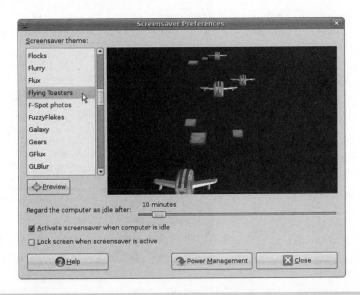

- **Sessions.** Mainly for Gnome desktop hounds, the Sessions tool lets you control which programs and services start up when you start up the netbook.

- **Sound.** Settings for all the computer's connected audio devices are here. You can also choose to hear system alert beeps and other warning noises for certain types of dialog boxes.

- **Sun Java 6 Plugin Control Panel/Java Policy Tool.** You can adjust the behavioral and security preferences for applications in Sun's Java programming language here.

- **Switch Desktop Mode.** Like the option at the bottom of the Applications menu, this option lets you change between the standard Ubuntu/ Gnome view of the system or the slick, simplified interface your netbook's maker may have provided.

- **Windows.** Settings for window behavior live here. For example, choose "Roll up" in the "Titlebar action" area to make window contents snap up and hide like a window shade when you double-click the window's title bar. There's also an option for selecting windows when the mouse passes over them.

Administration

When you need to adjust your network settings, add new users, change the computer's time and date, or make other system tweaks, visit the Administration menu. Linux doesn't like unauthorized people touching its stuff, so in order to get to many of these settings, you need to click the Unlock button and type your password.

- **Authorizations.** A tool for the system administrators, the Authorizations box lets you control who can change what on the computer and which actions need passwords.

- **Hardware Drivers.** This box contains a list of proprietary device drivers for added hardware like WiFi radios and LCD screens. Unlike open-source software, proprietary drivers are controlled by the people who make the hardware.

- **Hardware Testing.** Ubuntu maintains its own hardware database, and you can contribute to it by running the Hardware Testing program here. You run various tests to prove your hardware works (or doesn't work) with Ubuntu, and then upload the information to the Launch-pad hardware database.

- **Language Support.** Lets you choose the language Ubuntu uses to display your menus and dialog boxes.

- **Login Window.** If you're security-minded, you can choose to have the netbook ask you for your user name and password each time you turn it on. You can also change the look of the login screen, and even change its welcome message.

- **Network Manager.** See the available wired or wireless network connections here, set up a VPN (virtual private network) connection with your office, and delete outdated network connections you never use anymore (like the one from that conference last month).

- **Network Settings.** In these settings, you can specify *how* your netbook connects to the Internet—with or without wires. Click the Unlock button and type your password to adjust the settings for the types of networks you connect to. You can choose to have the netbook automatically discover available wireless networks or restrict it to a specific one.

- **Network Tools.** This box is a Swiss Army knife of programs to test and troubleshoot network connections.

- **Printing.** Set up a new printer connection, add a network printer, or share a printer connection here.

- **Services.** A somewhat geeky menu that lets you activate little helper programs here, like computer activity logs. It's best not to dabble in the Services box without knowing *exactly* what you're doing, as accidentally shutting down the wrong services makes for a very unhappy netbook.

- **Software Sources.** This box lets you set how often your Ubuntu system checks back to the Ubuntu mothership for system updates, as well as which software repositories it gets its wares from.

- **Synaptic Package Manager.** Like the Add/Remove box in the Applications menu, the Synaptic Package Manager lets you search, add, and remove software on the netbook safely, although the Add/Remove option is simpler.

- **System Log.** A sort of up-to-the-minute diary of everything your netbook's operating system has done lately, the System Log is helpful for troubleshooting techies but may not make much sense to Linux newcomers.

- **System Monitor.** Visit this box if you want to know specifics about your netbook, like what version of Ubuntu you're using, how much memory is in the machine, the type of processor, and how much disk space is left. You can also see a list of processes, or running programs (and force an unresponsive application to quit), as well a graphic depiction of how hard your processor is working.

- **Time and Date.** Set your netbook's date, time, and time zone here, or choose to have the system clock set itself to an Internet time server like the one at Purdue University or Penn State.

- **Update Manager.** Select the Update Manager when you want to manually check for system software update and patches.

- **Users and Groups.** Here, you can add new user accounts to the netbook (or gather a certain set of accounts into a group with restricted powers to keep the system safe) and also change system passwords.

Seeing How Much Hard Drive Space Is Left

Ubuntu gives you a quick way to see how much space you have left on your netbook: In any Nautilus file browser window, look at the bottom-left corner. The amount of free space is listed right there.

You have a couple of additional ways to see what's left on your drive:

- In a Nautilus window, right-click any folder and choose Properties from the shortcut menu.

- Choose System→Administration→System Monitor and click the File Systems tab to see how much disk space has been used and how much is available. (A file system is the way files are named, stored, and organized on a hard drive. Here, it can also refer to the hard drive and its partitions—separate areas divided up within the hard drive—as well.)

- If you fancy yourself a command-line sort of person, choose Applications→Terminal for command-line fun. At the command-line prompt, type *df* and press Enter to see a list of used and available disk space. (To do major system-changing commands, you need to type the administrator password.)

 Tip If you don't see the Terminal program in your Applications→Accessories menu, you may need to add it using the steps on page xx.

Ubuntu also comes with an extremely helpful program called the Disk Usage Analyzer that not only scans your drive space, but shows you exactly what's taking up all that room. To use it, choose Applications→Accessories→Disk Usage Analyzer and click the Scan Filesystem button on the toolbar. (You can also scan your Home folder or another folder using the toolbar's other buttons.)

The information is displayed in a colorful, circular graphic of a disc divided into blocks. Wave the cursor over a block to see what it is and how much real estate it's taking up. If you see that applications you never use are taking up precious hard-drive space, the decision to remove them (page 73) becomes that much easier.

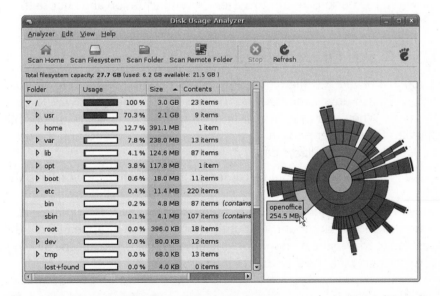

Backing Up Your Linux Netbook

If you live online in web-based mail and other applications while keeping relatively few files on your netbook's drive, backing up the computer may seem like a waste of time. But if you like to keep documents, photos, and music close to your Home folder (because you never know when the café WiFi will go down), backing it up is the sensible thing to do.

There are several ways and places to back up your stuff, each described below.

External Drive Backup

If the version of Ubuntu on your netbook doesn't include a back-up program in the Applications menu, you can snag one from the Ubuntu repository. Just choose Applications→Add/Remove. Using the software-installation steps described on page 71, search for backup and pick the program of your choice from the list of Ubuntu-friendly backup programs like Home User Backup. Once you install a backup

program, choose System→Administration, find it in the list of programs, and fire it up. You need to point the program to an external drive or another location where you plan to back up your files. If you need to restore files from the backup, return to System→Administration and choose the backup program's Restore component to retrieve the files.

USB Flash Drive Backup

If you just have a few files you want to back up, plugging in one of those tiny USB flash drives and copying the files to it is one quick way to back them up. When you plug in a flash drive to the netbook's USB port, the Nautilus file browser pops up to display the drive's contents and the drive itself appears in the Places pane.

In the Places pane, click your Documents folder (or wherever you keep the files you want to back up). Drag those files onto the USB drive's icon to copy them over. When you're done, right-click the drive's icon in the Places pane and choose Unmount. Wait until the drive's icon disappears from the desktop to make sure it's done copying any large files you may be moving. You can then yank the drive out of the netbook's USB port.

Online Backup

Renting space on someone else's server is another way to store your netbook's valuable files. Several online companies offer software and services especially for Linux backups. Some netbook makers, like Dell, even include online file storage and backup from sites like Box.net (*www.box.net*) to help add space to computers with small solid-state hard drives. Other Linux-friendly services include JungleDisk (*www.jungledisk.com*), which provides a network drive and backup software to get it there. Prices start at $2 a month, plus 15 cents per gigabyte stored. SpiderOak (*www.spideroak. com*) gives away 2 GB of online storage for free and will be happy to sell you more.

Closing Down Your Linux Netbook

When it's time to stop using the netbook for a while—when you're going to bed, getting on a plane, leaving for vacation without it—Ubuntu gives you several options for powering down. You can get to these options in a few different ways. Here are two of them:

- Choose System→Quit.

- Click the red Power icon in the top-right corner of the screen.

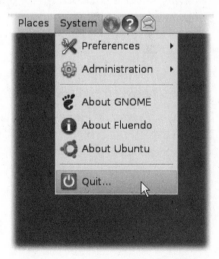

In either case, you'll see a box containing six different icons. The icons in the bottom row are the ones you want if you're ready to close down the netbook. Here's what they do:

- **Suspend.** Click this icon to put the netbook is a low-power "sleep" mode that turns off the screen and hard drive to consume much less power. Open files are still there when you press the Power key to wake up the netbook—unless there's been an electricity blackout that caused the computer to dump what was in its memory.

- **Restart.** Restart isn't really a power option. It shuts down all files and programs before turning the computer off and on again so you start out with fresh, clean memory. You might use Restart when trouble-shooting (page 279), or right after you install new software.

- **Shut Down.** This option closes all files and programs before turning the computer completely off.

 Some netbooks may also have a Hibernate option, which saves open files and programs before cutting off pretty much all the netbook's power.

But what about those icons in the top row of the Shut Down box? These three apply when you're sharing the computer with someone else. (Like Windows and Mac OS X, Linux lets you have multiple accounts on the same machine so all can have their own user names, passwords, and files.) Here's what they do:

- **Log Out.** When you are done using your account and want to make sure your files and settings are safe, choose Log Out to shut down your little corner of the netbook. This sends the machine back to its login screen without turning it off.

- **Lock Screen.** If you're not done using the netbook but need to step away, choose Lock Screen (or press Control+Alt+L on the keyboard) to password-protect your account. The netbook's screen saver descends and won't let anyone in without your password.

- **Switch User.** Lets you switch between netbook accounts, so you can quickly hand the machine over to your netbook-sharing buddy or jump between two accounts of your own.

Ubuntu is a versatile and ever-evolving system. If you want more information on the version you're using, click the question-mark-shaped Help icon in the top panel or visit *www.ubuntu.com/support*.

4 Connecting Devices to Your Netbook

Netbooks are built for portability. You grab yours and go—off to class, the coffee shop, the airport, wherever. But the tiny computer doesn't have to be just a lightweight way to browse the Web when you're out and about. As detailed in Chapter 1, most netbooks include USB ports, audio jacks, video connectors, and other places to plug in the same kind of hardware you use with a laptop or desktop computer.

Mice, printers, external monitors, music players, and USB drives—you can hook up just about any piece of hardware that works with a full-size machine. Attaching external devices is a bit more challenging on a computer that lacks a CD drive for installing driver software, but this chapter walks you through all of the steps. And since that netbook was meant for travel, you'll also find out what you need to take with you for comfortable computing no matter where you go.

Mice, Trackballs, and Tablets

Let's face it: That netbook's trackpad can feel a little small if you're using it for hours on end. Also, it may not be the most precise way to get around the screen if you're doing something like touching up digital photos or making art with a drawing program. Alternative *input devices*—mice, trackballs, and stylus-based tablets (like the ones Wacom makes for digital artists)—can ease the pain and give you more control over where you point on the screen.

Adding a Basic Mouse: The Easy Way

If you find yourself missing the mouse, there's no reason you can't add one to your netbook, as long as you have a spare USB port. The simplest (and cheapest) route is to plug in a regular ol' three-button USB mouse. With either Windows XP or Ubuntu Linux, it works right off the bat. You can point and click your way to netbook glory, and, in some cases, the scroll wheel works, too.

Adding a Mouse, Trackball, or Tablet

Fancier mice, trackballs, and tablets with programmable buttons are more complicated. Getting one of these to work correctly often involves installing the device's own *driver* software. The driver tells the operating system how to handle the special features of these devices—like the programmable buttons on a mouse.

On a Windows XP netbook, there are a few ways to get the hardware playing nicely together:

- If you have an external disc drive for your netbook, install the driver software from the CD that came with the mouse, trackball, or tablet, just as you would on any other computer.

- If you don't have a disc drive, take a stroll to the manufacturer's website. All device makers have them; check the packaging for the URL, but it's often something simple like *www.logitech.com*, *www.kensington.com*, or *www.wacom.com*. Check the Support area for a driver downloads page. You may have to click through a couple of screens and select your model number, but you'll eventually land on the download page for your device's driver. Just make sure you grab the one for your specific version of Windows XP. When the installer file finishes downloading, double-click it to install the driver software on the netbook.

- Using another computer, you may be able to copy installer files (usually a program called Setup.exe or something similar) from a CD onto a USB drive—and then connect the USB drive to the netbook to run the software. It may not work with all installers, though, as some are more complicated than others or need to be installed by CD for verification purposes.

On Linux, things can get a little more complicated since there are a lot of mice out there—and each one may have different needs. If you're buying a new mouse, check its specifications to see if it works on Linux.

Whether you're on the driver hunt for Windows or Linux machines, sites like *www.driverguide.com* and *www.softpedia.com* are great places to do a little research and maybe even pick up the software you need.

 Tip Other good sites to check for Linux hardware and information include Ubuntu's community-supported hardware page at *https://wiki.ubuntu.com/HardwareSupport* and the Linux-USB Device Overview page at *www.qbik.ch/usb/devices*.

One of the challenges of adding extra hardware to any Linux system is that there's a ton of mice, trackballs, and other input devices out there and the method for getting a particular one working with your netbook hardware and Ubuntu version can vary widely. In some cases, you have to do a bit of command-line work in the netbook's Terminal program (page 69). Still, there are plenty of instructions written by thoughtful people. Visit *www.missingmanuals.com/cds* for a roundup focused on the most popular makes and models.

 Tip Trying to get a Wacom pen and tablet working with your Ubuntu netbook? There's an entire open-source project devoted to the topic with helpful documentation at *http://linuxwacom.sourceforge.net*.

Adding a Bluetooth Mouse

Bluetooth—the wireless technology used to connect computers to hardware like mice, phones, and printers—is a feature of some netbook models. If your netbook has a Bluetooth chip, you can cut the cords.

To connect a Bluetooth-equipped netbook to a Bluetooth-equipped mouse or other gadget, you have to *pair* them. This process is sort of like introducing two friends at a party for the first time so they'll recognize each other every time they meet afterward.

Follow the instructions included with your mouse for putting it in pairing mode, which makes it visible to Bluetooth computers. Next, you have to help the netbook see and bond with the mouse.

Bluetooth in Windows XP

For Windows XP netbooks sporting a nifty Bluetooth radio under the hood:

1. Start the pairing by choosing Start→Control Panel→Bluetooth Devices (Classic view) or Start→Control Panel→Printers and Other Hardware→Bluetooth Devices (Category view).

   When the dialog box pops up, go to the Options tab.

2. Turn on the checkbox next to "Turn discovery on."

   This step lets the netbook *discover* (that is, notice) other Bluetooth devices within range of your netbook (usually 30 feet or less). While you're here, also turn on the checkboxes next to "Allow Bluetooth devices to connect to this computer" and "Alert me when a new Bluetooth device wants to connect" so your mouse can connect to the netbook. Click OK when finished.

 Tip If you want a taskbar shortcut to the Bluetooth settings, turn on the checkbox next to "Show the Bluetooth icon in the notification area" as well.

3. Click the Devices tab.

   After you've made sure the netbook can discover the mouse, you can add the mouse to the mix.

4. Click the Add button.

   When the Add Bluetooth Device Wizard pops up, turn on the checkbox next to "My device is set up and ready to be found." Click the Next button.

5. Select the mouse from the list of devices.

   Click the Next button to move on.

6. Type in the mouse's passkey.

   The passkey, which is included with the mouse's documentation, is its secret code that you need to share with the computer so the two can fully bond. Passkeys are often not too complicated (like *0000* or *1000*).

Once you type in the pass-key and the netbook accepts it, the computer and mouse are united in holy Bluetooth matrimony. If you want, you can also turn off the discovery mode on your way out of the wizard so no one else will discover your netbook when you're out and about.

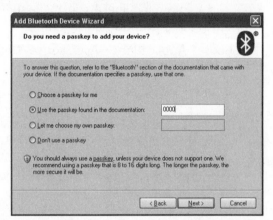

 Once you get the hang of pairing a Bluetooth mouse with your netbook, you can pair other Bluetooth-enabled hardware like mobile phones and printers to it as well by following the same steps.

Bluetooth in Ubuntu Linux

If you have an Ubuntu Linux netbook with a built-in Bluetooth radio, you're just a few steps away from your own wireless fun.

To pair up a Bluetooth mouse in Ubuntu, follow the mouse-maker's instructions for putting it into pairing mode and then:

1. In the top panel, right-click the Bluetooth icon and choose Preferences.

   The Bluetooth icon is at the right side of the top panel; it looks like a Viking rune version of the letter *B*.

2. Make sure the button next to "Visible and Connectable for Other Devices" is turned on. Click Close.

   This option means that other devices—like your mouse—can see the netbook.

3. Right-click the Bluetooth icon in the top panel and choose Browse Device.

   A box appears with a list of Bluetooth devices.

4. Select the mouse from the list and click Connect.

The mouse and the netbook begin to get to know each other.

5. When a window appears asking for a passkey, type in the one provided by the manufacturer and click OK.

Once you've provided the passkey, the mouse and netbook should be paired. However, if nothing happens, you may have to take the long way around: the command line. Again, make sure both the mouse and the netbook are in discover mode, and then:

1. Choose Applications→Accessories→Terminal. Type the following command:

```
sudo gedit /etc/default/bluetooth
```

 Note If you happen to already be using your powers of root, use this command instead:

```
gksu gedit /etc/default/bluetooth
```

A document opens in the text editor. It looks geeky, but brace yourself and look for a line that reads:

```
HIDD_ENABLED=0
```

And change the 0 to a 1 so that it looks like:

```
HIDD_ENABLED=1
```

Save the file.

2. In the top panel, right-click the Bluetooth icon and then choose Preferences.

On the line for Input Services, turn on the checkbox next to Running.

3. Click the Input Services line in the list.

An Input Devices section opens at the bottom of the box.

4. Click the Add button.

Choose the mouse in the Select Device list and click Connect.

5. Click the Enter Passkey button in the box that pops up.

The passkey is probably *0000*.

Once you type the passkey, the mouse and netbook should be paired. Close the Bluetooth preferences box and mouse away. If it doesn't work immediately, try rebooting the netbook.

 Note You may notice the word *root* in the command line when you use the Terminal program. No, it has nothing to do with trees or genealogy—root is the *superuser* account on any Linux system. Unlike other accounts on your netbook, the super-user has the power to change anything and everything on the system. Typing *sudo* before entering a command temporarily switches your user powers to root for just that one action.

Adjusting the Mouse

Want to fine-tune the mouse to adjust the double-click timing or con-figure it for a left-handed person? A quick trip to your netbook's mouse settings should take care of things. In Windows, choose Start→Control Panel→Mouse (in Classic view) or Start→Control Panel→Printers and Other Hardware→Mouse (in Category view) to get to the box with all your mouse-adjusting needs.

In Ubuntu, choose System→Preferences→Mouse to get to the settings.

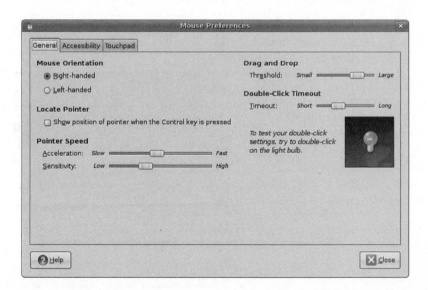

Connecting an External Monitor or TV

Let's face it: Netbook screens, even the larger ones, aren't all that big. And after staring at one all day, it can seem smaller and smaller by the minute. But if you have a spare external monitor or even a television and the right cables, you can connect the netbook to the big screen and stop squinting for a while.

As mentioned on page 18, most netbooks have a video port. This port can take a standard 15-pin VGA connection, which is the type of plug used on many external monitors and projectors. Connecting the monitor's cable to the netbook is the first step, but if your monitor or TV doesn't have a VGA connector, you can buy an adapter that bridges the gap. If your monitor has a DVI (digital video interface) connection, for example, get a VGA-to-DVI adapter.

Once you've connected the external monitor to the netbook, it's time to inform the operating system.

Connecting a Monitor in Windows XP

You tell Windows XP what you want to use for a monitor by editing the desktop settings.

1. Right-click the desktop and choose Properties from the shortcut menu. In the dialog box that opens, click the Settings tab.

   You'll see two rectangles: one representing your netbook screen and the other representing the external monitor.

2. Click Identify to have Windows assign a number to each monitor so you can tell which is which.

   For example, you might see a "1" on the rectangle for your netbook screen, and a "2" on the rectangle for your external monitor.

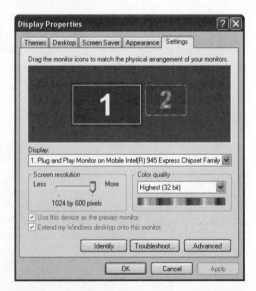

3. Now that you know which numbered monitor is which, click the menu under Display and choose between screens from the pop-up menu.

   You can also drag the screen icons into a new order that matches how the monitors are physically arranged on the desk.

4. Set your screen.

   If you just want to use the external monitor's screen right now, turn on the checkbox next to "Use this device as the primary monitor." If you want to use both monitors at the same time for a really expansive screen, turn on the box next to "Extend my Windows desktop to this monitor" and click OK.

Ubuntu Linux

If you bought a netbook with Ubuntu preinstalled, your manufacturer should have made sure that the video card can handle connecting an external monitor. In general, using multiple monitors in Ubuntu is notoriously unreliable, and with certain video cards you may have to do some serious tweaking to get the extra monitor working. If you're having problems for some reason, visit *www.missingmanuals.com/cds* for links to solutions for common video cards—or complain to your netbook's maker.

The following steps are how it's *supposed* to work:

1. Choose Applications→ Preferences→Screen Resolution.

   The Monitor Resolution Settings dialog box opens. If the Mirror Screens or Clone Screens checkbox is turned on, the dialog box shows one monitor called something like "Laptop 9."

2. Turn off this checkbox, and then drag the two monitor graphics to arrange them just as they are in front of you on the desk.

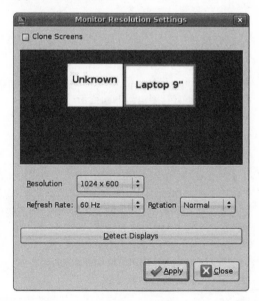

3. Adjust the screen resolution to that of the smaller screen. Click Apply.

   A warning box may appear to announce that the *xorg.conf* file will have to be changed. Click OK.

4. Log out and back into Ubuntu to see the changes take effect.

Setting Up a Printer

If you got your netbook to serve as your ultraportable window to online applications (page 175), you probably don't care too much about weighing yourself down with printed material. But there may be times when you do have to actually squeeze a piece of paper out of the machine—a report, a spreadsheet, or a PDF form to fill out and mail the old-fashioned way.

There are tons of printers out there, from inexpensive inkjets to pricey color laser machines. Although the parallel port used to rule the printer world, most printers these days come with USB connections, Ethernet ports, or both—just like your netbook. (The one thing the printer probably won't come with is a USB cable, which you have to purchase separately.)

This section shows you how to set up printers for both Windows XP and Linux. And since you may be on the go or on a wireless network, it also covers getting that netbook to see printers that aren't physically connected to it.

Adding a USB Printer in Windows XP

Most printers come with their own CDs for Windows XP that include the proper driver software and other utility programs—especially those high-falutin' models that also scan and copy as well as print. If you have an external disc drive attached to your netbook, install this software *before* you connect the printer. The installation program on the disc usually takes care of all your printer-adding needs for you.

If you don't have a disc drive, snag the drivers and installation software from the Support area of the manufacturer's website, as described back on page 14. If fact, installing the software from the Web usually means you're getting the absolute latest version of the drivers for your computer, because who knows how long that CD has been sitting around since it was made.

Adding a printer manually

If Windows XP doesn't recognize the printer or you can't find a download-able installation program for it from the manufacturer, there's always the manual way:

1. Choose Start→Control Panel→Printers and Other Hardware→Add a Printer (Category view) or Start→Control Panel→Printers and Other Faxes and then, in the task pane, click Add a Printer.

   The Add a Printer Wizard appears.

2. Click the option for "Local printer attached to this computer."

   If your printer is advertised as a Plug-and-Play model, turn on the checkbox next to "Automatically detect my Plug-and-Play printer" to have Windows try to find the printer on its own.

3. If Windows doesn't recognize the printer, click Next.

   This button starts you on your journey with the wizard. Select a printer port (Windows XP recommends one in the box) and click the Next button.

4. On the next screen, choose your printer's make and model.

   Click the Windows Update button if you want Windows to download what it finds for your printer. If you downloaded a driver, click the Have Disk button and direct the wizard to the files. Click Next.

5. On the wizard's final screen, name the printer and add other info.

   You can also tell Windows if this will be your default printer, and also if you plan to share it with other network users. You can also print a test page to make sure it all works.

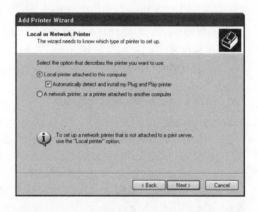

 If you have problems printing the test page, click the Troubleshoot button and walk through the Troubleshooting Wizard. (In case you haven't noticed, Windows XP has more wizards than a *Harry Potter* book.)

Adding a Network Printer in Windows XP

A printer can be part of a network in several different ways. It can be connected to a computer on the network and shared with the rest of the network. Or, the printer can be connected directly to the network, which actually makes it harder for your netbook to find it.

Adding a shared printer

If a computer on your home network is sharing a printer with your other computers, here's how to access it with your netbook:

1. Choose Start→Control Panel→Printers and Other Hardware→Add a Printer (Category view) or Start→Control Panel→Printers and Other Faxes and click Add a Printer from the task pane.

   The Add a Printer Wizard appears, just as it does when you want to add a local printer.

2. Click the button next to "A network printer, or a printer attached to another computer" and click Next.

3. Click "Browse for a printer."

   When you click the Next button, Windows XP searches for a shared printer on your network.

4. Select the shared printer and click Next.

   Windows asks if you're sure you want to connect to this printer. If you click Yes, the program installs the printer driver for you. Click Finish to wrap things up.

Adding a networked printer

Some printers are on the network through print servers or wireless devices like Apple's AirPort Express, which provides a handy USB port to give a regular ol' USB printer the powers of networking. To connect to one of these types of printers, you need to first get the printer's Internet Protocol (IP) address. An IP address is a series of numbers like 192.161.204.226 and is used to identify a device on a network. Here are some ways to find the printer's address:

- In office situations, the IP address is often taped to the side of the printer, or listed when you print out a test or configuration page.

- On AirPort networks, you can see the printer's IP address by using the AirPort Admin Utility program that came with the AirPort router.

- Try choosing Start→All Programs→Accessories→Command Prompt. Type in *net view* and press Enter. If the printer is visible, type *ping [name of printer]* and press Enter to see the IP address.

Once you have the printer's IP address, follow these dance steps:

1. Choose Start→Control Panel→Printers and Other Hardware→Add a Printer (Category view) or Start→Control Panel→Printers and Other Faxes and, in the task pane, click Add a Printer.

   The Add Printer Wizard appears. Click the Next button to get started.

2. On the next screen, click the button for "Local printer attached to this computer" and turn off the checkbox for "Automatically detect and install my Plug and Play printer." Click Next.

3. On the Select a Printer Port screen, choose "Create a new port."

   In the pop-up menu, choose Standard TCP/ IP Port and then click Next. Then click the fol- lowing Next button to start off the Welcome to the Add Standard TCP/IP Printer Port Wizard.

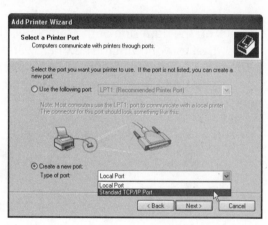

4. In the Add Port box, type the printer's IP address, which you collected earlier. Just type it in the first box, the one called "Printer Name or IP Address"; the Port Name box will fill in by itself. Click Next.

   Windows XP hunts around the network, finds the printer at the ad- dress you gave it, and adds it.

5. Click Finish to leave that wizard and go back to the one where you pick the printer driver and provide other information as described in steps 4 and 5 on page 97.

   Once you've added the printer, it's there, and you shouldn't have to do all these steps ever again.

Adding a USB Printer in Ubuntu Linux

Ubuntu automatically recognizes most standard printers when you plug the printer's cable into the computer's USB port.

Adding a USB printer automatically

If Ubuntu recognizes your printer right off the bat, a small printer icon appears on the right side of the top panel. The system automatically configures itself to work with the new hardware and pops up a message when it's done. If Ubuntu can't find the exact driver for your printer model, it suggests a substitute. To see if that actually works, take the suggestion and print a test page to see if it looks normal. If it does, you're all set.

Adding a USB printer manually

If the easy road to Printerville doesn't work for you—or you want to have some control over the setup—you can also configure a printer manually:

1. Choose System→Administration→Printing. In the Printer Configuration box that opens, click the New Printer button.

   The Add a Printer Wizard starts up and searches for your connected printer. If yours is listed in the pane on the left side of the window, select it and click the Forward button. The system now searches for the correct printer driver.

2. Select the printer manufacturer and model number.

   The system usually selects the correct manufacturer for you, but you can choose another if needed. Choose the model number for your printer (listed on the top or front of the device) and click Forward. (If it's a really old or obscure model and you happen to have a PPD—Post-Script Printer Description—file for it, you can also copy that file onto the netbook and then select it in this screen.)

3. Fill in the name and location of the printer (if you want to) on the last screen.

   In case you have multiple printers or plan to make the printer available for network sharing, you can give this newly added printer a name (like "HP 1012") and location ("Basement office"). Click the Apply button when finished. The freshly added printer now appears in the printers list.

4. Print a test page.

   Just to make sure the selected printer driver and your netbook are all good to go, select the new printer in the list and click the Print Test Page button. If the page (a series of grayscale boxes) looks funky, try another printer driver.

If you're still having printer woes, there are several online resources to consult for reference and driver information, including *https://help.ubuntu. com/community/Printers* and *www.linuxfoundation.org/en/OpenPrinting*.

 Tip Ubuntu also lets you save web pages and other open documents as PDF files for later printing. With the web page or document open, choose File→Print and then select PDF from the list of printers. After you click Print, Ubuntu saves the file in Home→PDF, where you can read it, print it, or delete it whenever you want.

Adding a Network Printer in Ubuntu Linux

If you're on a home network with Windows machines, and one of them has a shared a printer, you can use it with your Linux netbook—unless the printer is incorrectly configured. If you see the shared printer available on your netbook without having to do anything, Ubuntu may have even sensed it on the network and automatically set it up for you. In that case, start printing!

But if you see no shared printer and you know it's out there, it's time for some manual labor:

1. Choose System→Administration→Printing.

   This command brings up the Printer Configuration box.

2. In the Printer Configuration window, click the New Printer button to start up the Add a Printer Wizard.

   Ubuntu searches for your connected printer. If it doesn't find one, the New Printer window appears.

3. Select the option for "Windows Printer via SAMBA." Then, at top right, click Browse.

   The SMB Browser box pops up.

4. Select the shared printer you want to use and click OK.

   Click the Verify button to make sure you're allowed to use the printer. If you get rejected, you may need a user name and password. Ask whoever set the printer up for this information, and then turn on the Authentication Required checkbox and type the user name and password.

Now you just have to select the printer driver and all that other stuff in steps 2–4 on page 101.

If you have a printer on the network shared by way of a print server or its own connection with an Apple AirPort base station or other router, you can connect to it via its IP address; page 98 has tips for finding it.

 Note Many laser printers made by Brother use the LPD (Line Printer Daemon) protocol for printing. The New Printer box in Ubuntu offers a LPD/LPR Host or Printer option and Brother itself has a page of Linux setup and troubleshooting tips for its assorted printing and scanning devices at *http://solutions.brother.com/linux/en_us*.

Once you have the IP address written down:

1. Choose System→Administration→Printing. When the Printer Configuration box pops up, click the New Printer button to start up the Add Printer Wizard.

   Ubuntu searches for your connected printer. When it doesn't find one, the New Printer window appears.

2. Select the option for AppSocket/HP Jet Direct. In the Host box, type the printer's IP address.

   The default Host number—probably 9100—should work fine. Click Forward when you're done.

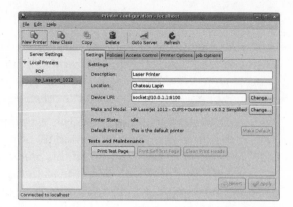

Once the netbook finds the printer, you can select the printer driver and related options in steps 2–4 back on page 101.

Storing Data on External Drives

Most external drives are USB-based these days, which means it's easy to connect them to your Windows XP or Linux netbook. In most cases, you just plug them in and the system recognizes the drive. This feature works for both the small, pocket-sized flash-memory drives as well as the larger, hard-drive based USB drives meant for system backups (page 54, Windows; page 84, Linux).

Windows XP

Adding an external drive in Windows is almost as easy as plugging a lamp into an electrical outlet. Connect the drive to a USB port on the netbook and wait for it to go through the Found New Hardware dance and show up in My Computer (page 53).

You can then drag files onto the drive's icon to copy them over. You can also right-click files and folders and choose Send To→[Name of Drive] to copy them to the external drive.

When it comes time to disconnect the external drive, however, do it safely, by clicking the Safely Remove Hardware icon in the taskbar. Simply yanking the drive's USB connection from the netbook can lead to scrambled files and an unhappy external drive.

Ubuntu Linux

Make sure the drive you're using is formatted with the FAT32 file system so Linux can read it. Most drives are, which means you can also connect the same drive to Windows or Mac computers to transfer large files between machines or back up each one to the drive.

Plug the drive into the netbook. The Nautilus file browser pops up to display the drive's contents in a window of its own. (If you close the file browser window or have turned off this preference, you can find the drive in Places→[Name of Drive].) With the Nautilus file browser open, you can navigate through your netbook's drive and drag files onto the external drive's icon to copy them.

You can also use those time-honored copy-and-paste moves to transfer files. Just right-click a file or folder you want to copy to the drive and choose Copy from the shortcut menu. Jump to the external drive by choosing Places→[Name of Drive] or by navigating there in Nautilus; right-click and choose Paste to deposit a backup of the item to the external drive.

When you're ready to disconnect the drive, right-click its icon in the Nautilus window or on the desktop and choose Unmount Drive from the shortcut menu before you unplug the USB connection.

 Tip If you intend to use the USB hard drive only with your Linux netbook, reformatting it from FAT32 to the ext3 file system will make it faster. One way to reformat the drive—and even divide it up into different partitions (page xx)—is to use GParted, or the Gnome Partition Editor program. GParted is available in the Ubuntu software repository; just search for it with Applications→Add/Remove and install it. When it's up and running, GParted displays all the drives you can partition or reformat. Make *sure* you've selected the external USB drive and choose Partition→Reformat→ext3 to reformat it. You can learn all about using GParted at *http://gparted.sourceforge.net*.

Connecting an External CD/DVD Drive

If you plan to install a whole bunch of software from discs or plan to burn your own CDs, think about buying an external CD/DVD drive. If you didn't buy the drive when you bought your netbook (page 16), buying it from same manufacturer helps ensure compatibility with your system. If the company doesn't sell one as an accessory, just shop for one that lists your operating system in its specifications. (Most USB disc drives usually just *work*, but Amazon sells several external models aimed specifically at netbook owners.)

Both Windows XP and Ubuntu Linux should be able to recognize modern external USB-based disc drives when you plug them in—most external drives are designed to work Plug-and-Play with Windows anyway and often come with their own slick disc-creation software. While these programs generally don't run on Linux, Ubuntu is fairly good at automatically recognizing USB hardware and comes with its own CD/DVD Creator program (page 70) to handle the burning chores.

 Tip External drives have been around for years. Plugging in an ancient USB 1.1 drive that you've had in the back of the closet may or may not work, but it never hurts to try.

Capturing Images: Connecting Scanners and Webcams

Digital photos and videos have become a part of everyday life for the average computer user, and there's no reason to miss out just because you have a netbook. If your camera or scanner is USB-based, you can probably get it working on the little laptop. And many netbooks even include their own built-in webcams for videochat on the go.

Adding a Scanner in Windows XP

Installing a scanner in a Windows XP netbook is much like installing a printer (page 96). In fact, with all the multifunction (and cheap) printer-scanner-copiers out there, you may have already done the installing when you hooked up the printer. In any case, it's basically a two-step process:

1. Find the driver from the CD and connected external disc drive or download it from the manufacturer's site on the Web.

2. Connect the hardware so Windows can find it. Review the steps on page 97 for manually installing a printer if you have trouble installing a scanner.

Once you get the scanner connected to the netbook and the photo or document you want to scan on the glass, you can use either the scanner's own software or Windows'. If you want to go the Windows way, here's how:

1. Choose Start→All Programs→Accessories→Scanner and Camera Wizard.

   Click Next to move things along.

2. In the Scanning Preferences window, choose the type of picture you're trying to scan.

Here, you can select a color picture, a gray scale photo, a black-and-white photo (which is also the setting for B&W text documents), or Custom Settings if you want more control over the final product.

3. Click the Custom Settings button.

In this box, you can adjust the scanning resolution, brightness, and other factors.

4. Click the Preview button.

Before you commit to the full-on scan, you can see a small thumbnail preview of what you're scanning. If you want to crop out part of the photo or scan a specific part of it, drag the handles on the corners of the dotted line around the preview image to make those adjustments. Click Next.

5. Name the scanned image, pick a file format to save it in, and choose where to save it.

If you are scanning photographs to email or post on the Web, choose the JPEG format, which gives you a nice compact file size. Click Next.

6. The scanner scans the photo or document.

After you scan, a Windows dialog box gives you a chance to publish the pictures to the Web, order prints, or quit.

Adding a Scanner in Ubuntu Linux

Remember the XSane program back on page 69 during the Ubuntu Linux menu tour? It comes into play here as your netbook's scanner helper—unless you installed something else when setting up the scanner.

 The S-A-N-E in XSane stands for Scanner Access Now Easy.

XSane is a good place to start, though. Connect the scanner (or multifunction printer) to the netbook, put a photo or document on the scanner's glass bed, and then fire up XSane.

1. Choose Applications→Graphics→XSane Image Scanner.

   The XSane program opens and attempts to find your connected scanner. Some scanners automatically work with XSane, some don't. Check at *www.sane-project.org/sane-supported-devices.html*. If XSane can't see your scanner, you get a "no devices available" message. Once XSane recognizes your scanner, a whole bunch of windows pop up for your scanning and adjustment pleasure.

2. In the Preview window, click the Acquire Preview button.

   The scanner captures a quick preview of the item you want to scan.

3. Select the part of the image you want to scan by moving the dotted line around the live area.

   In the options on the left side, you can choose your scan settings.

4. Choose your desired resolution, file size, and color settings.

   The Color pop-up menu lets you choose gray scale, black-and-white line art, or artsy halftones. You can also specify a file name and place to save the final scan.

5. Click the Scan button.

   The scanner goes to work, popping up the finished image in a Viewer window. XSane saves the scanned image to your selected location.

XSane lets you do some basic image-tweaking here, but you can really spruce up your photos with a proper photo-editing program (Chapter 9).

Tip You may be able jumpstart XSane into seeing your scanner by dipping into Terminal (page xx). It's not a sure shot to scanning glory, but if you want to give it that
ol' college try, choose Applications→Graphics→Terminal. When the command-line
window pops up, type:

```
sudo xsane
```

Press Enter. If XSane finds the scanner (and complains about the dangers of running it this way as root), it should start up and let you get down to business.

Adding a Webcam to Windows XP

Many Windows laptops sold these days—including netbooks—come with
a tiny webcam embedded in the computer's lid, right over the top of the
LCD screen. It's a wonderful thing because (a) you don't have to *buy* extra
equipment and (b) you don't have to *install* extra equipment.

All you really need to do
here is fire up software that
uses the webcam and give it
a go. For example, choose
Start→All Programs→
Accessories→Scanner and
Camera Wizard. Take a close
look—that's you in the little
video window. Instant-
messaging programs like
AIM (page 200) that allow
video chat are also a good
way to take that webcam
for a spin.

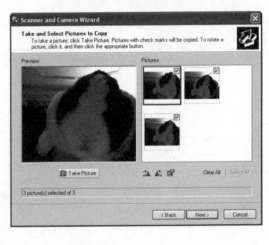

If you need to install an external webcam, you have your pick of models, as
the majority of them out there are USB-based and designed to work with
Windows. If you need to install driver software for the webcam and don't
have an external disc drive, try any of the driveless software installation
tips on page 46.

Adding a Webcam to Linux

If your Linux netbook came with a built-in webcam—look for the little circular lens peeping out above the screen—you don't have to worry about adding any new hardware. You can test our your camera with whatever webcam
program the manufacturer included (Applications→Internet→Dell Video
Chat, for example). Just fire up the program and let it find the webcam.

You can also try out the netbook's integrated web-cam with programs that come with Ubuntu like Applications→Internet→Ekiga Softphone, or install a different one from the Ubuntu software repositories (page 71). Some of these programs include VLC, xawtv, and the aptly named Cheese.

If your netbook didn't include a webcam, adding an external USB-based model isn't too difficult, thanks to a bit of webcam driver software included on Ubuntu. This software is called the Universal Video Class, so when shopping for a webcam to add to your netbook, getting one that's listed as *UVC-compatible* will save you a lot of headaches. Logitech (*www.logitech.com*) makes several Linux-compatible webcams, and you can find a list of others at *http://linux-uvc.berlios.de/*. Once you have a compatible camera, plug it into the USB port and Ubuntu will recognize it.

 Tip If the netbook and webcam aren't playing nicely together, you can find additional help at *https://help.ubuntu.com/community/Webcam* and *www.linuxwebcam.org*.

Listening to Music: MP3 Players and External Speakers

Along with pictures and video, your netbook can also play digital music files. Both Windows XP and Linux include at least one music-playing program and it's easy to get more. And if you have a portable music player like an iPod, Zune, or Creative Zen, you can even use it with your netbook. And thanks to the headphone jack, you can play your music privately with headphones or publicly with external speakers. Chapter 9 has more on netbook music management, but this section explains what types of players you can use with a netbook and where to find music.

MP3 Players with Windows XP

All major brands of portable digital music players work with Windows XP, so if you're thinking about buying one, the sky's the limit. Pretty much all of them connect with a USB cable and use software like Windows Media Player (included with Windows XP) or Apple's iTunes program (free to download at *www.apple.com/itunes*).

 Tip If you need to install custom software from a disc, say from a Phillips Electronics player or similar brand and don't have a CD drive, go to another computer and copy the CD's contents onto a USB drive. Then connect the USB drive to the netbook and run the software's setup program from there.

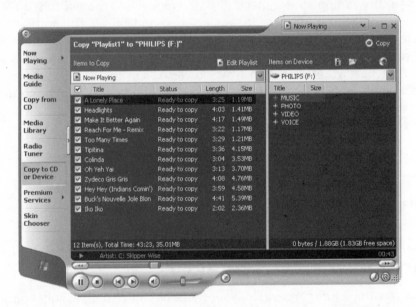

Depending on the player you have, you may have to load music onto it with a special program—like iTunes for an iPod. Some simple MP3 players let you add songs by dragging them from the computer into the player's Music folder.

In the early days before legal online music stores really took off in 2003, most people got music on their players by either *ripping* (that is, converting) songs from compact discs or illegally downloading MP3 files. If you don't have a CD drive (or a friend who's willing to rip for you), converting tracks from discs is a tad difficult, but there are plenty of online music stores to buy and download music from: Amazon, eMusic, iTunes, Rhapsody, the Zune Marketplace, and so on.

MP3 Players with Ubuntu Linux

Linux can also work with many MP3 players designed for Windows, including iPods. The iPod, however, must be formatted to work with Windows, not Mac, which uses a different file system.

When it senses an iPod getting plugged into the computer's USB port, Ubuntu's Rhythmbox Music Player jumps up to play the iPod's music. (Copy-protected files from the iTunes Store, however, don't play.) Another iPod-friendly music-management tool for Ubuntu is a program 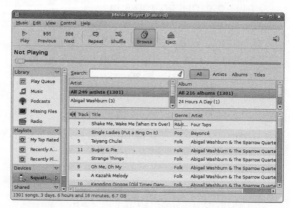 called gtkpod, which you can get from the Ubuntu software repository (page 71).

With some simple MP3 players—especially those that are basically just USB flash drives with folders for organizing music files, you may not even need a program like Rhythmbox. Just connect it to the netbook and drag the music files from your hard drive to the portable player in the Nautilus file browser (page 74).

Adding Headphones or External Speakers to the Netbook

To get started, just plug a pair of earbuds or headphones with a standard 3.5-millimter stereo connector into the netbook's headphone jack.

Some portable external speakers designed for laptops also connect to the computer's headphone jack—and many don't require any special software. These extra speakers may need batteries or electrical power to properly amplify the sound. Others may use USB connections and require more setup and fiddling, so check the documentation that came with your speakers.

You adjust the sound levels either in the music program you're using or by changing the netbook's overall volume. Most netbooks have shortcut keys on the keyboard for lowering and raising the volume—look for a little speaker horn with sound waves coming out of it. (The pictograph with lots of sound waves increases the volume and the one with one sound wave lowers it.)

You can also change the volume level onscreen:

- **Windows XP.** In the taskbar, click the speaker-shaped Volume Control icon and adjust the slider to raise or lower the volume. If you right-click this icon, you can set sound levels for headphone jack, speaker, and other audio components in the Volume Control panel.

- **Ubuntu.** In the top panel, click the speaker icon and drag the slider for quick volume adjustment. Right-click the icon to get independent sliders for the various audio components.

 Note Make sure not to blast the sound too loudly, as studies have shown that excessive sound levels, especially from earbuds, can cause long-term hearing damage. Keeping your headphone volume levels set to 70 percent (or lower) of the maximum volume can help preserve your ears.

On the Road: Cases and Cables

Netbooks were made to be light. While you probably don't want to haul around five pounds of extra stuff with your three-pound computer, you may need to have a few accessories on hand when you're working on the road.

Here are a few items to consider, and all of them can be found in your local computer-supply store:

- **A case or slipcover.** Your trim netbook doesn't really require a computer bag—just slip it into your purse, backpack, or briefcase. But to keep the netbook from getting scuffed up, you can get a slipcover to protect the netbook in transit. You can find these simple covers where laptop supplies are sold, and they come in everything from sporty, water-resistant neoprene to leather.

- **Ethernet cable.** Most hotels and airports now have their own wireless networks, but some offices, hotels, and other places still use wired Ethernet cables to get onto the network. For times like these, a three- to six-foot retractable Ethernet cable can save the day.

- **Extra power cord.** An extra AC cord means you don't have to drag cords back and forth between home and office. Buy one from the netbook's manufacturer to make sure you get the right one.

- **USB hub.** If you have a lot of USB devices to plug into your netbook and only two or three USB ports, using a small travel hub can give you enough places to connect everything.

- **Travel mouse.** Smaller than the typical mouse, and not tricked out with tons of programmable buttons, a travel-sized mouse takes up less room inside your bag. It's the computer pointer version of those tiny shampoo bottles in the drugstore. Many also have retractable cables so you don't spend your travel time untangling mouse cords.

- **Security cable.** If your netbook has a Kensington or security slot in the side (page 19), you can get a custom-fitted metal cable to connect to it and anchor the computer to a desk or chair so thieves have a much harder time making off with your laptop.

You can even find many of these items in one package like the Lenmar Laptop Computer Accessory Kit, which includes a retractable Ethernet cable, mini-mouse, 4-port USB hub, security cable, and one-gigabyte flash drive for about $70 or less. Verbatim's Notebook Essentials kit has a travel mouse, 4-port USB hub, and retractable USB, Ethernet, and phone cables, all for about $40.

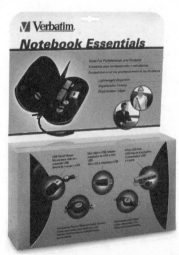

5   Getting Online

Now that you have your netbook customized to your liking, it's time to use it as it was *meant* to be used—on the Internet. The Internet is the home of the Cloud where you'll find online applications like Google Docs and Yahoo Mail, *30 Rock* episodes from Hulu.com, and vast datastreams from around the globe. You can have all this on your netbook as soon as you take care of a few details…like getting an Internet connection.

Getting online is a lot easier than it was just a few years ago, when stodgy dial-up modems were still in vogue and information waltzed along the wires at a leisurely 50 kilobits per second. These days, network service is streamlined. High-speed fiber-optic connections (like Verizon's FiOS service) can download data at a blazing 50 *mega*bits per second. (Since the old 56 kilobits-per-second dial-up modems of the 1990s can only move at a mere fraction of that speed, you can see why YouTube never really caught on until high-speed Internet became commonplace.)

Whether you use a wired or wireless network in your home, office, or on your travels, this chapter shows you how to get your netbook living up to its potential.

Ways to Connect to the Internet

Getting online means connecting your netbook to a local computer network, which in turn connects you to the giant network of networks known collectively as the Internet. Your netbook has at least two built-in ways to connect to a network—and there are a few others. Here are some of the possibilities:

- **A wired Ethernet network connection.** Still popular in offices and places where network security is an issue, an Ethernet network connection gives you a high-speed path to the Internet over a plastic-covered cable. Just about every netbook has an Ethernet jack, so all you need is the cable (page 118).

- **A wireless network connection.** The most popular way to get online these days, a wireless connection lets you get to the Internet over radio waves. Married to broadband Internet connections, wireless networks have flourished in homes where no one wants to see yards of unsightly cables slithering around the house. Wireless networks  are also ideal for those who like to travel and travel light, and all netbooks have a wireless chip inside. (See page 123.)

- **A mobile broadband card or USB dongle.** Not the cheapest way online, but one of the most versatile. Getting a mobile broadband card and service plan from a wireless phone carrier lets you get online pretty much anywhere you can get a cellphone signal. Some newer netbooks from wireless carriers include the card and service. You can even combine mobile broadband card with WiFi— Verizon's tiny MiFi router (*www.VzW.com/mobilehotspot*) pulls down a mobile broadband signal and shares it with up to five computers over its own WiFi connection, making it practically a pocket network. (See page 128.)

- **A cellphone connection.** Not every cellphone can pull double-duty as a data modem for linking your netbook to the Internet, but some can—even over a Bluetooth connection. (See page 129.)

- **An external dial-up modem.** Often derided by those in urban areas with faster network access, dial-up modems still have a place in the world—especially in rural areas where the phone line is the *only* pipeline to the Internet. (See page 130.)

You're not stuck with any one method, either. Sure, you may be floating along the wireless airwaves most of the time in the local café, but if you find yourself in a wired-only office or far away from a broadband connection of any kind, falling back to an Ethernet cable or pocket phone modem can still keep you connected with the rest of the world.

What You Need to Connect

Now that you've got the netbook in hand and know how you want to get online, you need to make sure you have a few other things:

- **An Internet service provider.** Most people already have one of these powering home or office Internet access. If you've never had Internet service at home, you'll need to sign up for a provider (page 118). If you're traveling, those hotel and airport WiFi networks take care of the ISP factor.

- **Passwords.** If you plan to tap into a secured wireless network—that is, one that requires a password to join—you must get the network's name and password from the network's administrator (the office computer guy, your 13-year-old daughter, or whoever is in charge of the network). If you're logging into a paid wireless hotspot at the airport or bookstore, your credit card number gets you on the network (ka-*ching!*).

- **Cables.** If you're connecting to a wired Ethernet network, you need an Ethernet cable if one is not provided at the desk you're using.

- **Cellphone kits/Modems.** If you plan to use your cellphone as a de facto data modem, you might need a data plan from your wireless carrier, along with a cable, unless your phone and netbook both do Bluetooth. If you're using a dial-up connection, you need an external phone modem to attach to the netbook's USB port, as most netbooks don't include a modem jack.

Once you have the necessary gear in hand, it's time to get it all together and get netbooking.

Getting an Internet Service Provider

To get Internet service on the netbook, you need an *Internet service provider*. (Makes sense, huh?) According to some surveys, an estimated 74 percent of adults are already online and using the Internet, so chances are you're among them. If not, or if you're considering a change of service or provider, here are a few things to keep in mind:

- **How much is it? No, really, how much is it?** Junk mail is full of colorful postcards from your local cable or phone company offering to give you TV, Internet, and telephone service for one low, *low* price. Be sure to read the fine print. How long does that rate stay in place? Do you have to sign a contract? Do you have to pay extra for equipment and installation? Do you want your home phone connected to the home network (which means no fun for anyone during an electrical blackout that lasts more than a few hours)?

- **What do other people think of it?** After you've read the company's information carefully to see what it says, see what its customers are saying. If you can go online—perhaps at a library if you don't have an ISP yet—read reviews of the service on sites like *www.theispguide.com* and *www.broadbandreports.com*.

- **How's the technical support?** Do you get 24/7 for those times of crisis, or does the Help Desk go off the hook at 5:00?

- **Can I use my service on the road?** If you're going for mobile broadband service, check the coverage map and make sure you can get online wherever you need to. People in the dial-up modem world should check to see if the ISP offers phone numbers around the country.

Even if you already have an ISP, you may be thinking of making a home network out of your Internet connection, especially if you already have a desktop computer in place and need to get the netbook online as well. The next few pages tackle that little project.

Setting Up a Wired Network

Setting up a wired home network typically consists of two separate phases:

- Installing a broadband connection, which brings fast Internet service to at least one computer in the house.

- Sharing that connection with the rest of the house by using a box called a *router* to allow multiple computers to tap into the fast Internet service.

Once you get the router, there are a couple different ways to get the Internet connection to the other computers. These ways include Ethernet cables—plastic-covered cords that leash each computer to the router—or *powerline networking*, which uses the home electrical system to carry data to the computers, which are plugged into special adapters.

Setting Up a Broadband Connection

Most home users go for high-speed Internet access from their residential cable or phone company. If you order from the cable people—places like Time Warner, Cox, or Comcast—you get your fast broadband Internet access by sharing the same wires that are bringing ESPN and Comedy Central to your TV. If you order from the phone company, say, Verizon, you usually get DSL (short for *digital subscriber line*) or the newer, faster, more expensive *fiber optic* service (FiOS) that's slowing rolling out around the country.

Once you order the service from your provider, there are two installation options:

- A technician from the company comes to your house and takes care of everything.
- You do it yourself (possibly with help from a friend or family member).

The latter option is becoming more common: Once you order the service, you get a connection kit with a modem, some Ethernet cables, a software CD, and a colorful step-by-step poster or setup guide. Follow your ISP's specific instructions for setup, but in general, it goes something like this:

1. Install any supplied software on the computer.

   If you're using a netbook with no disc drive, try copying the CD files to a USB drive on another computer and then installing them on the netbook from the USB drive.

2. Unpack the modem, cables, and other gear.

   If you ordered service from the cable company, you need to unscrew the thick coaxial cable from the back of the TV or cable box and attach a little device called a splitter (shown on the next page), which lets you plug two coaxial cables into the one coming out of the wall. With the splitter connected to the wall cable, use the extra supplied bit of coaxial cable to reconnect the TV or cable box and use the other to connect the splitter to the modem. You've just split one cable connection into two: one for the TV, one for the computer.

Tip If your TV picture quality suffers as a result, swapping out the cable company's cheap splitter for a powered splitter—also called a *broadband drop amplifier*—to boost the signal might help improve things. You can find powered splitters at Amazon, Radio Shack, and electronics shops.

If you ordered DSL service, you need to attach the supplied plastic filters to the other phone jacks in the house except for the one the modem will use. These filters screen out the screech of data traffic coming over the phone lines and make it possible to still use the phone while also using the computer. Plug the DSL modem into the wall with the supplied phone cable.

3. Connect the modem to the computer.

Use the supplied Ethernet cable to link the network port on the computer to the network port on the modem. At this point, you may need to type in user names and passwords from the ISP to finish the setup and get online at last, so have all your paperwork from the company handy.

Once you have the main Internet connection up and running, it's time to share it by making a home network.

Setting Up a Home Wired Network

Creating a home network lets you share your zippy Internet connection, but it has other perks, too. For instance, you can share printers and network drives, and even give online access to gadgets like your TiVo or game console. There are two main ways to make a wired network—Ethernet and powerline—and both of them require a *router*. A router is a box that takes one Internet connection and spreads it around to all the computers on the network. Routers sell for less than $40 and can be found at computer stores or sites like Amazon.com.

Ethernet

To make an Ethernet network, all you need are Ethernet cables and a router (like the D-Link model shown here and available at *www.dlink.com*). Ethernet cable prices vary based on length, but you can usually get a 25-foot cable for less than $10 if you shop around.

Unless you have a brand-new house prewired with Ethernet jacks in every room, you need an Ethernet cable that can stretch from the router to each computer on the network. That's usually not a problem if all the computers live in

a home office, but if you want to connect computers all over the house, you'll need a lot of Ethernet cables.

Once you set up the router according to the manufacturer's instructions, use an Ethernet cable to plug the broadband modem into the router. Then plug all the computers into the router's jacks (it should have four to eight of them) with Ethernet cable. If you don't want Ethernet cable snaking all over the house, consider setting up a wireless network (page 123) or using powerline networking.

Powerline networking

With powerline networking, you don't need Ethernet cords all over the place, because you use the electrical wires *inside your walls* as your network cables. To set up this type of network, you need to get a Powerline kit, which costs around $140. Most major network-equipment providers like Linksys, Netgear, and D-Link (shown here) sell them. The kits include

wall adapters that plug into the electrical outlets near the computers you want to connect. You still need a network router connected to your broadband modem, though.

Setting up a Powerline is pretty easy: Plug the Powerline adapter into the wall and then connect the router to it with an Ethernet cable. The adapter sends the router's Internet signal out through the electrical wires in the wall. Next, plug additional Powerline adapters into wall sockets near each computer in the house. Connect the computers to the Powerline adapters with a short length of Ethernet cable, and you're set.

Powerline networking isn't without its problems. It can be slow compared to a wired Ethernet connection and electrical fluctuations—like when someone fires up the hair dryer—can disrupt the network. And the house's wiring itself can affect a powerline network, particularly when there are circuits that are electrically isolated from each other.

Connecting to the Network

Once you've installed the hardware and plugged an Ethernet cable into each computer's network jack, your computers—including your net-book—should be networked. Both Windows XP and Ubuntu Linux should automatically sense the network connection and be ready to go. If you want to test this theory, start up your web browser program (page 151), and see if you can get to your favorite web page.

If you don't have an Internet connection, make sure both ends of the Ethernet cable are firmly plugged in and then check the computer's network settings.

- In Windows XP, choose Start→All Programs→Connect To→Show All Connections. Check to make sure the Local Area Connection is enabled. If not, try the Repair Connection option from the task pane.

- In Ubuntu Linux, right-click the Network Manager icon in the top panel (usually between the user name and battery indicator). On the menu, make sure Enable Networking is selected; if it's not, turn it on. Even if it *is* on, try deselecting Enable Networking from the menu, waiting a few seconds, and then turning it back on.

For either system, restarting the computer with the Ethernet cable plugged in may help the netbook realize that it's now connected to the home network.

Setting Up a Wireless Network

The steps for putting up a wireless network are almost the same as the steps needed for setting up a wired network. You need to have the broadband connection (page 119) already in place, but instead of a router and cables, you need a *wireless router*. Instead of sending the information along cables, a wireless router broadcasts the Internet signal over the airwaves, where computers equipped with wireless cards (your netbook included) can receive the signal.

And wireless routers aren't the ugly boxes they used to be—Cisco's line of home-networking gear (a sample is shown here) looks positively sleek.

To set up the wireless router, just follow the instructions that came with it. In many cases, configuring the wireless router means plugging it directly into the computer with an Ethernet cable, opening the web browser, and typing in the router's IP address along with a user name and password. These vary by manufacturer, but on Cisco-Linksys equipment, for example, you type *http://192.168.1.1* in the browser window to get to the router's configuration page, and then type *admin* for the user name and *admin* again for the password.

These settings are generic for every Cisco-Linksys router, and anybody can find them with a quick Google search, so change the router's user name and password while you're setting up the name of your new network and its password.

The network's name is also known as the *SSID* (service set identifier). If you live in a densely populated urban area, it's good idea to give it some sort of unique name like *PuppyNet* or *BaseStar* to make it stand out from all the *LinkSys* and *NETGEAR* networks that lazier people have set up in their own homes.

Wireless Network Security

Also turn on your router's wireless encryption feature. This step protects the data flying around the airwaves by scrambling it. It also forces people to type a password the first time they use your network. Depending on the brand of router you buy, you will probably have a choice of two different encryption systems: *WiFi Protected Access* (WPA) or the older, weaker *Wired Equivalent Privacy* (WEP).

Pick an encryption method and add a password for the network. Most computers can handle WPA (or the newer WPAZ) these days, but make note of the network's name, password, and type of encryption used. You then give this information with people you *want* to share your network with.

Some people may balk at setting a password for the network, because it can make it more difficult for friends and family to log in. But they really only have to use it the first time they connect, and can save the information in their own network settings so that future connections will seem practically automatic.

Connecting to a Wireless Network

Okay, you know the network is out there. It's time to jump online and have some fun. If it's a secure network, you need to know its name and the password to join it.

Windows XP

Windows XP may sense there is a wireless network within its range and alert you with one of those yellow balloons down in the taskbar's notification area. If it doesn't, right-click the wireless network icon (it looks like a PC beaming out radio waves) and choose View Available Wireless Networks. A box pops up showing you the networks within range.

Each network is also shown with its signal strength—weaker signals make for slower, less stable connections. The network's security status is also displayed: *Unsecured* means no password is needed; *security-enabled* means you need a password. Find your network in the list, click it, and then click Connect.

In the next box, type the network's password and then click Connect. After a second or two, your computer joins the network, and you can surf to your heart's content, free of wires.

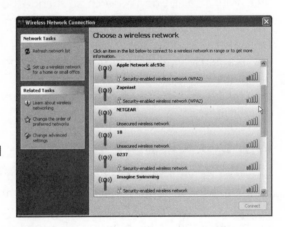

Ubuntu Linux

Choose System→Administration→Network Settings. Click the Unlock button and type your computer's password. Click Wireless Connection and then click the Properties button. Make sure the checkbox next to "Enable automatic mode" is turned on—unless you only want to connect to your home network. In that case, type the network's name, type of security encryption, and password. Under Connection Settings, choose "Automatic configuration (DHCP)." Click OK.

In the top panel of the Ubuntu desktop, right-click the Network Manager icon (to the left of the Battery icon) and make sure both Enable Networking and Enable Wireless are turned on. Now, click the Network Manager icon again to see a list of available networks.

A lock icon next to the network's name means the network requires a password to join. The horizontal bar next to the lock shows the strength of the network signal.

Click the button next to the name of the network you want to join and close the Network Manager menu. When presented with a password box, type the network's password. The netbook takes a couple of seconds to send the information to the router, and then you're online.

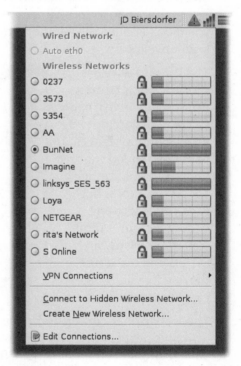

If you're having trouble connecting to the network, the next section offers some suggestions.

Common Wireless Network Problems

If your netbook doesn't magically connect to the wireless network, you can try a few basic things to troubleshoot the situation. Here are the most common things that can go wrong, and what to do about them, in order of difficulty:

- **You typed the wrong network password.** Even though you did it once, do it again just to make sure you entered it correctly. Remember, network passwords are case-sensitive. Also, it's a common security practice to mix letters and numbers together to make the password harder to crack, with numbers even substituting for letters. So make sure you're not typing *cooperstown500* when the password is really *c00perstown500*.

- **The wireless radio is turned off.** Netbooks have that handy button or key combination to turn off the wireless card in a hurry, so make sure you didn't accidentally hit the button yourself and turn off your wireless network card.

- **The Ubuntu wireless radio driver is turned off.** Sometimes installing software or fiddling with your Ubuntu system can have unintended consequences. If you can see wireless networks but can't connect to any, choose System→Administration→Hardware Drivers and make sure the one for your wireless card is not turned off.

- **The network is configured differently.** Most networks use DHCP (dynamic host configuration protocol) to dole out IP addresses (page 98) to computers wanting to join. But some networks use static IP addresses that you have to type into the network settings box. This setup makes the network more secure, but harder to join.

   If that's the case, ask your network administrator for the static IP address, plus the subnet mask and gateway numbers.

In Windows XP, choose Start→Control Panel→Network [and Internet] Connections. Right-click the wireless connection icon and choose Properties from the shortcut menu. In the Properties box, in the middle section of the General tab, under "This connection uses the following items," select Internet Protocol (TCP/IP) and click the Properties button. Click the button next to "Use the following IP address" and type the numbers you got from your network administrator or ISP.

In Ubuntu Linux, choose System→Administration→Network Settings. Click the Unlock button and type your computer's password. Click Wireless Connection and then click Properties. Under Connection Settings, choose "Static IP address" and type the numbers you got from your ISP or network administrator. Click OK when finished.

- **The network is down.** Can anybody else get on the network? Check the router. Sometimes *rebooting* it—unplugging the broadband modem and router for a few seconds before plugging them back in again—can get that wireless network back up where it belongs.

- **The network signal is weak.** Most WiFi networks have a range of at least 120 feet indoors, but obstructions like brick walls, windows, and metal file cabinets can sap signal strength. Try either moving the router or yourself to see if the connection improves.

Using Public Wireless Networks

Now that your netbook is all revved up for wireless action, you can use it on other networks besides your own. These include the free public networks at libraries, parks, jury-duty rooms, and other places where someone has thoughtfully connected a wireless router to a broadband Internet connection.

Commercial *WiFi hotspots*, or paid public networks, often found in airports and large chain bookstores are also an option—as long as you have a credit card or an account and password with the hotspot provider. T-Mobile (*http://hotspot.t-mobile.com*), for example, operates a lot of hotspots and has service plans that start at $20 a month.

To find a network on your Windows XP netbook, right-click the Wireless Network icon in the notification area and choose "View Available Wireless Networks" from the shortcut menu. On Ubuntu Linux, click the Network Manager icon on the right half of the top panel to see a list of nearby networks. Public wireless networks are generally unsecured, so you don't need a password to join them.

Public wireless networks are great for casual web surfing, but remember, they're *public*. You don't know who else is on the network. So take some safety precautions to keep your netbook's data safe from potential intruders. Page 262 has a list of tips for public network safety.

Getting Online with a Wireless Broadband Card

If a broadband network at home or work isn't enough Internet access for you, another option is a wireless mobile broadband card. These cards, available from wireless phone carriers like Sprint and Verizon, are tiny modems that let your netbook jump on to the same high-speed data networks used by smartphones to get to the Internet. Some netbooks even include the mobile card built right in.

In theory, anywhere you can get a cellphone signal, you can get online. Sounds great, doesn't it? You don't have to search out a WiFi network or hunt around for an Ethernet cable because you've got the Internet right there.

Of course, all these freedom does have a price, namely up to $350 for the mobile broadband card and then $40 to $60 per month for the service plan. Still, if you're on the go all the time—or better yet, have a job that will pay for the card—this option can be very liberating, even if the network speeds aren't quite as fast as WiFi or Ethernet.

If you have a cellphone, check and see if your carrier offers mobile broadband cards for laptops. You might get a deal if you already have an account with the company for your phone. If not, most wireless cellphone carriers offer some sort of *air card* or *broadband card*. And if you sign a contract, say for two years of monthly service, the company might even give you the card itself (or perhaps an entire netbook) for free—or nearly free. (These are cellphone carriers; they're used to doing this sort of thing.)

Before you seal the deal on your card, make sure you can get hardware that works with your netbook's operating system; Linux may be trickier than Windows. Most places offer a USB stick option that has the broadband modem built right in. AT&T, Verizon, and other wireless companies now sell netbooks with the mobile broadband chip right inside—and monthly service plans to go with them.

Some netbooks like the Lenovo S10 also have an ExpressCard slot, which is a smaller, flatter version of the old PCMCIA Type II card slots found on most full-sized laptops (but not so much on their smaller netbook cousins). If the card's driver software and connection program aren't available for download, you may also need to beg or borrow an external CD drive if you don't have one for your netbook.

Using Your Mobile Phone as a Modem

Over the past few years, cellular phone networks have been enhanced and upgraded to handle lots of data along with voice signals. These are sometimes referred to as *3G networks*, in reference to the current third generation of mobile communications standards. The next, even faster type of network is called 4G, but those new networks aren't expected until at least 2012. If you have a smartphone that sends email and surfs the Web in a flash, like an iPhone, Blackberry, or Windows Mobile model, you're probably using a 3G network.

And with this smartphone, you might be able to get your netbook online, too. You do this by *tethering* (connecting) your phone to your netbook and using the phone as an external data modem for the computer.

The exact tethering procedure depends on your phone, your netbook, and your wireless carrier. A quick search for tethering at *www.smartdevicecentral.com* brings up instructions for all the common wireless carriers.

As far as linking the phone to the netbook, your options include:

- **USB cable.** Many phones come with a USB cable for connecting it to a computer to transfer files. If your phone didn't come with a cable, you can find one online by searching for "USB phone data cable"; prices range between $20 to $60.

- **Bluetooth.** If you have Bluetooth chips in both the netbook and the phone, you can pair them (page 90) to make a wireless connection between the two. Make sure the computer and phone both have their Bluetooth radios turned on so they can discover each other. Page 90 has sample instructions for pairing Bluetooth devices, but refer to your phone's manual for specific steps.

- **WiFi.** If your phone has built-in WiFi, you might even be able to turn it into a pocket wireless hotspot. To do so, you need a program on your phone like WMWiFiRouter ($30 at *www.wmwifirouter.com*) or Walking-HotSpot ($25 a year; *www.walkinghotspot.com*).

The first step is connecting the phone to the netbook. Next, you have to get the phone onto the data network so it can share the goods with the netbook. If you plan to send email and other data over the connection, you need to get a data plan from your wireless carrier. This plan is separate from the one for the phone itself, and it's specifically designed to let you tether the phone to the laptop. Prices range from $40 to $60 a month. This may sound pricey, but it can get your netbook on the Internet if you don't have any other options.

 Note Be sure to read the fine print on your carrier's plan to make sure it includes tethering. With so many monthly service options available these days, it's easy to get the wrong one.

Using a Dial-Up Connection with Your Netbook

Ah, the noble telephone dial-up modem connection. The slow, simple lifeline that got millions of people on the Web in the mid-1990s has been largely tossed aside for better, stronger, faster broadband connections—except for folks who can't afford it or can't get high-speed Internet access where they live.

Dial-up is still around, costing as little as $5 to $10 a month, depending on the provider. National dial-up providers include NetZero (*www.netzero. net*), PeoplePC (*www.peoplepc.com*), and Earthlink (*www.earthlink.net*). You can sign up for an account on an office or friend's computer and order a CD of the software you need to connect to the ISP (if you have a disc drive) or possibly download the software from the site and install it from a USB drive.

Finding a dial-up ISP is the easy part. Because netbook hardware is so streamlined and designed for wireless Internet access, most models don't even include an internal phone modem. In this case, you can get a USB-based 56K modem for about $50 from a company like US Robotics (*www.usr.com*) or Zoom (*www.zoom.com*); both offer Windows *and* Linux-compatible modems.

Even if you don't have special connection software from the ISP, you can manually configure your netbook to get online. You need your ISP account information: your user name, password, and at least one access number for the modem to dial.

Windows XP

If you're using Windows XP, you can summon the New Connection Wizard to walk you through punching in the ISP's phone number. The wizard will even find you a dial-up provider if you don't know where to look.

Just plug the phone cord into the netbook's modem and then choose Start→All Programs→Accessories→Communications→New Connection Wizard. Select the Connect to the Internet option. On the next screen, you can tell Windows XP to let you choose an ISP from a list or guide you through setting up your connection using the username, password, and phone numbers you already have from your service provider. When you finish the wizard, you can get online in the future by choosing Start→Connect To→[ISP].

Ubuntu Linux

The most important step in getting Linux dial-up to work is to make sure the modem you get is actually Linux-compatible. Most aren't, so shop wisely and follow the installation instructions.

Although you can configure a modem connection (called a point-to-point connection) in Ubuntu's Network Settings box, there's an alternate method, which you may find easier. Choose Applications→Add/Remove, search for *gnome-ppp* and install the software.

Choose Applications→Internet→GNOME PPP. Click the Setup button. When the Setup screen appears, click the Detect button. Once the software has configured itself to use your modem, turn off "Wait for dialtone" checkbox and then click the Options tab. Turn on the "Dock in notification area" checkbox and then click Close. Back on the main screen, type your user name, password, and ISP access number. Click the Connect button to dial your way online.

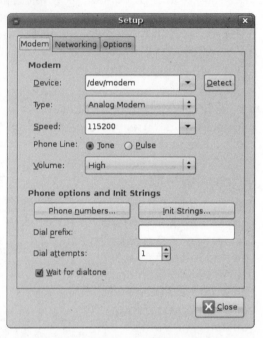

Tip Getting Linux and certain modems to play nice can take some fiddling and venturing deeper into Linux. If you're having trouble, check out the Ubuntu community support page on the topic at *https://help.ubuntu.com/community/DialupModemHowto*.

6 Email and Web Browsing

Email is the driving force that first motivated many people to invite computers and the Internet into their homes. The millions of electronic epistles that fly through the air between computers, smartphones, and handheld organizers have become an indispensable part of daily personal and professional life. No wonder the U.S. Postal Service has been losing business the past 15 years.

You may be surprised to know that the first email message was sent way back in 1971. Twenty years later, the *World Wide Web*—the interconnected system of electronic pages containing everything from academic papers on Johannes Gutenberg to video clips of dogs riding skateboards—became *another* reason to go out and buy a computer.

It's small wonder, then, that the netbook's ability to keep a near-constant connection to email and the Web makes them the hottest-selling computers on the market today. This chapter shows you how to get your netbook's email and web browser fired up and ready to go so you, too, won't miss a thing.

Setting Up an Email Program

You have two common ways to get email on your netbook: through a web-based mail (*webmail*) site like Yahoo, or from your Internet service provider and an email program like Outlook Express. Both methods have their pros and cons. But you may not have to choose *one* way to get email. You can, for example, download your Gmail email into an email program most of the time, so you can organize it better, but also check it on the Gmail website when you're on the road.

Here's a quick look at each basic mail-gathering method.

Using a Webmail Account

Most webmail systems work like this: You pick the service you want to use (Hotmail, Gmail, Yahoo, and so on) and sign up for an account. As part of this process, you select an email address and password. Whenever you want to engage in a little postal activity, you log into your account on your chosen webmail site and do all of your mailing activities through your web browser window. (Page 151 explains how web browsers work.)

Webmail is versatile, and it's always there for you to check and send messages on Internet-connected devices like desktop computers, netbooks, mobile phones—even on certain types of hotel television sets. Webmail also keeps

track of your email address book, so you've got your contact info right at hand. And, if you want to save any of your mail on your home computer, you can make copies from your web-based Inbox or even download it to a regular email program.

Webmail provides a stable, consistent address on the Internet. If you move to a new town and change ISPs, you have to get a new email address, but your webmail address stays the same no matter how you get online.

The downside to webmail is that many free services are advertiser-supported, so you and your correspondents get to look at little advertisements stuck at the bottom or along the sides of the messages. Another potential bummer: If the webmail site goes down, you can't get your mail. Mail delivery from your ISP (page 118) can be hindered by a server crash as well, but there's nothing like a Gmail outage to get a whole bunch of people going through email withdrawal at the same time. Google, however, has come up with a way to read Gmail even when you're offline (page 136).

Some services also limit the number of messages you have in your account (well, they *do* own the servers) or the size of the file attachments you're allowed to send. And if you don't log in for a few months, you may find your account (and any mail in it) deleted because the service thought you wandered off for good.

And speaking of servers, some people felt uneasy about having all their personal mail sitting around on someone else's webmail machines. The fact is, *all* email, not just webmail, bounces around along a series of different computers as it travels along the Internet. Unless you encrypt your messages with a program like PGP, a number of people could potentially read your mail.

 Note When it comes to email privacy, a good rule of thumb here is to never put anything into a plain email message that you wouldn't put on the back of a postcard. So avoid sending embarrassing personal revelations and valuable data like your Social Security digits, credit card numbers, or bank account info.

Webmail Providers

There are several webmail providers out there, and most of them give you at least 5 GB of server space to store your mailbox. Five gigabytes is plenty for most people—room enough to store at least half a million email messages—although that will fill up faster if you regularly send off megabytes of photo or video attachments and never delete anything. Here's a quick look at four of the big webmail services.

- **Gmail.** Since it debuted in 2004, Google's take on webmail has been consistently innovative, expansive, and downright fun. Gmail account holders get at least 5 GB of mail storage space storage, easy search, a killer filter to weed out junk mail, text-formatting tools, a spell checker, sortable labels, and clever add-ons from Gmail Labs like a program called Mail Goggles that stops you from sending email when you may have had a bit too much to drink. Google doesn't charge extra if you download the mail from your account with an email program. You just have to go to your Gmail settings, click the "Forwarding and POP/IMAP" tab, and tell Gmail to enable POP or IMAP downloads (page 140).

If you prefer to leave your Gmail on the Web but want to read it even when you're not connected to the Internet, click the Offline link at the top of your Inbox page and follow the steps to install Google Gears. Google Gears (page 177) snags copies of messages and lets you work even without the Web. And finally, Gmail also looks really good on a mobile phone. (*http://gmail.google.com*)

- **Yahoo Mail.** With the recent promise of unlimited mail storage, Yahoo attempts to separate itself from the rest of the herd. For example, it offers junk mail and virus blocking, it can play photo slideshows right in an email message, and it can serve up your local news headlines. If you  find Yahoo Mail's ads irritating, you can pay $20 a year for a Mail Plus account, which gives you ad-free messages, a better spam filter, and the ability to download Yahoo messages to an email program like Thunderbird. Paying for a Mail Plus account also ensures that Yahoo won't dump all the messages in your account if you don't log in for four months, which happens on free accounts. (*http://mail.yahoo.com*)

- **Windows Live Hotmail.** Microsoft currently has two different flavors of webmail: regular free Windows Live Hotmail and $20-a-year Windows Live Hotmail Plus. The free account gives you a 5-gigabyte mailbox, junk mail and phish filters, virus-scanning, plus fancy backgrounds, fonts, and layout styles for your messages. Windows Live Hotmail Plus gets you a 10-gigabyte mailbox, ad-free messages, and an account that won't disappear into the mists if you don't check it for a month or so. (*www.hotmail.com*)

- **AOL.** Once the biggest members-only dial-up ISP in the United States, AOL has pretty much dropped its proprietary software and monthly fees. Anyone can now sign up for a free, web-based AOL email account on the company's site. Spam and virus protection are included with every account, and there's always a link to AOL's news and entertainment pages. (*www.aol.com*)

 Just about every major webmail provider now offers additional services like instant-messaging and online calendar programs you can get to and use right from your main email window. These sort of things really work well together. For example, if your best friend sends you an email message about having dinner, you can send him an instant message (if you see he's online) to confirm the date and then update your schedule right in your web calendar so you don't forget. Want to know more abut instant messages and web calendars? Visit pages 199 and 189, respectively.

Using ISP Email

When you signed up for your Internet service provider (page 118) to get on-line, odds are the company gave you at least one email address. Unless the company has its own webmail service, you need to collect the mail sent to that address in a dedicated email program on your computer. These types of programs download your mail, display it for you, and let you send you own messages. Email programs, sometimes referred to as email *clients*, live on your computer and generally keep all your messages (or at least the message header information) on your hard drive, not on some unknown server.

Once you choose a program, you have to set up the software to work with your ISP's mail server. You simply start your email program, select the New Account option, and then type all the information you got from your ISP when you signed up (like your user name, password, and the names of the mail servers) so your email program knows where to look for your mail.

Although they take longer to set up, email programs typically let you be much more creative in composing your messages. Compared to some on-line webmail sites, email programs usually make it much easier to do things like change the type style and color or drag and drop photos into your messages. (Services like Gmail, however, have caught up considerably with standalone email programs in the word processing department.)

But in some cases, you don't even have to make the choice. If your webmail service allows it, you can download the messages from your web-based account with the same email client you use to snag your ISP mail.

Popular (and free) email programs

Email is such a standard now that just about every computer operating system includes some sort of email program. Here's a quick look at the most popular ones.

- **Outlook Express.** You don't have to go any further than your Windows XP Start menu to find Outlook Express right there waiting for you. It's not the slickest email program ever invented, but it does all the basics: sending, receiving, sorting, and storing messages and file attachments. As old as it is, millions of people still use Outlook Express so you can find plenty of add-ons and other programs that work with it. For example, iTunes 8 even lets you export your OE contacts to your iPod.

 Note Outlook Express is a big target for virus writers and other evildoers who want to fool it into opening messages tainted with malicious code. Still, it's free and adding an antivirus program (page 264) to your Windows XP netbook is a good idea anyway.

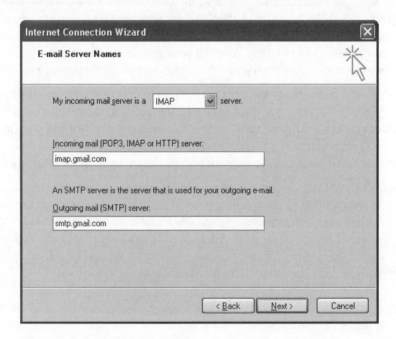

— **Evolution.** Included with Ubuntu Linux, Evolution does much more than send and receive email. It also serves as a calendar, organizer, and electronic address book. Like Linux itself, Evolution is an open source program, so all of its programming code is right out there on the Web where anyone can see it, improve it, or fix it. Linux systems aren't as vulnerable to the same viruses and worms that plague Windows machines, but junk mail is universal, so Evolution offers a serious spam filter to weed out the garbage.

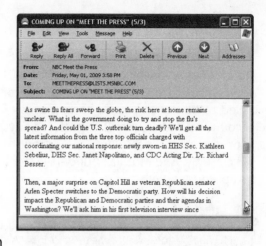

— **Thunderbird.** If you don't like the mail program that came with your netbook, you can pick out one of your own. Mozilla's Thunderbird is available for both Windows XP and Ubuntu Linux and makes a nice, open-source alternative. Another good thing to come out of Thunderbird's open-sourcefulness are the extensions (add-on programs) you can get to make it even more useful. You can find extensions for enhancing your address book, weeding out duplicate entries, or even smacking down more spam than what Thunderbird's built-in filter already does. You can get Thunderbird extensions by going to Tools→Extensions→Get More Extensions when you have the program open in front of you. Windows people can download a copy at *www.mozilla.com/thunderbird*, while Linux netbookers can find it in the Ubuntu repository (page 71).

Setting Up an ISP Mail Account

The word *configure* is flung around by computer geeks quite a bit, but it's nothing to be afraid of. It just means "to set up." If you can put together a tricycle or follow a recipe to make brownies, you can configure an email program. During the process, you have to supply a few basic pieces of information so that the mail program knows where to look for your mail and how to handle the messages you send to other people.

Since Outlook Express comes with Windows XP, it's a good one to use as an example. To get rolling, go to your Windows Start menu. If Outlook Express is not listed up top there, choose Start →All Programs→Outlook Express.

Ubuntu Linux machines come with the Evolution mail software, which is very similar to set up: Choose Applications→Internet→Evolution. You're asked to fill out the same basic pieces of information about your email account as with Outlook Express or any other email program, so have your user name, password, and account settings information from your ISP close by. And Mozilla Thunderbird for Windows and Linux uses similar setup steps as well.

 Tip Microsoft's successor to Outlook Express is called Windows Live Mail, and it works on Windows XP as well as the newer Windows Vista. Windows Live Mail has an updated look and lets you check accounts from several providers—including Yahoo, Gmail, and Hotmail all in one place. If you want to try it out, you can download it for free at *http://download.live.com/wlmail*.

If you've never opened Outlook Express before, the Internet Connection Wizard comes roaring in to help. After you answer each of the questions the wizard asks, click the Next button.

1. Screen 1: Your Name.

   Type your *real* name, or whatever you want to appear in the message's From: field. Many email programs and address books grab your name from Outlook Express and file it away for your recipients to keep as your contact information, so don't call yourself Zaphod Beeblebrox unless you want to be filed in all your friends' contact files that way.

2. Screen 2: Internet E-mail Address.

   When you signed up, your ISP either let you pick your own user name or assigned you a not-too-clever variation on your real name. Your email address is your user name, followed by the @ sign, and then the ISP's domain name, so it'll look something like *adama@caprica.com* or *bob.harris726@comcast.net*.

3. Screen 3: E-Mail Server Names.

   Now things get a wee bit trickier. You have to tell Outlook Express what kind of mail server your ISP uses to receive (incoming) and to send (outgoing) mail and the addresses of those servers. Your choices are usually POP (Post Office Protocol, where your mail downloads from the server to your computer once) or IMAP (Internet Message Access Protocol, where your mail stays on the server). This information is more technical than what you've typed so far.

— **Type.** If your ISP uses a POP3 sever like most of them do, you don't have to touch the "My incoming mail server" menu. If your ISP uses IMAP, though, select "IMAP" on the drop-down menu.

— **Server name.** Your incoming mail server is probably named something like *mail.comcast.net* or *imap.aol.com* and your outgoing mail server is likely named something like *smtp.comcast.net*. Since some ISPs try to organize things further with incoming mail servers called *pop.central.cox.net* or *pop-server@fish.net*, make sure you know the exact addresses or you won't be able to send and receive email.

If you can't find your paperwork from the ISP, check its website and look for a Technical Support or Frequently Asked Questions area where you might find pages on "Mail setup," "POP Access," or "Server names."

 Tip IMAP is quite handy if you check mail in multiple places, like on your netbook *and* your phone.

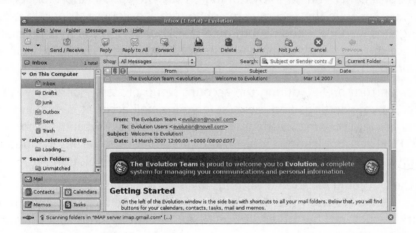

4. Screen 4: Internet Mail Logon.

Type your email account name and password.

— **Account Name.** In this box, only enter your account name—the part of your email address before the @ sign. So if your email address is *starbuck@galactica.com*, just enter *starbuck*.

— **Password.** Your password is the one you chose—or that the ISP assigned you—when you signed up for an Internet account. Despite the fact that you're typing your password here, don't turn on the box next to "Log on using Secure Password Authentication (SPA)" unless the account setup instructions from your ISP specifically tell you to do so.

When you're done, the wizard deposits you on the Outlook Express mail screen, which shows your mailboxes and folders. If you want to test it out, click Create to make a new message, address it to your email address, type *Hello World*, and click Send/Receive to fire it off. Click the same button again to see if your message appears in your new mailbox. If it doesn't, go back and recheck your settings in Tools→Accounts→Mail→Properties and make sure you correctly typed in all server addresses from the ISP.

Adding SSL Security

Outlook Express, Evolution, and Thunderbird all give you a chance during setup to encrypt your incoming and outgoing messages to add an extra layer of security. You do so by turning on *SSL encryption* (short for Secure Sockets Layer) in the Security area of your mail account settings. In most programs, you just need to turn on a checkbox telling the mail program to use the same user name and password settings for outgoing mail as incoming mail.

You can turn on SSL during the account setup process—or after you've filled in your settings and made sure your email account is working. To get back into your mail settings for any reason after you've initially configured the account, choose Tools→Accounts→Mail→Properties in Outlook Express or Edit→Preferences→Mail Accounts→Edit in Evolution.

In the Outgoing Mail Server settings in Outlook Express, for example, you just need to turn on the "My server requires authentication" checkbox. Click the Settings button and select "Use the same settings as my incoming mail server."

In Evolution's Receiving Email and Sending Email settings, select SSL Encryption from the Use Secure Connection pop-up menu and choose Password for the Authentication Type. (Turn on the Remember Password checkbox unless you really like typing it all the time.)

In Thunderbird for Windows, you can find the SSL settings at Tools→Account Settings→Server Settings; for Linux, choose Edit→Account→Settings→ Server Settings. Under Security Settings, select SSL and turn on the "Use secure authentication" checkbox.

Depending on your ISP, you may have to specify port numbers to use with SSL authentication. Check with your ISP's technical support or online account setup guide for the information. Most of the time, IMAP connections use port 993, while POP accounts use port 995.

Email Basics

No matter how you get your email—on the Web or downloaded to your netbook's mail program, the concept behind email remains the same. You read it, reply to it, send new messages, organize it, and so on. The next few pages offer a quick Email 101 refresher course.

Reading Email

Each time your mail program collects your mail, it deposits the fresh batch of new messages into your mail program's Inbox. Until you delete or move the message, it stays in your Inbox. To help you tell the old from the new, most mail programs highlight the new mail's subject lines with bold text or place dots next to the unread messages.

Most mail programs offer you a couple ways to view a message: inside a preview pane or open in its very own window.

Outlook Express, Evolution, Thunderbird, and other mail programs divide their main windows into multiple sections called *panes*, and the preview pane is the horizontal section below the Inbox list. When you click a message's subject line in the Inbox, the body of the message appears in the preview pane. If you want more room to see the message preview and less of your Inbox, drag the divider bar up or down.

When you open a message in its own window, it's easier to see all the *header* information, which is the top part of the message with all the To:, From:, Subject:, and other address stuff. The part of the message with the text is typically called the *body*.

If you have a stack of mail to plow through, you can blast through them in preview mode by tapping the up and down arrows on the keyboard to display each one's contents in the preview pane.

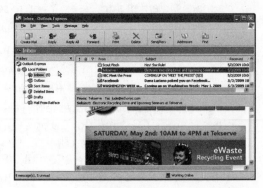

Sending Email

Once you've gone to all the trouble to set up and configure your email account, odds are you're going to want to tell everyone you know. If you've never done it before, here's how to make and send a message.

1. In your email program (webmail or ISP client) create a new, blank message.

   Look for a New or Create Mail button on your program's toolbar. Likewise, you can choose File→New Message (or however your program phrases it). An empty message form opens.

2. Address the message.

   In the message's To: field, type your recipient's email address. If you've written the person before or your computer's address book has a matching entry, your mail program may recognize the name as you type it and complete the task automatically. If you're typing the address manually, be sure to enter it exactly and remember, there are  no spaces in email addresses. If you're sending the message to multiple people, separate each address on the To: line with a comma.

3. Add additional recipients to the CC: or BCC: fields in the message header.

   If you need to keep someone else in the loop besides your main recipient(s), type those addresses on the CC: line. As with old-fashioned office memos, CC stands for Carbon Copy and means all the people involved get the exact same copy of the message, and everyone knows it. Putting addresses in the BCC: field (Blind Carbon Copy) means that nobody in the To: or CC: fields can see the address and don't know that you're sending the message to other people.

4. Summarize the message body with a few short words in the Subject line.

   Give your recipient a quick tip-off to what your message is about, which can contribute to how quickly your message is opened and read. Subject lines are increasingly important for spotting spam in your Inbox, and many spammers resort to crafty tactics go get the message read with lines like "Did you see my video?" "Important warning from the bank," or "Account update information."

5. Choose a format.

   Mail messages can come in different styles, including plain, unvarnished text or laden with fancy styling like different colors, fonts, and backgrounds. Most modern mail programs can display these messages in *rich* (formatted) text or HTML, but some can't. If you don't know what mail program your recipient uses, stick with plain text for best results. Check your mail program's menus for the commands to change your message style; most keep this info under the Format menu.

6. Type your message.

   Click in the message body below the header and start typing. You can also cut and paste clickable web links or chunks of text from other documents. If your mail program has a spell checker, you can run it to weed out embarrassing typos. Most programs let you attach a *signature file* to the bottom of each message you send. A signature file is like your letterhead (except it's at the bottom of the message). You can set one up in your program's preferences to save yourself the trouble of manually typing out your contact information on the bottom of every message.

7. Send your message.

   Click the Send button on the message to shoot it across the Net and into your recipient's Inbox.

After you send your message, a copy of it resides in your Sent mailbox, where you can refer to it if needed.

 Tip If you're on dial-up, you can address and compose a bunch of messages at once, which collect in your Outbox. When you go online, the messages in your Outbox actually go *out*.

Exploring Your Mail Program

Email programs don't just have an Inbox, but also have a few different folders depending on if the message is coming or going and what type of message it is. Outlook Express, for example, has five folders in the vertical pane in the mail program's main window, as do most other email programs. To see what's inside any of these folders, click an icon in the vertical pane to reveal its contents in the main pane. These folders include:

- **Inbox.** This box holds all the messages you've received, both read and unread, until you delete them. New messages show up in bold.

- **Outbox.** Like an outgoing box on your desk with a stack of interoffice memos waiting to be picked up, the Outbox holds messages that you've written, but that haven't been delivered yet. Click the Send/Receive button (or its equivalent in the program you use), to shoot the message out to the Internet and on its way.

- **Sent Items.** Once your message is sent, your copy of it moves to the Sent folder. Some mail programs don't start out set up to keep outgoing copies of your messages, so if your Sent folder never has anything in it, check your program's settings.

- **Deleted Items.** When you select a message you don't want anymore and click Delete, it goes here. As with the Windows Recycle Bin, the contents stay in here until you manually empty the folder. This setup can be good if you accidentally tossed something you need during a fit of spring cleaning, but it also means these messages are taking up space on your drive because they're not really gone. Look for a menu command that says something like "Empty Deleted Items folder."

- **Drafts.** This folder holds the messages you've started but not yet completed because it was time for dinner when you were still writing them. To go back and finish, go to the Drafts folder and select the message you were writing at the time you stopped.

- **Junk** (optional). Mail programs like Thunderbird and Evolution come with a built-in Junk filter that automatically routes obvious spam into its own festering holding pen so you can dump it all at once. If junk mail lands in your regular Inbox, you can teach your mail program what's junk by tagging it with the Junk button or command so the filter knows what to look out for in future deliveries.

You'll also see any other mail folders that you created in the list. Just as you can make new folders on your computer to store specific or related files, most mail programs let you create and name mail folders so you can store and organize messages. Check your mail program's menus for a "New" or "New Mailbox" option.

Once you make a special folder, you can store messages in it. These messages can be all on a certain topic or from certain people. Most mail programs let you make a *filter* that automatically routes messages from specified senders or with particular words in the subject line into your special new mailbox.

A filter, also called a *rule*, is a standing command you set up to reroute mail to a designated place, like your Quarterly Report folder, your Love Notes folder, or if it's junk mail— right into the Deleted Items or Junk folder. To set up filters or rules, go to your mail program's preferences area and look for a New Rule or New Filter option. Type the criteria for your filter (someone's email address, for example, or certain words in the message Subject line), tell the mail program which folder you want to use for these types of messages, and click OK.

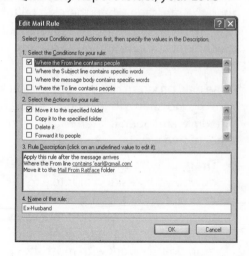

Using File Attachments

To attach a file to your open message-in-progress—like a photo, document, or video clip—just look for an Attach button in your mail program's toolbar or an Attach File link on the webmail page. Paperclips are usually the chosen icon marking an Attach File com-

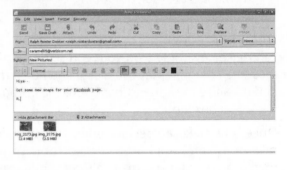

mand. Once you click the button or link, locate the file you want to send on your hard drive and then click Attach. You see the attached file's icon on your message. Finish your message and send it off.

You can tell if someone has sent you a file attachment before you even open the message when there's a telltale paperclip icon next to the message's name in the Inbox. When you double-click to open the message, the attachment appears under the message text or in the Attachments: field at the bottom of the message window.

Some mail programs let you double-click the attachment and open it right from the message, while others require you to save the attachment to your hard drive and open it later. You can free the file from its email envelope in either of two ways:

- **Drag and drop.** Drag the attached file's icon from the message window to your desktop or into a folder of your choice. If the sender went nuts with the attaching and sent a bunch of files at once, click one and press Ctrl+A to select them all so you can do a group-drag. (If you're using a webmail service, look for a Download link instead, as drag-and-drop doesn't work with most sites.)

- **Click and save.** Right-click the attached file and choose Save As from the shortcut menu. When the Save As box pops open, navigate to the folder where you want to put the attachment and click Save to dump it in. For multiple attachments, click one and press Ctrl+A to select them all. Then right-click and select Save All.

Outlook Express and Windows XP may block your attempt at seeing, opening, or saving an attachment. Due to the swarm of worms and viruses aimed at Outlook Express, Windows XP stops about 70 different file types that could *potentially* carry a virus at the gate to your Inbox by graying out the file name or displaying a warning banner to stop you from downloading the attachment. (Microsoft is not alone in its paranoia: Gmail also blocks attachments with an *.exe* file extension on the grounds that it could be a virus.)

Of course, a lot of people are probably sending you attachments that are perfectly fine, and it can be frustrating when Outlook Express butts in between you and that file you really need to open. If you have an antivirus program installed on your computer, you can safely tell Outlook Express to back off. Choose Tools→Options→Security and on the Security tab, turn off the option called "Do not allow attachments to be saved or opened that could potentially be a virus." Click OK. Restart Outlook Express if it still stubbornly refuses to let you see the attachment.

Managing Your Mail

You can do lots of things with an email message besides read it: reply to it, forward it, print it, save it, file it, or send it straight to the trash if it turned out to be spam. Here's a rundown of the basic ways to do all of these in most mail programs:

- **Replying to a message.** Writing back to someone is quick and easy with email. Just click Reply, and your mail program creates a new message already addressed to the person you're responding to. Most email programs include a copy of the text from the original message so you can respond point-by-point or just leave in the message body to refresh your correspondent's memory. In the Subject line, "Re:" prefaces the message's original subject so your friend knows you're responding to that particular message. If the message was addressed to multiple people, click the Reply All button on the message to respond to everyone at once.

- **Forwarding a message.** Clicking the Forward button on a message creates a new copy of the text in a fresh message form that you can address to other people with your own personal note at the top. Many people forward jokes around the Internet this way, but many bosses like the Forward command to delegate requests to their employees.

- **Printing a message.** Click the Print icon at the top of a message to send a copy to your printer. You can also use the standard print keyboard commands (Ctrl+P) or choose File→Print in most mail programs. Most programs include the message header (page 143) with the sender's name, subject, and time stamp up top. Text messages usually print without problems, but messages formatted in HTML may be too wide to fit on a regular piece of paper and you may have to do some tinkering in your print preferences, like rotating the paper orientation from Portrait to Landscape or shrinking the message to fit on one page.

- **Sorting a message.** All your mail doesn't have to live in your Inbox, and you can have several other mail folders to sort and store messages, as described on page 147. You can drag messages into newly-created folders or pull out messages that were accidentally sent to the Junk folder and place them where you want them.

- **Deleting a message.** When you want to trash an obsolete, unneeded, or unwanted message in a standalone email program, you have plenty of options for zapping it out of your Inbox. You can right-click its name in the Inbox and choose Delete from the menu, click the Delete button in the toolbar, or can select it in the window and press the Delete key on the keyboard. This key sends the messages to the Deleted Items or Trash folder, which doesn't mean that it's gone permanently from your computer. If you threw it out accidentally, you can get it back by opening Deleted Items or Trash, and then dragging it back to your Inbox. If you want the messages gone for good, right-click the Deleted Items or Trash folder and choose the option to delete or erase all the messages within. You can delete one message at a time here by selecting it and pressing the Delete key on the keyboard. To toss out messages in most webmail services, turn on the checkbox next to the unwanted message and click the Delete button on the toolbar. There's often a Select All option at the top of the mailbox that lets you turn on all the checkboxes at once for mass deletion.

Before long, your netbook will be humming with email flying in and out of it. If you need to take a break from all that work, a little Web browsing can be very relaxing…

Using a Web Browser

As mentioned earlier in this chapter, the World Wide Web—or just *Web* as it's known to friends—is a vast repository of collected human knowledge, complete with pictures of strawberry Pop-Tarts bursting into flame. All of this comes to your netbook through the web browser, a handy piece of software that comes with the system.

If you have a Windows XP netbook, you start out with Microsoft's Internet Explorer as your browser. Ubuntu Linux users start out with Mozilla Firefox. Firefox is available in a Windows version at *www.getfirefox.com* as well, and XP netbook owners can also opt for Google Chrome (*www.google.com/chrome*), Opera (*www.opera.com*), and Apple's Safari browser (*www.apple.com/safari*).

But no matter which browser you use, they all pretty much work the same way. The basic anatomy of a web browser includes:

1. **Title bar.** This strip across the very top of the browser window shows the name of the page like "Technology News — The New York Times" or "Facebook | Home." Click the title bar to drag it around the screen if you need to move the browser window out of the way.

2. **Menu bar.** Like most other programs, web browsers have their own menus, with commands to Print or to display the history list of all the sites you've looked at recently.

3. **Button bar.** A row of big clickable buttons below the Menu bar are shortcuts for navigating backward and forward through a series of web pages you've visited, to reload the current page, or to return to your Home page—the first site you see when you start your browser (page 157).

4. **Address bar.** Every page on the Web has its own address, also known as a URL (Uniform Resource Locator, if you want to get all Mr. Spock about it). This address starts with *http://* and continues on with the rest of the address, like *www.microsoft.com*. Once you type or paste the URL into the address bar, hit Enter to go there.

5. **Search box.** In the old days, whenever you wanted to go to a search engine, (a website like *www.google.com* or *www.ask.com* that's devoted to matching up web pages with whatever search keywords you type into it), you had to go to the search engine's own web page. Thanks to the search bar in most web browsers, you can start your search right in the browser window. Click the arrow next to the icon to change search engine sites.

6. **Links bar.** When you find a site you want to visit regularly, drag its address out of the Address bar onto the Links bar to make a one-click shortcut for return. The Links bar is called the Bookmarks bar in some circles.

7. **Tabs.** When you want to have several different web pages open at once, you can open them in tabs, which gives each one a little file-folder-like tab within the window. Click each open page's tab to reveal it in the main browser window.

8. **Main window.** Displays the web page in all its glory.

9. **Scroll bar.** If the page's contents are too long or wide to be seen all at once in the browser's window, drag the scroll bars on the side or bottom of the window to see what you're missing.

10. **Status bar.** This little strip down at the very bottom of the browser window tells you whatt the program is currently doing, like *contacting news.bbc.co.uk* or *loading http://papercuts.blogs.nytimes.com*, and can be informative if you think the browser isn't paying attention to your clicking.

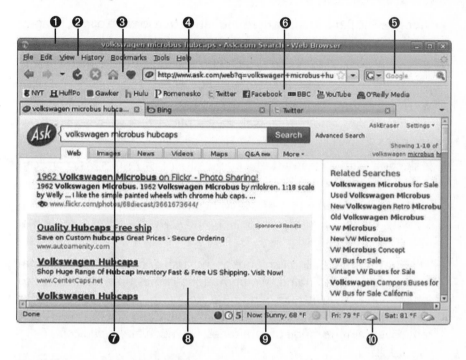

Tip Netbook screens may be on the small side, but that doesn't mean the text in your browser window has to be tiny, too. If you come across a page that needs a boost to make it readable, press the Ctrl and plus (+) keys to zoom in on the page's contents. Press the Ctrl and minus (–) keys to zoom back out, or Ctrl and zero (0) to return the page to its normal size.

Searching the Web

The Web is so vast, finding the information you seek would be impossible if it weren't for a handy group of sites called *search engines*. Most search engines work exactly the same: You type in *keywords*—search terms relating to the subject you want to read about (like *West Highland terrier breeders* or *sugar cream pie recipe*). Once you hit Enter, the search engine consults its vast index of the Web and presents you with a list of pages that contain your keywords.

Many browsers now include a shortcut Search box at the toolbar's top-right corner. This search box may be set to use a particular search engine, like Yahoo or Google. You can choose a different one by clicking the small triangle next to the box and selecting from the pop-up menu.

Popular search engines include:

- **Google.** The Big Kahuna, where you can search for web pages, images, books, news headlines, and more. (*www.google.com*)

- **Yahoo.** This time-honored search site is actually older than Google and is still a good resource. (*www.yahoo.com*)

- **Microsoft Bing.** Also able to run searches on specific categories like images, videos, and regular web pages, Microsoft's speedy search vehicle has its uses. (*www.bing.com*)

- **Ask.com.** With a clean interface and super-fast results, Ask.com can help you find what you're looking for in a flash. (*www.ask.com*)

- **Webcrawler.** Short on time? Use Webcrawler to search for results from Google, Yahoo, Microsoft Live Search, and Ask.com—all at once. (*www.webcrawler.com*)

- **Wolfram Alpha.** Billing itself not as a search engine, but a "computational knowledge engine," Wolfram Alpha comes up with answers to queries on its own instead of running around the Web looking for links to other sites. It's especially helpful for math and science questions, but covers a huge range of categories. (*www.wolframalpha.com*)

 Tip Want to find even more search engines? Go to your favorite search page and type, well, *search engines*.

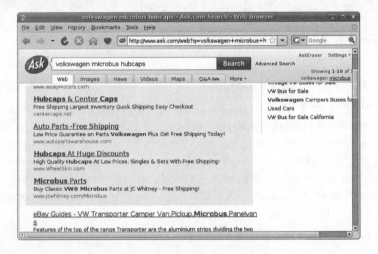

Navigating the Web

Getting around the Web is easy, given the number of different ways you have to jump from page to page. Here are the most common ways to surf the electronic waves:

- **Address.** As described in the previous section, you can go directly to a web page if you know its address. Just type it into the Address bar and hit the netbook's Enter key.

- **Link.** Those underlined or colored words on a web page are hyperlinks: shortcuts to another web page. Click the link, and you're down the rabbit hole to a whole new page.

- **Button.** The navigational icons in the browser's Button bar let you advance or retreat through web pages you've previously looked at during your surfing session.

- **History.** The browser's History list, which can get quite long if you're an avid Web walker, contains a list of all the pages you've looked at today, yesterday, and often the day before. You can specify how much history the browser remembers in the program's preferences or settings area. Press Ctrl+H to view your History on most browsers.

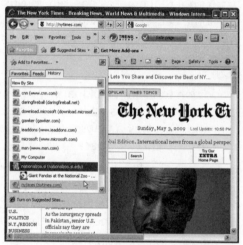

- **Bookmarks.** Like their analog counterpoints, bookmarks (also known as favorites) take you back to places you want to remember. But where having 400 bookmarks in an actual book doesn't do you much good, having 400 bookmarks in your web browser means you have 400 quick links to jump back to sites you want to revisit.

Bookmarks are an important part of the web browsing experience. The next section sells you how to make them.

Adding Bookmarks

Whatever you call them, bookmarks and favorites are incredible time savers. When you come upon a site you want to see again, bookmarking it gives you an easy link back to it—and the luxury of not having to type the address.

To make a bookmark for the page you're currently browsing, go to the Bookmarks or Favorites menu in the menu bar and choose the command that reads something like, "Add Bookmark" or "Bookmark this link" or "Add page to Favorites." In most browsers, you can also right-click the page to get a shortcut menu with a bookmarking option, and some include buttons with plus signs or stars you can click to bookmark the page.

When you opt to save a bookmark, you get the option to edit its name and even save it to the Links/Bookmarks bar. If you decline to put it in the Links bar (it's not *that* great a page, but you just might want to go back there and buy some beef summer sausage gift packs for the holidays), the link lands in the browser's Bookmarks or Favorites menu.

RSS

In addition to saving bookmarks, you can also subscribe to *RSS feeds* from icons in the browser's address bar. RSS stands for Really Simple Syndication, and it's a way a website can tell you that it's changed so you don't have to keep checking back to see if there's anything new.

When you subscribe to a feed, you get notified when the page is updated, usually by a little number next to the page's bookmark in the Links bar or Bookmarks menu indicating the number of updates. RSS is great for keeping up with blogs and news sites that change frequently.

To subscribe to a feed, just click the orange icon with the curvy white radio waves on the right side of the address bar. Now the website notifies you when it has something new to show.

To read your feeds in Internet Explorer, click the Favorites button on the toolbar and then the Feeds button or tab; click a feed name to see the newest updates. If you choose to subscribe to your feeds with Firefox's Live Bookmarks feature, you'll see a submenu with all the latest news when you select the bookmark.

If you find yourself truly hungry for feeds, consider Google Reader—a free service that lets you easily subscribe to, browse, and share news items and RSS feeds. Once you create your Google Reader account at *www.google.com/reader*, your favorite feeds also show up when you log in from your mobile phone or other wireless gadget.

Tip Want to have your browser automatically start up and land on your favorite news site, sports team home page, or blog? In Internet Explorer, choose Tools→Internet Options→General and in the box for Home Page, type or paste in your favorite site's address and click OK. In Firefox for Windows, choose Tools→Options→General to get there, or Edit→Preferences→Main for Firefox on Linux.

Transfering Bookmarks from Another Computer

If you bought your netbook to serve as a secondary or traveling computer, you probably already have a whole bunch of bookmarks in the web browser on your primary machine. Wouldn't you rather bring them along to the netbook instead of having to painstakingly recreate them? Not a problem.

Most modern browsers now include an import/export function that lets you save your bookmarks to a file that you can then transfer to a second browser. The exported bookmarks file is typically just an HTML document (*HyperText Markup Language*; the lingua franca web page code), that you can email to yourself, copy to a USB drive, or transfer over a home network to get from the old computer to the new computer. (And if you used the Windows XP Files and Settings Transfer Wizard described back on page 22, your bookmarks are probably already waiting for you on the netbook.)

If you need to move your bookmarks, here's how:

- **Internet Explorer.** Choose File→Import and Export to start the Import/Export Wizard. Click Next to kick it off and on the next screen, click Export Favorites from the list. Click Next again and choose the Favorites folder or subfolder you want to copy. Click Next, save the HTML file to the desktop, and 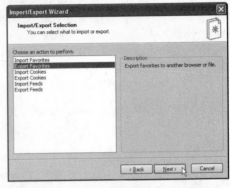 click Next one last time to finish the job. Copy the HTML file (probably called *bookmark.htm*) to the netbook. If you're using Internet Explorer on the netbook, too, choose File→Import and Export to start the Import/Export Wizard again, but select Import Favorites instead of Export and point the wizard to the HTML file you just copied to the netbook. If you're bringing them into Firefox, choose Bookmarks→ Organize Bookmarks→Import and Backup→Import HTML and pull in the file.

- **Firefox.** Choose Book- marks→Organize Bookmarks→Import and Backup→Export HTML. Pick where you want to save the *bookmarks.htm* file and click the Save but- ton. Copy the file from the saved location and transfer it to the netbook. If you're using Internet Explorer on 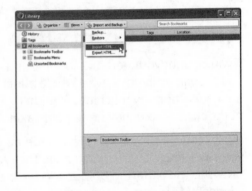 the netbook, choose File→Import and Export to start the Import/ Export Wizard again and select Import Favorites. Point the wizard to the HTML file you just copied to the netbook. If you're bringing them into Firefox, choose Bookmarks→Organize Bookmarks→Import and Backup→Import HTML and pull in the file.

 Tip If you have more bookmarks than the Library of Congress gift shop and add more every day, a program that automatically synchronizes your bookmarks across all your browsers might be in order. Free programs like SyncIT for Windows (*www. sync2it.com*) can help, as can some Firefox utilities mentioned in the next section.

Adding Tools to Your Web Browser

Your browser program is not just your window to the Web. With handy tools and mini-programs called **add-ons**, you can teach your browser new tricks. Add-ons can do things like show the weather forecast in the status bar or display buttons to control your MP3 jukebox software so you can pause the music without having to switch to the jukebox window.

Both Internet Explorer and Mozilla Firefox make it easy to add cool stuff to your browser.

- In Internet Explorer, choose Tools→Manage Add-ons→Find More Add-ons. You end up at the Internet Explorer Add-ons Gallery, where you can stroll through neatly categorized lists of IE helper programs and install them on your browser with a click of the "Add to Internet Explorer" button.

- In Firefox, choose Tools→Add-ons→Get Add-ons to see a list of available and recommended goodies. (You can also click the Browse All Add-ons link in the box to jump put to Mozilla's official Add-ons site for Firefox.) Select the add-ons you want and click the "Add to Firefox" button to install them.

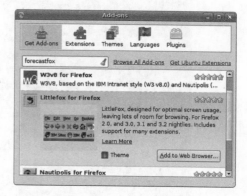

One word of caution, though: Piling up too many add-ons may slow down your browser or cause it to crash. If you're having problems, you can turn off or uninstall add-ins in the same browser menu you added them from. In IE, choose Tools→Manage Add-ons→Enable or Disable Add-ons and turn off the misbehaving code. In Firefox, choose Tools→Add-ons, find the bad one in the clickable Extensions, Themes, or Plug-ins lists, and click either the Disable or Uninstall button.

 Tip Netbook screens are on the puny side, and sometimes browsing can feel like you're looking at the Web through a pair of binoculars. To see a little bit more of the page, press the F11 key to ditch the address bar and expand the main browser window into full-screen mode. If you feel lost without your toolbars, though, there are other solutions. The Littlefox or Classic Compact add-ons for Firefox can help a bit—both squish the toolbars and other browser elements into a tighter space so you have more room for your main Web window.

You can also find browser add-ons by searching the Web. For example, if you're into social networking, Yoono (*www.yoono.com*) for IE and Firefox puts a pane on the left side of the browser window that keeps a running list of status updates from people you know on Facebook and other social sites—and it keeps your bookmarks in sync with other computers you may use. Photos your thing? The Cooliris add-in (*www.cooliris.com*) turns your browser into a 3-D wall of images. Although an add-on's website can tell you more about the software, it's generally safer to get the add-on from the IE Gallery, Mozilla Firefox Add-Ons page, or other closely monitored browser repository.

Tip The XMarks add-on for Firefox is another way to keep your bookmarks up to date across your various computers. Just install it from the Get Add-ons list on each of your Firefox-equipped computers to keep your bookmarks backed up and in sync across machines.

Browser toolbars

In addition to browser add-ons, you can enhance your browser with additional toolbars, especially if you're using Windows. (On Linux, check the toolbar's system requirements before getting too excited.) These toolbars usually add things like search shortcuts, links to maps, pop-up ad blockers, and more. In fact, most of the major search engines have their own toolbars available that do things like highlight your search terms on pages or make suggestions for relayed searches. Here's where to find more info on each of these toolbars:

- The Google Toolbar (*http://toolbar.google.com*)
- The Yahoo! Toolbar (*http://toolbar.yahoo.com*)
- The Windows Live Toolbar (*http://live.toolbar.com*)
- The Ask.com Toolbar (*http://toolbar.ask.com*)
- The AOL Toolbar (*http://toolbar.aol.com*)

People not into searching may just be annoyed by the extra buttons gunking up the top of the browser. But for people serious about the ability to search, these types of toolbars can help you dig around the Web more efficiently.

Tip One very popular browser add-on is StumbleUpon (*www.stumbleupon.com*). Just click the Stumble button in the toolbar to land on a random site that other people have really, really liked. It's a lot of fun and you never know what you might find.

7 Business Basics: Word Processing and More

Got a quarterly report, monster spreadsheet, or 100-slide presentation you need to check over while you're on the road? Netbooks may not have the most powerful videogame-churning processors, but there's more than enough mojo under the keyboard to handle standard office chores like word processing, number crunching, and slideshow creation.

As described in earlier chapters, netbooks come with the basic software like WordPad to let you do light word processing and other texty stuff. But you're not stuck with only these simple tools—you can use much more powerful productivity software (like the nearly universal Microsoft Office) on your netbook. Ubuntu Linux machines come with the OpenOffice.org suite (think Microsoft Office, but free) already installed and ready for you to dig into a document or worksheet.

But you don't have to limit yourself to using programs installed on your netbook. With the Web within reach, you can do your office homework online and even *keep* it there using tools like Google Docs & Spreadsheets and other free services designed to let you stay productive on the run. This chapter shows you what's out there, software-wise, if you need to get a little work done between Facebook visits.

Microsoft Office for Windows Netbooks

The core programs in Microsoft Office's suite—Word, Excel, and Power-Point—have been around in some form for 20 years and have enjoyed something close to world domination for much of them. For much of the corporate and academic world, Microsoft Word is *the* standard for word processing; Excel owns the spreadsheet world, and even third-graders in suburban America are composing their book reports exclusively in PowerPoint.

So it's probably safe to say that if you have a Windows netbook for business travel or school use, you might want to run at least one or two of the Office programs on it. You can write your papers or reports and format them nicely in Word, check your inventory in Excel, or proofread the latest company sales presentation in PowerPoint.

Microsoft Office has gotten more diverse since the early days of the suite. Programs in the various Office versions can include:

- **Word** for word processing, basic graphic design, and simple Web-page creation.

- **Excel** for spreadsheets, charts, formulas, and other ways to sort and manage data.

- **PowerPoint** for creating slideshows and presentations.

- **Outlook** for email, contact management, and appointment scheduling.

- **Access** for database work.

- **Publisher** for creating custom flyers, brochures, stationery, and other company-branded materials.

- **OneNote** for creating a digital shoebox where you can stash and organize text, images, and other files for the projects you're working on.

Although you don't have to have Office installed on your netbook to open and view Office files you've been sent, having the suite makes it easier, since you have the full Office toolbox at your disposal. (See page 174 for instructions on how to open Office files without actually having Office.)

 Tip Although it's the most common, Microsoft Office isn't the only business software game in town. ThinkFree Office (http://*product.thinkfree.com*) has a $50 suite that works with Office file formats and even comes in a netbook edition (page xx). Corel makes the WordPerfect word processing program and has its own office suite (you can get a free trial version at *www.corel.com*). And if you want something free that lasts longer than 30 or 60 days, OpenOffice.org also comes in a Windows version at *www.openoffice.org*. See page 171 for details.

Installing Microsoft Office

Before you go to Installationtown, there are a few things to keep in mind about putting Office on your netbook, namely *speed* and *space*.

On the speed side, although the system requirements for Office 2007 say you need at least 256 MB of memory in the netbook, 512 MB makes the program less sluggish. More memory is also recommended for Office features like Instant Search, so having more memory installed in your netbook helps zip things along.

As for space matters, the Office installation files need at least 1.5 GB of your netbook's disk space. If you have a regular 80 or 160 GB hard drive, this isn't as painful as someone with an 8 or 16 GB solid-state drive. (After you install Office, though, you can dump the downloaded installer files and grab some of that disk turf back. Just trash the Downloads folder left behind on your desktop or in whichever folder you use to store downloaded files.)

You have at least a couple ways to get the Office programs on your little laptop:

- Use the Office installation disc and an external disc drive. You also need a valid license code, so check your particular edition to see on how many computers you can install the software; the Home and Student Edition of Office 2007, for example, lets you install the programs on up to three non-commercial home computers. Insert the installer disc into the netbook's attached drive and follow the onscreen guide.

- You can download the whole enchilada from Microsoft at *office.microsoft.com*, use it free for 60 days, and then pay for it if you decide to keep it. The process works like this: You fill out a short form on the Office download site, Microsoft emails you a temporary activation code, and you download a small file called the Microsoft Download Manager to your netbook's desktop. If it doesn't automatically run after it downloads, double-click this file to kick off the download marathon and get the other 650 MB or so of Office program files. Downloading can take a couple of hours, depending on the speed of your broadband connection. When the download is complete, the installer asks you if you'd like to install Microsoft Office.

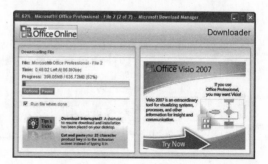

Microsoft has a thing for multiple editions of its programs: two editions of Windows XP, four main editions of Windows Vista, six assorted worldwide editions of Windows 7, and four versions of Microsoft Office 2007. The Office editions vary by the different combinations of included programs. But even the most basic one—Home and Student Edition—comes with Word, Excel, and PowerPoint. The more expensive business-oriented Office packages include corporate tools like the Access database program.

But remember that you can choose what gets installed. Click the Install Now button if you want to put everything on the netbook. Click the Customize button on the installer's dialog box if you want to get picky. Want Word but feel the need to leave Excel and PowerPoint at home? Just tell the installer so.

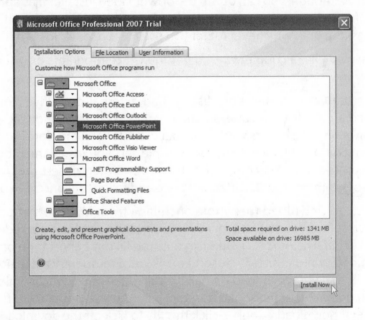

Tip If you downloaded Office as a free trial and want to go ahead and buy it before your 60 days are up, you can pay anytime. Just click the round Office button in the top-left corner. Click the Options button (which is called Word Options, Excel Options, and so on, depending on which room in the suite you happen to be in). Click Resources in the left pane and then, next to Activate Microsoft Office, click the Activate button to open the Activation Wizard. Click the Convert button and get out your credit card to pay for your official product key that unlocks the Office software permanently.

Getting Around Microsoft Office

Once you install Office, summon your program of choice from Start→All Programs→ Microsoft Office→Microsoft Office Word 2007 (or Excel, or PowerPoint) to get rolling. Or, if you want to add your most-used programs to your Start menu where you can easily find them, right-click each pro-gram's name in the All Programs submenu and choose "Pin to Start Menu."

Microsoft Office on the netbook works just like Microsoft Office on a desk-top or full-sized laptop except that you have less of a screen to see it on. And it may be a tad slower, depending on the amount of memory you have installed on the netbook.

If you're already an Office power user, you're ready to jump right in now. If you're still a bit of a novice, check out one of many large, heavy books on the subject, like *Office 2007: The Missing Manual* (*www.missingmanuals. com*). No matter what your familiarity, here are some quick tricks you can do right now to make Office 2007 on the netbook a little easier to use:

- **Minimize the ribbon.** The ribbon is that massive dashboard-like panel of icons and menus along the top of the screen in Office programs like Word and Excel. See how much of your netbook's screen that stuff takes up? To roll up the ribbon while you work, click the small black arrow at the top of the screen on the left and choose "Minimize the Ribbon" to make all that stuff disappear until you go back to this menu and reverse course.

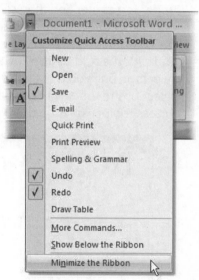

- **Make keyboard shortcuts.** Office programs have more menu items than an all-night diner, but the good news is that you can assign many of them to keyboard shortcuts. This means you can just press a couple of keys to, say, check spelling or call up the box where you can add a border to a document. To make your own keyboard shortcuts—or see which ones Microsoft has already assigned—click the round Office button in the upper-left corner and then click the Options button at the bottom of the box. Click Customize in the left panel. At the bottom of the box next to Keyboard Shortcuts, click the Customize button there to see all the menu items that are (or can be) assigned to keyboard shortcuts. Select a menu item—if it has a shortcut, it's displayed in Current Keys area. If it doesn't have a shortcut, click in the Press New Shortcut Key box and press the key combination you want to use.

- **Customize toolbars.** You can also design your own toolbars and opt to display only the icons you want to see in the Quick Access Toolbar at the top of the screen. To do so, click the round Office button in the upper-left corner and then click the Options button at the bottom of the box. Click Customize in the left panel. In the left column, select the commands and icons you want to see in the Quick Access Toolbar and click the Add button. If you make a mistake, in the right column, select the one you don't want and click Remove. Click OK to add your selections to the tiny toolbar at the top of the screen. (The Quick Access Toolbar stays up there even if you minimize the Ribbon.)

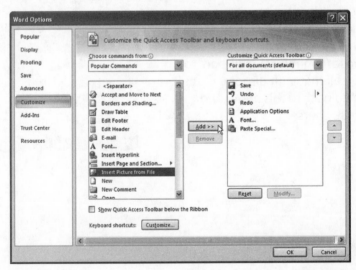

Older versions of Office let you swap different toolbars on and off the screen, depending on what you want to see. Check under the View menu for each program to see what your options are.

Tip Microsoft offers several other free programs you can download and try out for a couple months. These include Groove for collaborating, Visio for making flow-charts and other business graphics, and Project for managing complex projects. You can find them all at *http://us20.trymicrosoftoffice.com/default.aspx*.

Microsoft Office Live Workspace

Ever run off to a meeting on Monday morning and realize that the mas-sive Word report you spent all weekend slaving over is...*still at home on the netbook?* The downside to working on multiple computers is that you tend to have files scattered across various machines. Sure, you can email them to yourself or pop them onto a USB pocket drive to tote around, but Microsoft has another solution for you.

It's a little something they call Microsoft Office Live Workspace. And it's free. You get your own little corner on one of Microsoft's servers to store your Word, Excel, and other Office files. You can get to them from any Inter-net-connected computer—or even give other people permission to see or edit your files.

You can also create *workspaces*—shared online collections of documents, calendars, and other files—and collaborate with coworkers or family members. You don't even have to think too hard about what to put on-line—the Office Live site has a number of preconfigured workspaces, like a household-themed one with a grocery list, calendar, emergency con-tact sheet, and so on. Workspaces for sports teams, office projects, school classes, events, job searches, travel, and other situations are also available on Office Live Workspace.

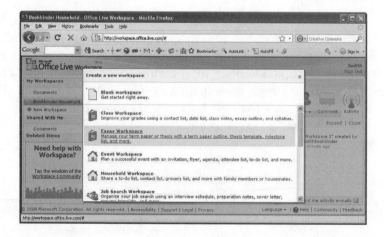

Setting Up Your Office Live Workspace

Getting your own chunk of the Office Live Workspace action is simple:

1. Point your web browser to *www.officelive.com* and sign up.

   If you already have a Windows Live ID (that is, an account with Microsoft, like a Hotmail address, Xbox Live account, or other Microsoftian product), sign in. If you don't have an account, head over to *www.live.com* and sign up. Next, click the Get Started Now button. You need to be using either Internet Explorer or Firefox for Windows. (Sorry, Linux peeps.) Once you get your Office Live account set up, you can store up to 5 MB of stuff there, courtesy of Microsoft.

2. After you land in your newly created Office Live account, download the Microsoft Office update offered on the main page.

   Click the onscreen button for the Microsoft Office update. This downloads a small setup program that gives you menu options in your netbook's Office programs to save files right to your online workspace instead of having to copy them manually.

3. Create a new workspace.

   The main screen offers a three-step tutorial and little explanatory videos on making workspaces and adding files to them. You can follow along there or just go rogue by clicking the green plus (+) button next to Add Workspace in the left pane of the browser window. A window pops up, asking what type of workspace you want to create and offering you several preformatted choices—or even a free-form blank workspace to get you started.

4. Add documents.

   On the top row of your workspace, click the Add Document button. From the menu, you can choose to add a single file—or multiple documents. A box pops up and asks you to locate the files on your hard drive. You can upload Office files, pictures, audio clips…just about anything. You can even make your own files right here in the Office Live Workspace. Click the New button and choose the type of file you want to make, like an Excel spreadsheet, an Event list, or even a Note to yourself.

 Note Microsoft plans to replace *both* Office 2007 and Office Live Workspace in the first half of 2010 with Microsoft Office 2010. In addition to the new desktop software, Office 2010 will have a free-for-everyone Web component with stripped-down versions of Word, Excel, and the gang. Take that, Google Docs! Keep tabs on the software at *http://www.microsoft.com/office/2010*.

5. Share with others.

   Chapter 8 of this book is all about sharing documents and collaborating with others online, but who wants to wait until Chapter 8? Click the Share icon on your workspace page. Here, you can give friends, family, or coworkers permission to visit your workspace, share your files, and see what you're up to. Choose Share Workspace (unless you want to Share the Screen with someone, which is your other option here) and when the message form pops up, add the people's email addresses. They get a message with a link to your workspace, and soon everyone's sharing.

   When you're in the message form, you can also set privileges for people to edit or just view the files—handy if you want to prevent the kids from adding unhealthy items to the grocery list.

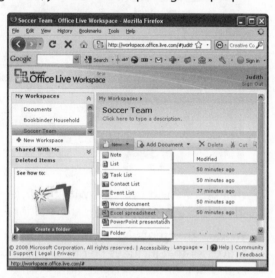

When you're done using your workspace for the day, log out. You can always come back to it by signing in at *http://workspace. officelive.com* with the name and password you used when you set up your Office Live Workspace account.

 If you have questions about how Office Live Workspace works or what you're allowed to do with it, visit the question-and-answers page at *http://workspace. officelive.com/FAQ*.

OpenOffice.org: Free Word Processing, Spreadsheets, and More

As powerful and ubiquitous as Microsoft Office is, it still costs money— about $100 to $150, and that's for the bargain-basement edition. But what if you don't have that kind of cash, or don't need complete compatibility with other people's Office files?

Consider OpenOffice.org, a free, open-source alternative to Microsoft's ubiquity. But don't worry, being a maverick won't make you a pariah: OpenOffice.org can open and save files in Microsoft Office's own formats. You can exchange those files with people using Word or Excel without having to buy those programs yourself. Pretty cool, eh?

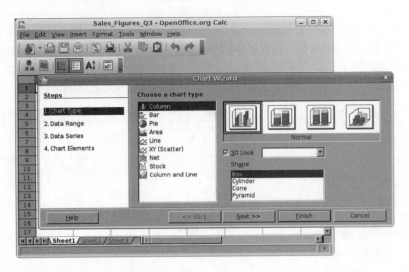

So what programs do you get with the OpenOffice.org suite? As with Microsoft Office, you get the standard toolbox for business work:

- **Writer.** An alternative to Microsoft Word, Writer is a powerful word processor that includes plenty of text and document formatting tools and other writing aids like auto-correction. You can insert graphics, tables, and other images into your documents—or just use it to make an artfully styled family holiday newsletter.

- **Calc.** If you need to crunch numbers, run formulas, make charts, and generally mine the depths of your data, use Calc instead of Microsoft Excel.

- **Impress.** You can create multimedia presentations that rival those of Microsoft PowerPoint with Impress, which lets you use animations, fonts, drawing tools, plus 2-D and 3-D clip art in your work.

- **Draw.** Edging into Microsoft Visio territory, Draw is a graphics program that you can use to make diagrams, flowcharts, org charts, and even free-form illustrations. You can open files in common formats like JPG, TIF, GIF, BMP, and PNG, and save your work in the OpenDocument format, which Microsoft Office (and most other office-software collections) can open.

- **Base.** If you have a database or want to make one, the Base program that comes with OpenOffice.org can handle the job. Due to its more corporate nature, Base is sometimes not included in OpenOffice.org on some netbooks, but you can certainly download and install it from the Internet.

If you've been using similar programs, OpenOffice.org will seem vaguely familiar, as the text-formatting tools of Writer, rows and cells of Calc, and the slides of Impress all work basically the same way as those in other business programs. And face it: You can't beat the price.

 Tip Need a spell checker for ancient Greek or an Australian medical dictionary to enhance your OpenOffice.org productivity? Programmers have come up with lots of little helper apps and other cool tools that work as add-ons to OpenOffice.org. Visit the collection at *http://extensions.services.openoffice.org* to see the vast range of stuff you can add to your suite.

Installing OpenOffice.org

The good news for Ubuntu Linux netbookers is that OpenOffice.org is already installed on your computer. It's part of Ubuntu, and you can find it on your system at Applications→Office (or Applications→Graphics if you're looking for the Draw program).

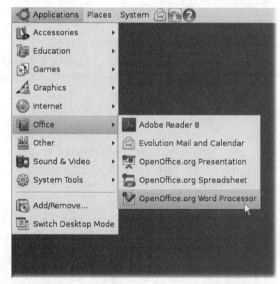

If you have a Windows netbook, you can download the suite at *http://download.openoffice.org*. You need at least 650 MB of drive space to handle the installation files, but after you install OpenOffice.org, you can toss those installers and only give up 44 MB. The suite can run on 256 MB of memory, but 512 MB is recommended. Once you install it, choose Start→All Programs→OpenOffice.org and open the program within the suite you want to use.

As with an open-source software project, there are a couple things to remember when using OpenOffice.org. First, the software is still a work-in-progress—a very advanced work-in-progress, but a few bugs and glitches may remain. Second, there's no free 90-day phone and email support like Microsoft offers.

OpenOffice.org has tons of support documents, forums, and a Frequently Asked Questions page at *http://support.openoffice.org/index.html*, but no nice person on the other end of the telephone line to gently guide you through your problem, even at $49 a call like Microsoft charges after the first 90 days. (The OpenOffice.org support page lists consultants you can hire, though.)

 Tip Need some training? You can find free OpenOffice.org tutorials online for everything from installing the software to using specific programs in the suite at *www.tutorialsforopenoffice.org*.

Using OpenOffice.org 3 to Open Microsoft Office Files

With so many major corporations, schools, and individuals using Microsoft Word, chances are someday someone will send you a Word doc. If you have Version 3 of OpenOffice.org, double-click the document and see if Writer jumps up to open it. If it doesn't, choose File→Open in Writer, navigate to the document, and open it that way. Documents in older versions of Word should open just fine in OpenOffice.org 3 as well.

But while OpenOffice.org lets you open and edit the files, it doesn't let you save files in Word 2007's *.docx* format. You can, however, save them in the old standby *.doc* format, which just about every version of Microsoft Word can open.

 Tip As handy as OpenOffice.org is, it sometimes has trouble translating intensive formatting, charts, and other complex things Word lets you do to a document. You may find borders and tables messed up, fonts looking weird, and other anomalies. If that's the case, take a browser stroll to the OpenOffice.org Ninja site at *www.oooninja.com*. In addition to tips and tutorials, you can also find converter programs that make heavily formatted Word 2007 files translate more accurately, plus versions of Office 2007 fonts for Linux and Windows XP.

Google Docs: An Online Alternative

Google started out as a simple, powerful search engine in the late 1990s, and boy, has it grown. Google now offers dozens of web-based services and an online warehouse of free software like Google Earth and Picasa (page 227).

Among these goodies is Google Docs & Spreadsheets, an online word-processor, spreadsheet, and presentation suite that lets you make and edit files right in your web browser. Your files live on the Web, where you can get to them from any Internet-connected computer. From here, you can send files by email, share them with other users, or save them on your netbook in several common formats like plain text, PDF (page 191), Web-page code, or Microsoft Word's own *.doc* format.

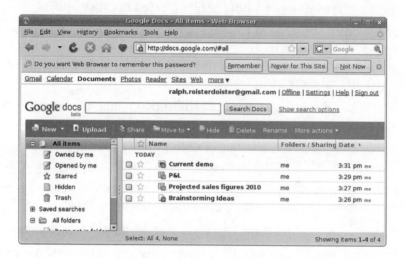

You can even collaborate with coworkers on the same file at the very same time (page 211) while chatting over Google Talk (page 200)—eliminating the need for expensive long-distance phone calls. As flexible as it is, Google Docs doesn't yet have the advanced features that Microsoft Office and OpenOffice.org give you for complex documents.

Like OpenOffice,org, Google Docs & Spreadsheets is free as long as you sign up for an equally free Google account. (If you have a Gmail address, you can use that.) Then all you need is a compatible web browser, like the current versions of Internet Explorer and Firefox. Hop to *docs.google.com* and get started.

Using Google Docs & Spreadsheets

Once you log in, you see your own little workspace. The pane on the left shows the location and ownership of all your files, while the main part of the browser window displays all the file names. The blue menu bar above it all offers the following choices:

- **New.** Click here to create a new document, presentation, spreadsheet, or form—or a folder to keep them all in. The last option, From Template, lets you make a new file based on a collection of online templates created by Google and other companies.

- **Upload.** Select this option to move copies of existing files like Word documents, Excel spreadsheets, or PowerPoint presentations to Google Docs. If you don't actually own Microsoft Office, this feature gives you a way to open and see files created in Office apps.

- **Share.** Click this button to invite other people via email to view selected files. You can make them collaborators (which means they can make changes to your files) or mere viewers (look, don't touch). More on all that on page 211.

- **Move to.** Use this command to shift documents into other folders you've created on your Google Docs workspace.

- **Hide.** Sweep selected files out of sight (from you and others) with the Hide command. You can always undo this move if you change your mind.

- **Delete.** Dump the selected file into the Trash bin. You need to empty the Trash to flush the discarded file out to the virtual sea.

- **Rename.** Choose this command to change the name of the selected file.

- **More actions.** This collection of commands lets you control the sharing of a file (and who's in charge of it), see the revisions made to it, or save it in a number of different formats.

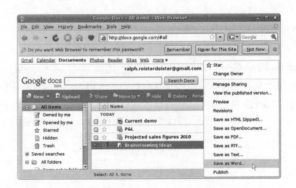

When you create a new document, spreadsheet, or presentation, the browser window becomes a blank canvas, ready for you to type text or enter formulas. The menus along the top of the screen offer most of the standard commands you'd expect to find in office software (cut, copy, paste, save, check spelling, word count, and so on), plus text-formatting tools and commands for inserting tables, comments, images, and links into the file.

Google Docs Offline

"Sure," you say, "Google Docs is great—as long as you have an Internet connection. But when you can't get on the Web, you're *toast*."

Well, not exactly. Thanks to some nifty technology powered by the Google Gears software, you can have copies of your Google Docs files synchronized between the Web and your hard drive. So if the Internet goes down (or you're on an airplane), you can still work on your documents.

To use Google Docs offline, first get Google Gears going on your netbook:

1. Log into your Google Docs page and click the Offline link up at the top of the screen.

   A box pops up offering to install "offline access" for Google Docs.

2. At the bottom of the box, click the "Get Google Gears now" button.

   A box pops up asking you to allow *https://docs.google.com* as a trusted site. Turn on the checkbox saying you trust the site and click Allow. When the process is finished, the site asks if it can put a shortcut for Google Docs on your desktop as well.

Google Gears is now ready to go, snagging copies of your files behind the scenes as you work. Even if you're cut off from the Internet, you can still get to your files by clicking the Google Docs shortcut on your desktop or by pointing your web browser to *http://docs.google.com*. When you regain Internet access, the document on your netbook updates itself on the Google Docs site.

Working with Contacts

Unless you're talking about corrective eyewear, the word *contacts* sounds impersonal and businesslike. Sure, a contact can be a potential client you met at the sales conference last month, but a contact can also be your brother, mother, or sorority sister. A contact is pretty much anybody you email, call, or visit.

A contact file for someone can contain as little or as much information as you can cram in about the person, including:

- First and last name
- Email addresses
- Postal addresses (work, home)
- Phone numbers (home, work, cell, weekend cabin in Tahoe)
- Fax number
- Instant message screen name

Depending on the program, you may also have places to fill in other random bits of information about the person like a birthday, anniversary, or short notes like "use Vero Beach phone number from November to April."

Just about every computer operating system has some sort of built-in program that saves and sorts contact information like an electronic Rolodex. Contacts programs let you look someone up by typing in the name (or part of the name), and you can often set up an email message to the selected contact with just a click.

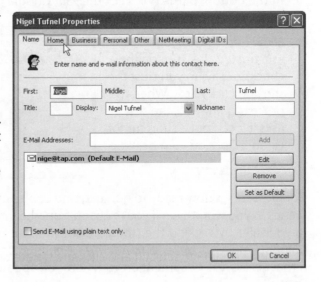

Making New Contacts

Whether you realize it or not, your netbook has at least one address book on it already. Here, you can add new contacts or import ones from other computers and programs (page 181).

- **Windows XP.** The Windows Address Book (which integrates with Outlook Express) comes with XP; later versions of Windows have Windows Contacts. To see it, choose Start→All Programs→Accessories→Address Book. When you open it, you see the names of people you've collected with the "Add Sender to Address Book" command in Outlook Express. To make a new contact file for someone, choose New→New Contact and fill in as much (or as little) information as you want about the person by clicking through the Name, Home, Business, Personal, and Other tabs along the box. To add more information (or update existing info), double-click the entry. When it's time to clean out the Address Book, select unwanted entries and click the Delete button at the top of the window.

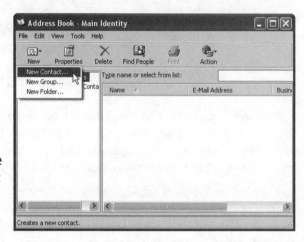

- **Ubuntu Linux.** Evolution, the email program that comes with Ubuntu Linux, keeps its own contacts file. To see it, choose Applications→ Internet→Evolution Mail and click the Contacts button on the left side of the screen. To make a new contact file for someone, choose New→Contact. A tabbed box pops up where you can fill in details like name, email address, various phone numbers, and plenty of miscellaneous information like the contact's spouse's name or a video chat screen name. To edit or add information, just double-click the entry. To remove a contact, select it and click the Delete button.

If you have Microsoft Office on your netbook, you probably use Outlook, the suite's email and personal organizer program. If you haven't used Outlook before, start up the program and click the Contacts button, then choose New→Contact to create a contact file.

If you use a web-based email service like Yahoo Mail, Hotmail, America Online, or Gmail, your contacts are right there, whenever you log into your account. In fact, web-based mail is the easiest way to corral your contacts, because they live in the magic cloud and you can get the same fully updated information with your netbook, or indeed, any Internet-connected computer.

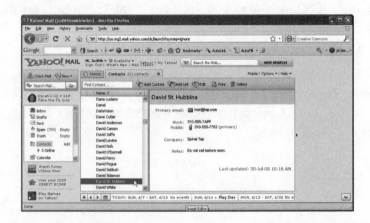

To get to the contacts area of most webmail services, log into your mail account and click the Contacts link or tab. To add a new person to the list, click the Add or New button in the contacts area to pull up a blank form that you can then fill in with all of the person's information.

Managing Contacts Between Web and Netbook

Are your contacts where you need them to be? If you want to get existing contacts onto your netbook, you probably fall into one of three categories:

- **Your contacts are on the Web.** If you've been using Yahoo Address Book or whatever contacts program comes with your Webmail account, you can use that on your netbook with no extra work.

- **Your contacts are on another computer, and you want to move them to the netbook.** You have a little work to do. See the next section for instructions on exporting your contacts from their current program and into the contacts program on your netbook.

- **Your contacts are on another computer and you want to move them up to the Web.** Even if you have your contacts in a program on your netbook, putting them on the Web as well lets you see them whenever you have an Internet connection. See page 183 for instructions. You can also find online services that let you keep everything in sync between the computer and the Web.

The next few pages tell you how to sling that address book around to the Web and back—or just onto the netbook if you want.

Transferring Contacts Between Computers

If you use the same email-and-contacts program in both places, copying your contacts between computers is a breeze. For example, you may have Microsoft Outlook on both your desktop PC and your spiffy little netbook. If so, moving a copy of your contacts files goes something like this:

1. Open Outlook on the first computer (the one with all the contacts files), and choose File→Import and Export.

2. Select "Export to a file" and click Next.

3. Since you're going from Outlook to Outlook, choose "Personal Folder File (.pst)" and click Next.

4. From the list of stuff in Outlook's Personal Folders list, select Contacts, and click Next.

5. Save the file to a USB drive or to the desktop so you can transfer it by email or server.

6. Move the exported file to the netbook via USB drive, email, or network server.

7. Open Outlook on the netbook and choose File→Import and Export.

8. Select "Import from another program or file" and click Next.

9. Select "Personal Folder File (.pst)" from the list and click Next.

10. Locate the file on the netbook and import it into its copy of Outlook, which now has all of the contacts from your desktop's version of Outlook.

The steps are slightly different if you're transferring contacts between different programs, but the concept is the same. There's a format that most contacts program can read, called **Comma Separated Values**, or CSV for short. (As you might expect from the name, the individual bits of information in a *.csv* file—like first name, last name, email address, and so on—are separated by commas.)

In many cases, you can export your contacts as a big *.csv* file from one program, copy it onto a USB drive, connect that drive to the netbook, and then use the mail program's import command to pull in that same *.csv* file.

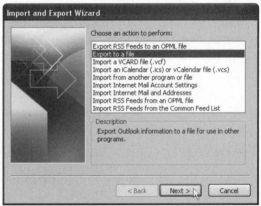

Tip Another format you may encounter in the contacts world is vCard, or *.vcf*. You often see vCard (also known as electronic business cards) stuck to the end of messages as attachment files. When you get one of these in Outlook or any program that can import vCards, right click the vCard attachment and choose "Add to Contacts" to add the person to your address book.

Transferring Contacts from Computer to Web

Having your contacts on your netbook's hard drive means they're always at your fingertips, even without an Internet connection. But say you want to put them up on the Web too, either as a backup or to move more of your life online. Even if you haven't done much with the contacts in your Gmail, AOL, Yahoo, or Hotmail account, you can pull the contacts out of Outlook (or wherever you keep them) and import the names and addresses into your webmail account.

Gmail, Yahoo, and Hotmail let you import contacts from other programs as long as you've exported the information as a *.csv* file. Here's how:

1. Open your contacts file in your email program or address book. Look for an Export option under the File menu and choose Comma Separated Values or CSV as the file type.

2. Export the file to the computer's desktop or another easy-to-find location.

3. Log on to your webmail account and click the Contacts link or tab.

4. Click the Import or Import Contacts link. In Gmail, for example, the Import link is on the upper-right side of the Gmail contacts window.

5. The site asks you to locate the *.csv* file you exported from your mail program.

6. Select the *.csv* file and import the contacts into your webmail account.

Now, when you open your webmail's contacts file, you should find plenty of friends there.

Syncing Contacts and Calendars to Devices

If you have a smartphone or personal organizer that you want to connect and sync to your Windows netbook, you shouldn't have a problem as long as you can run the device's synching software on your netbook. If you don't have a CD drive for the netbook, you can download the software:

- Blackberry Desktop Manager (*http://na.blackberry.com/eng/services/desktop*)

- Palm Desktop for Palm and Treo devices (*http://kb.palm.com/wps/portal/kb/common/article/33529_en.html*)

- Microsoft ActiveSync for Windows Mobile smartphones (*http://www.microsoft.com/windowsmobile/en-us/help/synchronize/activesync-download.mspx*)

- iTunes for iPhone (*http://www.apple.com/itunes*)

If you want to sync the gadget with two computers (the netbook and your other one), check the sync program's settings or manual for using the device with multiple machines. Some may just sync up automatically and use timestamps to sort things out, while others may need more fiddling to add the device and, say, have it work with multiple Outlook profiles.

 Note Palm's latest smartphone, the Palm Pre, skips desktop synchronization in favor of keeping your online data up-to-date. The support area of Palm's website has information about setting that up at *www.palm.com/us/support/downloads/pre/migration/index.html*. If you pine for a way to keep your data closer to home on the netbook, companies like Chapura (*www.chapura.com*) and CompanionLink (*www.companionlink.com*) have desktop sync solutions for the Pre.

Connecting a phone or PDA to an Ubuntu Linux netbook is considerably trickier, and some devices like the Blackberry don't work at all (unless you do some major tinkering). However, Ubuntu does come with a program called the Gnome Pilot for setting up and syncing with Palm devices with the Evolution program. Connect your Palm handheld and choose System →Preferences→PalmOS Devices to get started with the Gnome Pilot setup assistant.

Online Contact Syncing

Even if you don't use a webmail service, there are plenty of ways to keep your address book online where you can always get to it. There are also services, both free and paid, that synchronize your contacts across multiple computers so your address book is current, no matter where you update it.

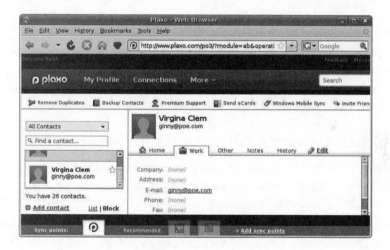

Here are some of the options out there:

- **Plaxo.** A free service, Plaxo has an online address book that synchronizes with Outlook Express, Outlook, Gmail, LinkedIn, Hotmail, the Mac OS X Address Book, America Online, and Windows Mail. The Pulse feature serves as a dashboard for all your social-networking sites, pulling in updates from your friends on Facebook, Flickr, and other popular gathering places (page 215). Plaxo has software for Windows netbooks and a version for Linux machines using the Mozilla Thunderbird email program. (*www.plaxo.com*)

- **MobileMe.** At $100 a year, Apple's life-syncing service that keeps contacts, calendars, and mail all up to date between PCs, Macs, and iPhones is not cheap. But you also get 20 GB of space on Apple's servers to use for online galleries to show off your photos and videos, plus mail and file storage. MobileMe, however, does not play well with Linux browsers. (*www.apple.com/mobileme*)

- **Google Sync.** Although it's still in the early stages, Google now has a service that synchronizes online Gmail contacts and Google Calendar information with your iPhone, Blackberry, Windows Mobile device, and a number of other smartphones You don't need to sync the phone to the netbook to transfer the info because Google Sync keeps track of new entries no matter where you make them. And it's free. (*www.google.com/sync*)

Plenty of other online address books are out there, and your mobile phone carrier may even have a syncing solution as well, like Nokia's Ovi service (*www.ovi.com*). And where there are contacts, there are usually calendars.

Staying on Track with Calendars

In addition to serving as your electronic address book, the netbook can also step up to the plate as your personal appointment diary. Even if you don't have a dedicated calendar program on the computer to keep track of events and schedules, you have plenty of options on the Web.

Desktop Calendar Programs for Windows

Windows XP doesn't include a calendar program (Outlook Express is sadly lacking in this department compared to its beefier, more expensive cousin, Outlook), but you can find plenty of freebies at shareware download sites.

If you've ponied up the big bucks for Microsoft Office, then you have the mighty Outlook at you disposal. You can see your daily, weekly, and monthly schedules with the click of the Outlook window's Calendar button. You make a new entry on the calendar by choosing New→Appointment and filling out the box with the date, time, name of the event, notes, and so on.

The toolbar in the Appointment window has controls that let you set an alarm to warn you—five minutes to two days ahead of time—that this event's looming. If it's a standing meeting or appointment, click the Recurrence button in the toolbar to schedule it in advance—and all at once.

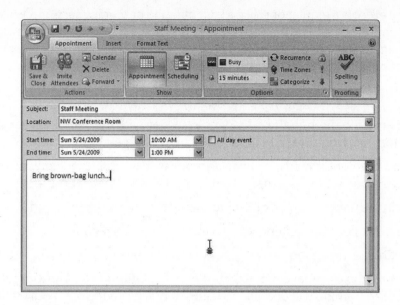

Outlook has a handy search box that lets you rifle through your schedule to see where you were on a given day or where you'll be a few days from now. Like contacts, Outlook calendars can sync up with a number of portable gadgets, including Windows Mobile devices and iPhones.

 Tip You can use Google Calendar Sync to keep your Outlook and online Google Calendars (page 186) up to date with each other. Just download and install the Google Calendar Sync software—you can find a link to it, along with thorough instructions, at *http://snipurl.com/ims8g*. Type your Google name and password when prompted to get Google Calendar and Outlook sharing nicely. Don't have a Google Calendar? See page 189.

Evolution Calendar for Ubuntu Linux

Basically the open-source version of Outlook for Linux, Evolution handles mail, contacts, and calendars—plus other digital scraps of information like memos and task lists. If you need to start making sense of your schedule, choose Applications→Office→Evolution and click the Calendars button in the main window. Choose New→Appointment to make a new entry and fill out all the pertinent information like date, time, and location.

If the event is a regular one, like a staff meeting or therapy session, click the Recurrence button at the top of the window. A box opens where you can automatically schedule the appointment at the proper intervals instead of plotting it on the calendar one instance at a time.

Buttons along the top of the Evolution Calendar toolbar let you see your day, work week, overall week, and month. You can search for appointments by name, flip through the calendar day by day with the Next and Previous buttons, and jump back to the present by clicking the Today button.

If you have one already, you can also pull in a synchronized copy of your online Google Calendar (page 189) to display within Evolution, too:

1. In the Calendars area of Evolution, choose File→New→Calendar.

    A box pops up, inviting you to select a type of calendar to make.

2. Choose Type: Google.

    Give the calendar a name to display in Evolution's list—*My Google Life* or something will do. Next to Username, type your Gmail address. Under Refresh, pick a frequency for how often Evolution updates itself with your Google Calendar information. Turn on the checkbox for SSL (it's a security thing) and pick a color for your calendar to make it stand out against others in Evolution. Turn on the checkbox next to "Copy calendar contents locally for offline operation" if you want to see your schedule without being connected to the Internet. Finally, click OK.

3. Enter your Gmail password when prompted.

    Providing you typed the password correctly, Evolution now pulls in your Google Calendar events and displays the events onscreen in its main window.

Because they're accessible from any number of computers and by any number of people, online calendars have become very popular over the past few years. The next section describes some of the more popular options, in case you'd like to sign up for one yourself.

 Tip If you work a non-traditional schedule like Tuesday to Saturday or from noon to 9:00 p.m., you can adjust your calendar views and what day your "week" starts in your calendar program's preferences area.

Online Calendars

If you gather your mail through Yahoo, Gmail, America Online, or Microsoft Hotmail, you've probably noticed a link to a calendar somewhere on your mailbox page. It makes sense—say you get an email dinner invitation and want to mark it down. Boom! The calendar program's right there within reach.

And needless to say, the *online* part of online calendars makes them incredibly convenient for viewing on a number of machines. You can update your daily schedule on your netbook before you leave the hotel for the day and then check your appointments on your mobile phone. Most online calendar services now have streamlined views that fit nicely on mobile phones and wireless organizers.

If you don't use webmail, you can still sign up for a free account just to use the calendar part of the package.

- **Google Calendar.** Like everything Google, Calendar is full of nice touches, like icons displaying the four-day weather forecast. There's also a Quick Add box: You type in a short phrase like "dinner at Brick Lane Curry House Monday at 7pm" and Google automatically sticks the event right in there the following Monday at 7:00 p.m., without you having to navigate to that day square to make the entry. If you use Gmail, Google also notices things that look like invitations and events in your messages and gives you a link to add them to the calendar with one click. (*http://calendar.google.com*)

- **Yahoo Calendar.** Just a click away from your Yahoo mailbox, Yahoo Calendar has some nice features of its own—once you're in the Calendar area, click the Options link to check them out. You can easily add horoscopes, weather, and holidays. You can import and export Yahoo Calendar information to Palm and Outlook. (*http://calendar.yahoo.com*)

- **America Online.** AOL's calendar offering is fairly uncomplicated, making it easy to add events like holidays and moon phases. You can also install a plug-in that syncs up the calendar between AOL, Outlook, and a Windows Mobile phone, iPod Touch, or iPhone; click the Sync button on the main calendar screen to get the software. (*http://calendar.aol.com*)

- **Windows Live Calendar.** Microsoft's online calendar comes with a clean design and big easy-to-click tabs for showing your different views. You can make a Birthday Calendar for your contacts to keep those special days in mind ahead of time. The Outlook Connector plug-in lets you see your Live calendar events alongside your boring old work calendar in Outlook. (*http://calendar.live.com*)

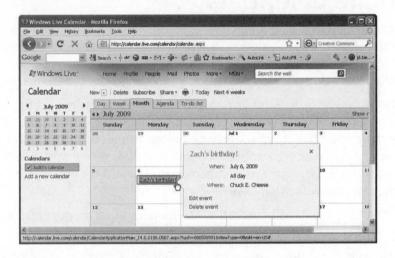

Once you get used to the portability and convenience of online calendars, you'll probably never want to deal with the spiral-bound paper versions again.

Calendars: Sharing and Subscribing

Another thing online calendars are good at? *Sharing.* Each one described in the previous section offers a link or tab that lets you share your calendar online with specified friends, people on your contacts list, or the world at large.

With most calendar sites, you can also *subscribe* to public calendars other people have put on the Web. These calendars can be of anything—shared calendars from friends and family, Federal holidays, religious holidays, World Cup match schedules (which are religious holidays for some people), rock-band tour dates, and more.

You can also add public calendars (even to programs like Outlook and Evolution) by supplying the calendar's URL when you add a new calendar. Apple's iCal program has inspired a number of public calendars that you can download as an *.ics* file, (the common format used for shared online calendars) and import into other online calendar sites at *http://www.apple.com/downloads/macosx/calendars/*.

To add a public calendar, look for a Subscribe link on your calendar page and see what the site has to choose from. In Google Calendar, for example, you add a public calendar in the Other Calendars area on the left side of the screen. Click the Add button and choose "Add a public calendar" to see a catalog of calendars you can subscribe to. In Windows Live Calendar, click the Subscribe link at the top of the page to go to a page that lets you paste in a public calendar's URL or import an *.ics* file.

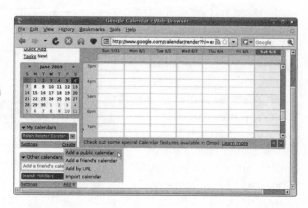

Tip In Outlook 2007, click the Search Calendars Online link in the left pane of the Calendar screen to see Microsoft's roundup of fun, wacky, and even helpful public calendars.

Viewing PDFs with Adobe Reader

Way back in the closing years of the 20th century, sending and sharing files around the Internet was something of challenge. Even if you were just emailing a document in a common format like Microsoft Word, you had to worry about the little things: Does my recipient have the same fonts that are in the document? Do they have the right version of Word? Do they even *have* Word?

Fortunately, Adobe Systems came along and invented the Portable Document Format, or PDF for short. When a file is converted to a PDF, it retains the look of the original layout, fonts, and other graphic elements used in whatever program was used to make it in the first place—and it can do so in a much smaller file size that's usually pretty manageable for email. (Page 100 tells you how to make your own PDF files from your documents.)

Almost everyone—including the U.S. government—is using PDF files now, doing things like converting forms to PDF files that you can download, print, fill in, and mail. Music labels are putting CD liner notes in PDF files.

And thanks to free software called Adobe Reader, you can easily open and view PDF files on your netbook and in your web browser. Adobe Reader comes preinstalled on many netbooks, but you can always snag the latest version at *www.adobe.com*. Check your All Programs or Applications menus to see if it's listed.

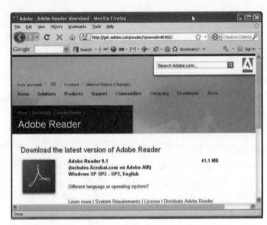

As long as you have Reader installed, you're set. Now you don't have to worry if someone emails you a PDF file, or if you need to grab the 1040EZ on April 14th from *www.irs.gov*. Just double-click the file to open it in all its glory.

Versions of Adobe Reader are available for just about every operating system out there (which adds to the format's near-universal compatibility), including Linux. But it's not the only thing that can open and display PDF files these days, either.

There are plenty of other PDF programs for Windows out there like Foxit Reader at *www.foxitsoftware.com/pdf/reader*. Ubuntu users can install a variety of other PDF reader programs by choosing Applications→Add/Remove and searching for *pdf* in the Search box to see what's in the software repository. (Page 71 has more information on installing Linux software.)

Working with Graphics

Graphics can be anything from a basic bar chart to a complex illustration, so the programs that make graphics tend to range widely in price and power. The netbook's small screen (and low-powered processor) may not make it the best choice for doing detailed work, but for times when you need to whip out a quick graph or illustration, you do have some options beyond Window's XP's simple Paint program (page 43).

Here are some options:

- **OpenOffice.org Draw.** The Open-Office.org suite included in Ubuntu includes a full-featured graphics program called Draw (page 172), which can save images in the OpenDocument format. OpenOffice. org comes in a Windows version as well, available for download from *www.openoffice.org*.

- **Microsoft Visio.** If you need to make flowcharts or map data, Microsoft's Visio software for Windows might be your best buddy. At $260, it's not cheap, but you can download a free 60-day trial version or test it out in sample form in a web browser at *http://office.microsoft.com/visio*.

- **SmartDraw.** Need a Windows business graphics program? Organizational charts, project timelines, forms, floor plans, and charts? Smart-Draw can handle all of that, and you can insert these files into Microsoft Office or Corel WordPerfect documents. The program costs $200, but you can download a free trial at *www.smartdraw.com*.

- **DrawPlus.** If you need a simple drawing program to make hand-drawn illustrations on your Windows netbook, DrawPlus 4 might do the trick—and it's free. For a mere $10, you can upgrade to DrawPlus 6, which includes more filters, effects, and features. Free Serif Software also has free 3-D graphics and page-layout software at *www.freeserif-software.com*.

- **Scribus Desktop Publishing.** Scribus is a free, open-source page layout program for Windows and Linux. A Windows installer is available, and the site has instructions for installing Scribus in Ubuntu, which is a little more complicated. (*www.scribus.net*)

- **KompoZer.** For budding web designers, this free program lets you make web pages without having to wade around in a river of HTML code or expensive programs. (*http://kompozer.net*)

- **Google Docs Draw.** If you need a simple set of lines, charts, or free-form squiggles for a Google Doc in progress, just choose Insert→Drawing to open up the Drawing Editor palette. (*docs.google.com*)

- **Inkscape.** An open-source alternative to Adobe Illustrator and Corel-Draw, Inkscape can create art like company logos, maps, web page graphics, diagrams, and freeform illustrations. It's available in versions for Windows, Linux, and the Mac OS. (*www.inkscape.org*)

- **The GIMP.** Although it's more of a photo-manipulation program, the GIMP (the Gnu Image Manipulation Project) can make photo illustrations by adding type and funky effects. It's included with Ubuntu Linux; a work-in-progress version for Windows is available at *http://gimp-win. sourceforge.net/stable.html*.

Chapter 9 has more about working with photos and the GIMP. One word of caution, if you plan to do a lot of graphics work on your netbook: Get a mouse, trackball, or tablet (page 88) to save your clicking hand from turning into a cramped claw from doing detailed work on such a tiny machine.

> **Tip** If you already have Microsoft Office installed on your netbook, don't overlook the page-layout and drawing tools built into Word. Although it's not as powerful or as flexible as a full-blown graphics and layout collection like Adobe Creative Suite (Illustrator, Photoshop, Flash, and Dreamweaver for a mere $1800), Word's basic toolbox is often enough. To get a taste, click the Insert tab in Word 2007 to see the types of clip art, tables, charts, and other graphic elements you can put into a Word document.

Welcome to the Free World: Software

Free software is not an unknown concept to Linux people. After all, the system is available for free all over the world and it's been updated, improved, and lovingly distributed by thousands of people over the years. And adding new free software is easy in Ubuntu: Choose Applications→Add/Remove and search the repository for new and cool programs. (If you don't find what you're looking for there, search through the repository at System→Administration→Synaptic Package Manager, which lets you find and install new programs in a similar way.)

Since it's the most popular and widely used operating system in the world, Windows has even more software to choose from. Although there are some really, really expensive programs for Windows out there, many of the available programs are free (or really inexpensive).

Unlike open source software in the Linux world, however, free and cheap Windows programs tend to be demo or stripped-down versions of larger, more expensive programs or software written by independent developers. Some programmers charge a fee; others give away their software but humbly ask for a small donation.

You can find many of these gems, usually referred to as *shareware* or *freeware*, on websites called *shareware archives*. These sites collect free or nearly free programs—everything from games to business tools like currency converters—for Windows and other systems.

There are a few things to remember with freeware and shareware, though. For starters, you're probably not getting any one-on-one technical support aside from a Frequently Asked Questions Page or maybe a simple user guide posted on the programmer's website. Then again, many free programs have dedicated mailing lists, active discussion forums on the developer's website, or links to ask the programmer a question directly. So with a little extra effort, you might actually get better help than from Big Software's technical support representative on the other side of the world.

More importantly, however, are safety concerns. Malicious software gets passed around the Web disguised as cool games or helpful utilities and can wreck your netbook—or even steal valuable information like bank-account passwords and Social Security numbers.

To help keep yourself safe, only download shareware from well-known sites (like the ones listed here) that test the programs for spyware. And by all means, if you plan to download a lot of software, install antivirus and antispyware programs on your netbook (page 264).

That said, here are some of the better-known shareware archives to explore:

- **Download.com.** The name says it all, and this site (owned now by CBS Interactive) is a vast treasure trove of free and cheap software for Windows, Mac, mobile phones, and even Web-based wares. (*www.download.com*)

- **TuCows.** With its distinctive double-headed bovine logo (Two Cows, get it?) is one of the oldest and largest shareware sites on the Web, hosting 40,000 programs from around the world. Not everything is free here, but it's easy to find the stuff that is—just click the Freeware tab. (*www.tucows.com*)

- **VersionTracker.** Neatly designed with minimal graphics, VersionTracker is a great site to browse for Windows, Mac, Palm, and iPhone freeware, with links to news and reviews from the world of software. (*www.versiontracker.com*)

- **SourceForge.** This site has information on many open-source software projects. It's a little geekier than most software sites, but you can find really inventive and interesting works-on-progress here. (*http://sourceforge.net*)

Remember, if you really like a piece of software you find on the Web—open-source project or a free program—making a small contribution to the developer (through PayPal, for example) can help show your appreciation. Shareware and free software sites often provide links to the programmer's own website, where most will cheerfully accept donations.

8 Collaborating with Others

I f the Internet has accomplished one thing, it's bringing people around the world together faster and easier than ever before. You can send an email message in seconds compared to the days or weeks it takes to mail information on paper. But even email has given way to more immediate forms of online communication: instant messaging, voice chat, and video conferencing. And when you buy a netbook, you already have the hardware (computer, webcam) and often the software to do it all for no more than the cost of the Internet connection that you probably also already have.

That's right—your netbook can make long-distance phone calls or let you say goodnight to the kids when you're stuck in a hotel room a couple continents away. It also lets you see who's online right this moment with an instant messaging program.

This chapter shows you how to set up your netbook to connect with the people in your life in real time. If the colleague you're working with isn't always online when you are, this chapter also takes a look at sites designed for long-distance collaboration. You can work together on a document, file, or project even when one of you is in Sydney and the other is in San Antonio.

What You Can Do Online

Online collaboration can be as simple as shooting a lunch invitation to your coworker in the next cubicle via instant message. It can be a video chat with your boss that jumps 12 different time zones. Or it can be three college buddies all working on a screenplay by editing the same online document—even though they live in three different states.

To do all of those things, the only software you need is an instant-messaging program and a web browser, both of which probably came on your netbook. On the hardware list, your netbook (with its built-in webcam or an external clip-on one) and a broadband Internet connection should suffice. Except for exchanging plain old text-based instant messages, a broadband connection is pretty essential here, especially if you want to have smooth video chats with friends.

- **Instant messaging.** Just because your netbook has built-in instant messaging and web browsing software doesn't mean you're stuck with it. You can install your own favorite instant message program (page 200) or browser (page 151).

  Here are some of the things you can do with a regular ol' free IM program:

  — Exchange text messages with people online

  — Invite two or more people into a group chat

  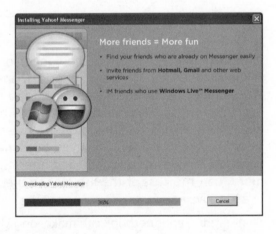

  — Participate in voice chats from computer to computer

  — Conduct video chats with webcam-equipped pals

  — Directly transfer files too big to email from computer to computer

- **Online document sharing.** With the help of sites like Google Docs (page 211), Microsoft Live Workspace (page 169), or Zoho Writer (page 213), you can work on the same files with other people. The files are stored in a central area that's accessible to everyone via web browser. Some sites, like Basecamp (page 213), include organizational tools like project-planning calendars and to-do lists to help keep everyone on track.

- **Voice chats/phone calls.** Voice chats from computer to computer are one thing, but if you want to also call regular phones around the world from your netbook for low rates and decent audio quality, a program like Skype (page 208) lets you make the connection. The program also alllows video chat between other Skype users now as well.

- **Social networking.** If you really want to share your life with your friends, general social-networking sites (page 215) like Facebook or MySpace let you post photos, videos, notes, whimsical updates about your recent doings, and more for all your connected buddies to see. And if you have more focused interests, like photography or business networking, places like Flickr and LinkedIn are where you want to be.

Setting Up Instant Message Software

When it comes to instant messaging (IM, as its known to its friends), there are two things to consider: the *network* or service you want to use and the *software* you use to get to it. Each IM network has its own software you use to chat up your associates.

To use IM, you sign up for an account with a service, install the software (if needed), and then pick your screen name and password. Your screen name is how you appear to other people in their IM program windows.

Now, back in the old days, if you signed up for a particular instant-messaging service like AIM (AOL Instant Messenger) or Yahoo Messenger, you could only talk to people who were using that same service. AIM members could only yap with other AIM members, and so on.

This system led people to sign up for the service that most of their friends happened to use and that was that. If you wanted to talk to a friend using another IM service, you had to go sign up for another IM account with that service just to talk to that *one* friend. So most people just signed up for AIM (the largest of the bunch) and stayed there.

In recent years, a notion called *interoperability* has taken hold, meaning you can IM with people on different services. For example, AIM members can now let the messages fly with users of Apple's iChat IM program with .Mac and MobileMe accounts. And if the two services still don't interoperate with each other, you can get an IM software program like Trillian that connects the various IM services itself, letting AIM users talk to people on Yahoo Messenger.

The most common IM services include:

- **AIM.** Still an IM behemoth, AIM has millions of members and its own ad-laden IM software you can download from its website. The AIM software comes in versions for Windows, Mac, and Linux, but Ubuntu users should stick with Pidgin, described on page 201. (*www.aim.com*)

- **Windows Live Messenger.** Known in its earlier life as MSN Messenger, Microsoft's IM service lets its members talk to people using Yahoo Messenger. Windows Live Messenger 2009 lets you include AIM and Google Talk members into your contacts list as well. Needless to say, this software is for Windows. (*messenger.live.com*)

- **Yahoo Messenger.** Yahoo members don't need to download a separate program to chat with other Yahooligans and Windows Live people—you can IM directly within the web browser by typing *web.im* in the address bar. You need to be using Internet Explorer or Firefox with the Flash 9.0 plug-in (page 159) installed. Windows people can also download a traditional IM software program for much faster performance. (*messenger.yahoo.com*)

- **Google Talk.** The search giant has its own IM service as well, with a Windows program to download. Gmail users can also do voice and video chat right inside their Gmail windows in the Internet Explorer, Firefox, Chrome, and Safari web browsers. People with AIM accounts can also link them to their Gmail addresses for chatting within the mail window. (*www.google.com/talk*).

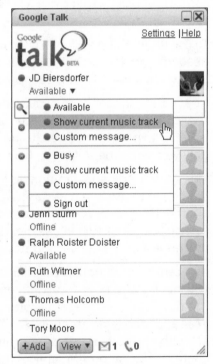

- **Jabber.** An open-source IM network, Jabber works with a number of software programs on all types of computer systems. Pidgin, described next, works with Jabber networks. (*www.jabber.org*)

Each IM service has its own software, but if you just want a program that talks to everyone on the various services, here are some options:

- **Pidgin.** Already installed for Ubuntu Linux users, the Pidgin IM software also comes in a Windows version and can link AIM, Yahoo, Windows Live, Google Talk, Jabber, and oodles of other IM services together. It's shown here and it's free. (*www.pidgin.im*)

- **Trillian.** Another all-purpose program that links AIM, Windows Live, and Yahoo members together in one window. The basic version of Trillian is free. (*www. ceruleanstudios.com*)

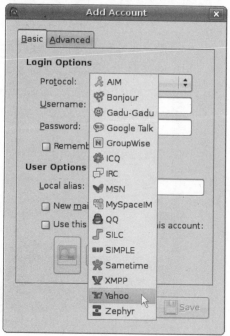

Once you have selected an IM service and installed the software, you're just a couple of steps away from the fun part. First, you need to make a Buddy List—your approved list of people to exchange messages with.

The Buddy List/Contacts List

If you already use an IM service on another computer, your existing Buddy List pops up on the netbook as soon as you log into your account. If you've never used an instant message program before, you need to add some *buddies*. To do so, you need your friend's IM screen names. If you don't know their screen names, ask them.

Methods for adding buddies to your Buddy or Contacts List vary, but most programs have an "Add Buddy" or "Add Contact" icon on the IM window. When the box to add a new buddy pops up, type your pal's screen name and click Add.

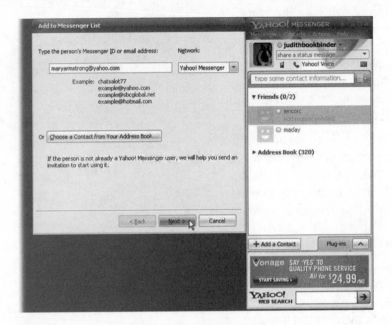

Most IM programs also let you add a pal's mobile phone number to your buddy list; for U.S. and Canadian pals, just type +1 before the phone number's 10 digits. When you send a message to the number from your IM program, it shows up as a SMS text message on the cellphone. (For international numbers, you need to add the country code instead of +1; there's a list of codes at *www.smsmac.com/coverage*.)

To send a message to someone on your buddy list, double-click the person's screen name in the list. A box pops up that lets you type the initial message. Once the person accepts your invitation to gab, the conversation unfolds like movie-script dialogue in the IM window. When you're done, close the window, log out of the service, or quit the IM program.

You can also set your *status line* from a pop-up menu under your name in the Buddy List window. This little caption lets your online pals know when you're too busy to talk, away from the computer, and so on.

Many IM programs also let you link your status line to whatever song is playing on your computer from Windows Media Player, iTunes, or whatever music program you use. Just be prepared for some ribbing from the music critics on your contacts list if you spend the afternoon listening to Rod Stewart croaking out "It Had to Be You" or Ethel Merman's disco album (yes, she made one in 1979 and it's still for sale online today).

 Note Chat is similar to instant messaging, except you can carry on a conversation with more than just one person. To set up a chat in your IM program, just select some people from your Buddy List and choose the program's Chat command. In AIM, for example, choose Actions→Chat→Buddy Chat.

Voice Chat by Instant Messenger

Instant messages don't have to be terse typed exchanges. If your netbook has a microphone (either built in or an external accessory from Radio Shack), decent speakers, or a headset microphone, you can turn your tiny computer into a rectangular telephone.

Starting a voice chat in the most popular IM programs is fairly straightforward, as most programs include a telephone icon or Voice Chat menu command to get the conversation started:

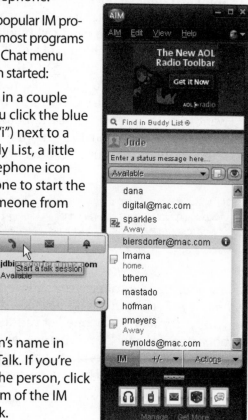

- **AIM.** You can chat out loud in a couple different ways on AIM. If you click the blue Info button (the lowercase "i") next to a friend's name on your Buddy List, a little window pops up with a telephone icon along the top. Click the phone to start the call. You can also call up someone from the Actions menu at the bottom of the Buddy List window: Click a name on the list and choose Actions→Talk. Or just right-click the person's name in the Buddy List and choose Talk. If you're already text-chatting with the person, click the Talk button at the bottom of the IM window to add a soundtrack.

- **Windows Live Messenger.** Microsoft's instant message software also has voice and video chat built right in. To get started, select a contact from your list and open a new chat window. In the Chat window, choose Call→Call Computer. Once the person you're calling accepts your invitation to gab, you can both start talking. Microsoft also has a Windows Live Call service that lets you call a regular phone number by choosing Call→Call a Phone (this service is not worldwide, and you have to pay to use it).

- **Google Talk.** Google recently added voice and video chat for Gmail users and other folks who've signed up for Google Talk. The feature only works on Windows netbooks at the moment, and requires you to download and install a small piece of software on the computer. After you install the software, sign back into Gmail and click the name of the person you want to call. If the buddy's screen name has a video camera next to it, you can do voice and video by clicking Video & More. If the pal doesn't have a webcam attached, you can still do a voice call, as long as the other person also has Google Talk.

- **Yahoo.** The Messenger program lets you make free PC-to-PC voice calls, and if you sign up for the company's low-cost Yahoo Voice Phone Out program, you can even call regular phones and cellphones. You can also leave a recorded "voicemail" if your pal isn't online at the time—Yahoo sends a message to the person's email account with an audio file attached. To place a PC-to-PC call, go to your Messenger Contacts List, wave the mouse cursor over the name of the person you want to chat up, and then click the phone icon to start the call. You can also start a call from the Actions menu: Choose Call Computer and select the name of your co-chatter from the Contacts list.

 Note: Pidgin, the IM program that comes with Ubuntu Linux, does not yet offer voice or video chat. Linux users can do voice chat over Skype (page 208) or with the Ekiga Softphone program (page 109) included with Ubuntu.

Calling your buddies directly through the IM program can save time— and money, if you're in a long-distance situation. Granted, this probably won't be a crystal-clear phone conversation. After all, your voice signals are bouncing along the same Internet pathways (known as "tubes" in some parts of Congress) as video, photos, and other big chunks of data, and your call quality is also affected by your own connection strength and speed.

If you like the idea of Internet phone calls, however, skip ahead to page 208 to read about Skype, a program designed to make free and cheap calls around the world.

Video Chat by Instant Messenger

While hearing someone's voice is much more personal than typing back and forth, getting to *see* your friend or family member live, right on your netbook screen, is even more personal. And, since most netbooks come with a built-in webcam, they're naturals for video chats—which most IM programs also offer these days.

 Even if your netbook didn't come with its own webcam at the top of the screen, you can add one of those clip-on models—which are often shaped like giant eyeballs—for as little as $30. Page 108 has information about adding an external webcam to your netbook's arsenal.

One thing you definitely want to have with that webcam and IM program: a broadband connection. Video data takes up a lot of bandwidth, and even on slower DSL and cable hookups, you may see some skippy, choppy pictures. It's definitely not fluid high-def digital TV.

Most IM programs have the video chat settings in the message window or nearby:

- **AIM.** Click the name of the buddy you want to see and choose Actions→Video to send a video chat invitation. You can also right-click the person's name in the Buddy List and choose Video. When the person accepts, you see the video feed. (Like some TVs, AIM has a picture-in-picture feature that lets you see how you look in a small window as well) You can also switch to videoconference mode in an existing IM text session by clicking the Video button at the bottom of the window.

- **Windows Live Messenger.** Select the person on your list of friends. In the chat window, click the Video button to request a video chat. When your friend accepts, the video window reveals the person on the other side of the connection and the chat begins.

- **Google Talk.** Still currently available only for Windows (and Mac)—but keep checking, Ubuntu faithful!—Google's voice and video chat feature uses its own software (page 200). Once installed, just look for a webcam-equipped pal on your Contacts list and choose the Video & More menu option to start the camera rolling.

- **Yahoo Messenger.** Fire up Yahoo's IM program and choose Messenger→View webcam. Next, on the Actions menu, choose "Invite to View My webcam" and pick a pal from the Contacts list. Click OK, and you invite the person to see the feed from your webcam. Now, choose Actions→View Webcam. Pick the person from the Contacts list and click OK. Now you're set to see her webcam. Choose Actions→Call Computer, click the name of your pal on the Contacts list, and click OK to start the video chat.

If you have trouble connecting, your firewall (either on your netbook or your network, especially if you're in an office) might be blocking the video feed. Check your IM program's Help section to see what port you need to use for video. Yahoo Messenger, for instance, recommends adjusting your firewall settings to allow a connection using the *TCP protocol* on *Port 5100*. If you're on an office network, check with your systems guru to see if video chat is allowed through the corporate firewall.

 Tip One video chat alternative for Ubuntu Linux fans to chat with each other is Wengo-phone (*www.wengophone.com*), an Internet phone and videoconference program from a small company in France. The basic computer-to-computer services are free, but like Skype (page 208 and another IM service that happens to make good-quality voice calls most of the time), Wengophone lets you call regular phones from your netbook. Just search for *wengo* in Applications→Add/Remove.

File Transfer by Instant Messenger

Ever have a really cool file that's just too big to email? Giant PowerPoint presentations, video clips, podcast audio tracks—all of these may exceed the file-attachment limit set by your email provider.

But there's an easy way to get that big honkin' file to that special someone, especially if you both use compatible instant-messaging services. Just use the program's *file transfer* function to create a direct connection from your netbook to the other person's computer. Another way IM one-ups email? The person gets the file as soon as the transfer is complete, instead of having to wait for your email programs to upload, send, and then download the file.

 Tip If you have trouble getting the file to go through, you may have to burrow into your firewall settings to allow the transfer. And if you're behind a corporate firewall, file transfers may be blocked for security reasons, so check with your systems administrator.

Here's how to transfer files in the common IM programs:

- **AIM.** In an open message session with your buddy, click the Send Files button at the bottom of the IM window. You have the option to send one file or a whole folder of stuff. You can also set up a file transfer by right-clicking the person's name in the Buddy List and choosing Send File, or by choosing Actions→Send File. Now you just have to select the file to send.

- **Windows Live Messenger.** If you're already chatting away with a contact and want to send over a file, click the window-menu button on the right, choose Send File, locate the file, and wait for the other person to accept. You can also just go to the window menu button, choose Send File, and then pick someone from your Live Messenger Contacts. Windows Live Messenger also sets up a shared folder with a contact, so that anything you drop in the folder is automatically available to that person. Click the Sharing Files folder icon at the top of the Contacts list window and then select the contact you want to share with. (The Sharing Folder has been replaced with Windows Live SkyDrive in recent versions of the program.)

- **Yahoo Messenger.** You can send up to two gigabytes of stuff to a fellow Yahoo Messenger user by just dragging the file into the IM window. You can also choose Actions→Send a File. If you see the contact online and haven't started an IM session, you can drag the file onto the person's name in the Messenger contacts list.

- **Pidgin.** Right-click a buddy in your list and choose Send File. In the box that pops up, find the file you want to send on your drive and click Open. The file transfer begins. Click Stop if you need to halt the exchange.

Many programs let you start a file transfer by simply dragging the file from the computer's desktop into the same box that you type in your message text. Hit the Enter key to start the transfer.

 Note Google Talk can do file transfers as well, but only between computers using the official Google Talk software for Windows (*www.google.com/talk*). If you're tapping into Talk from your Gmail window or another program, file transfer is a no-go. If you and your pal both have the Google Talk program, just click the Send Files button on an open chat window, locate the file on your hard drive that you want to send, and click OK to start the transfer.

Making Phone Calls with Skype

Skype—once primarily known as a service that let you make decent-sounding phone calls from computer-to-computer over the Internet—has become something of an all-around messaging program that lets you also do video chat, send instant messages, fire off text messages to mobile phones, or even send and receive calls from mobile and regular phones.

Windows users can get Skype at *www.skype.com*. Download the Skype installer and run the program, just as you would install any other bit of downloaded software (page 46).

Ubuntu Linux users can snag the Skype software through an online repository by choosing System→Administration→Synaptic Package Manager (which works much like the Add/Remove software feature under the Applications menu). Type *Skype* in the Search box and turn on the checkboxes to install the program.

The Skype software and basic computer-to-computer service are free, but you do have to sign up for a calling plan with Skype if you want to call regular phone numbers. The plan can be a monthly subscription (unlimited calls to 40 countries around the world for $13 a month), or Skype Credits charged to your credit card.

To use Skype, you need the free software, a free Skype account, and a netbook with at least a microphone and speakers. If the idea of talking to a computer makes you uneasy, you can also use a headset-microphone or a USB-connected phone handset; all are available at *www.skype.com/shop*. Using a headset also cuts down the feedback effect you might experience with audio signals from the computer's speakers echoing back into the computer's microphone. For video with the Windows version, the Skype site also sells compatible webcams.

When you open the program for the first time, you're prompted to create a Skype name and account, which is just like creating a screen name for an instant-message program. Once you have your Skype name, you can log in and start adding other people's names to your Skype contacts list so you can call them up. If you don't know a person's Skype name, check your netbook's address book (page 178) to see if the information is listed there—or just ask the person. You're friends, right?

Like most instant-message programs, you can set your current status to be displayed in the Skype window for all to see. If you're working hard and don't have time to take a call, change your status to *Do Not Disturb*. Lonely and want someone to talk to—anybody at all? Change your status to *Skype Me*.

Making Calls with Skype

To place a computer-to-computer call, click a name in your contacts list and then click the green Call button. To hang up after you've finished chatting, click the red End button.

To call a regular phone number using Skype on your netbook, click the Call Phones tab in the Skype window. A telephone dial-pad pops up, along with a box to buy Skype Credits, which you need to pay for the call. Have your credit card or PayPal account ready.

Once you've paid up, click the flag pop-up menu and select the flag of the country you're calling, and then type the phone number. (Click the Save button to have Skype retain all this information so you don't have to type it in every time you want to call your friend Max in Brighton.) Click the green Call button to start the call and click the red End button when you're done.

If you want to dial it up video-style, click a person in your Skype contacts list and click the green Video Call button. You can even do text and video chat at the same time—just click the Show Messages link at the top of the video window to start up a regular instant-message textfest while you talk to your friend in the video window.

 Tip Need to keep an official copy of a Skype call for future reference? Windows programs like vEmotion (*www.voiceemotion.com*), Pamela for Skype (*www.pamela.biz*), or Skype Call Recorder for Linux (*http://atdot.ch/scr*) let you record the call right to an audio file on your hard drive. Before you record, though, check the local laws for recording phone calls at *www.rcfp.org/taping*.

Working Together with Google Docs

If you're gung-ho about Google Docs after reading about it in the last chapter (page 175), you can share your love—and your Google Docs—with other people. You can even invite them to collaborate online with you. (Microsoft has something similar for Office workers, as described on page 169.)

Once you have a document, spreadsheet, or presentation you want to share with others in your online list of Google Docs, turn on the checkbox next to the files you want to share, and then click the Share button in the blue bar at the top of the window. Add the email addresses of people you want to work with on this file—you can choose to make them Collaborators (able to make changes to your file) or Viewers (read-only pals) from the pop-up list.

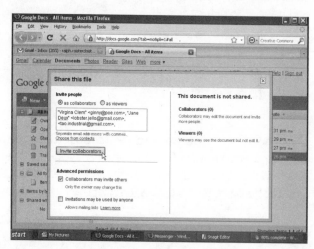

If you want to, you can type a short note telling everyone why you're sharing or what you want them to do with the file. Click Send Invitation when you're done. When people accept your invite, they can see the document by clicking the link in the message.

To actually edit the document, your collaborators need Google accounts (or be willing to sign up for one; there's a link at the top of the page to do so). Viewers can read without signing up.

Tracking Revisions to Documents

Up to 10 people can edit the same document at the same time. With all these people invited to paw over your documents, spreadsheets, and presentations, you may want to keep track of who does what to the files. (Just to give credit where credit it due, as well as to have someone to blame for the lame changes.)

If you need to revert to an earlier (that is, less-ravaged) version of your file, open it and choose Tools→Revision History. A list of all the revisions to the file appears, showing the date and time of the revision, the changes to the file, and the name of the person who made them.

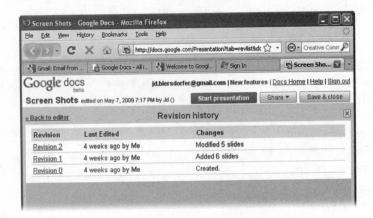

Click the version you want to see (choose Older or Newer to move backward or forward in the file's history until you find the one you want). When you find the right version of the file, click the "Revert to this one" link on the side of the page to make this version the live working file.

 Tip The Chat window on the Google Spreadsheets screen shows you who else is working on the file. You can also use it to instant-message your fellow collaborators about the changes everyone is making to the file. You may be on the same screen, but perhaps not everyone is on the same page.

Online Collaboration Sites

Google Docs & Spreadsheets, Microsoft Office Live Workspace, or Microsoft SharePoint (if you work in a collaborative corporation with a SharePoint server) are great for keeping your work-in-progress safely tucked away on the Web. But you don't have to be a Microsoft maven or a Google groupie to find a wide choice of online collaboration, word-processing, and project-management sites. Because everything is kept online, you and your co-conspirators can check into the web branch of the office from wherever you and your Internet-connected netbook happen to be.

Some sites are free—or offer free entry-level accounts with the option to upgrade to more services and storage space. Some require payment on a monthly or yearly basis. But all of them let you work totally online and collaborate with your associates for a particular project, or several of them. Here's a quick look at just a few of the many options out there.

Zoho

Free for personal use (and with a discount for nonprofit organizations), Zoho's tagline is "Work. Online." Like other sites, Zoho offers its own online word-processor, spreadsheet app, and presentation program that you can share with others. But where Zoho really excels is its collaboration tools. You can make a *wiki* (sort of an online group blog/reference document that everyone can contribute to) with Zoho Wiki, store files in the online repository of Zoho Share, organize the project's timeline and To-Do Lists with Zoho Planner, and even discuss matters with your collaborators in real-time using Zoho Chat. The site also has a wealth of business-oriented apps for things like creating invoices, setting up web conferencing, and managing large, unwieldy projects. (*www.zoho.com*)

37 Signals

With web-based apps called Basecamp, Backpack, Highrise, and Campfire, you'd think 37 Signals specializes in some sort of urban-hiking experience. In a way, it does: Thanks to the company's software, you can hike all over city and country and still make sure everyone is meeting their project deadlines, even if you're checking in from your netbook via a mobile broadband card (page 128) in Yellowstone National Park. Most of the company's services cost money, but you can sign up for a free 30-day trial to see if it's all going to be worth it to you and your team's productivity. The services include:

- **Basecamp.** For group projects and planning, Basecamp provides an online workspace with file sharing, message boards, to-do-lists, deadline calendars, and more. Prices start at $24 a month for a space where you can work on up to 15 projects and store 3 GB of stuff online. (*www.basecamphq.com*)

- **Backpack.** Sort of a mini office intranet, Backpack lets you store company documents, tutorials, and schedules in a safe place online. Everybody on the team can get to the files, and you don't even have to bug the company IT department to set it up for you. (*www.backpackit.com*)

- **Campfire.** If everyone's on a different IM service, you can skip the incompatibilities and herd the gang together on Campfire, a web-based chat space that can be password-protected from the outside world. What happens in Campfire, stays in Campfire. (*www.campfirenow.com*)

- **Highrise.** Think of it as a giant Rolodex on the Web that not only stores the names and address of all the people on your contacts list, but lets you keep track of when you last spoke, wrote, or communicated with them. Highrise can also serve as a centralized address book. (*www. highrisehq.com*)

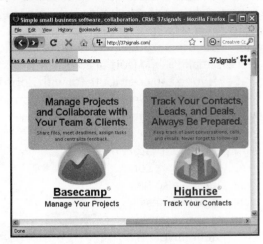

37 Signals has other software services as well, including Ta-Da Lists (free, über To-Do Lists at *www.tadalist.com*) and Writeboard (free, web-based text documents to compose or share at *www.writeboard.com*).

Huddle

Another online workspace site, Huddle offers document management, discussion forums, project alerts, and digital whiteboards and wikis for online brainstorming. And it also gives you one workspace with a gigabyte of file storage for free. If you need more space for your stuff or have multiple projects in need of multiple workspaces, you can level up with a paid plan—price start at $15 a month for 5 workspaces and 2.5-gigabytes of space. (*www.huddle.net*)

ThinkFree Mobile Netbook Edition

The ThinkFree site has its own $50 Office-like suite of programs that are compatible with Microsoft's power trio of Word, Excel, and PowerPoint—and the software works on Windows, Mac, and Ubuntu Linux systems. A free gigabyte of online file storage is included in the deal and the software can even sync documents across multiple computers. What's really cool, though, is that ThinkFree has come up with a slick, streamlined version of the suite just for *netbooks*. The intuitive, clutter-free screens let you get going quickly, especially when you and your netbook are already on the go. (*product.thinkfree.com/mobile/netbook*)

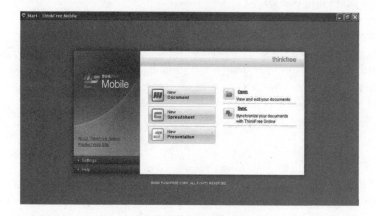

Social Networking Sites

All work and no play makes for a very dull netbook experience. C'mon, admit it—part of the reason you bought the little laptop was to keep up with your Facebook friends when you're on the road, isn't it? *Isn't it?*

Even though you can get to most popular social-networking sites on a mobile phone, it's much easier to use a netbook, where you can see the real site rather than the abbreviated version you get on some mobile apps. (Well, except for Twitter, since 140 text characters are going to look about the same on any device.) Also, some phones can't deal with some of the software these sites use, like Flash and JavaScript.

If you haven't yet joined up with a social-networking site, here are a few to consider.

Facebook

Once merely an online directory for Harvard students back in 2004, Facebook has exploded into a collective of 200 million (and counting) members connect-ing and reconnecting to friends and family around the world. Once you set up your free profile page, you can start collecting *friends* (people you'd like to share your page with and vice versa), uploading photos, links, and videos to share, participating in games and forums, and a whole lot more. (*www.facebook.com*)

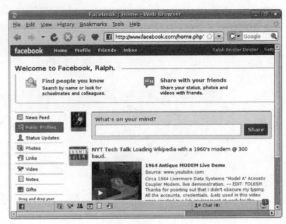

MySpace

Once king of the social-networking sites, MySpace has lost some ground to Facebook but still maintains a healthy membership. It, too, offers free profile pages that let you share your life with all your confirmed pals on the site. One thing that currently sets it apart from Facebook, though, is MySpace's vast online music offerings, from indie bands needing exposure to established acts trying to stay in the public eye. You can stream tons of music, and even download and buy tracks if the bands have made the music available for purchase. (*www.myspace.com*)

Flickr

A massive photo-sharing site used by millions of photographers from around the world, Flickr is a great place to search out and see great pictures, post your own, and even learn about photography and digital cameras. On the social side, photographers from all walks of life can add their work to pools of similar photos and participate in online discussions. You can also upload short video clips to your Flicker page. You can get a free account that lets you upload 100 megabytes of photos and two videos a month, or pony up $25 a year for unlimited photo and video uploads to share with the world. (*www.flickr.com*)

LinkedIn

A social network for the business-minded, LinkedIn provides a place to display your resumé, provide recommendations for colleagues, and see what your contacts are up to, work-wise. The site also serves as a database for recruiters and other people looking to fill jobs. A basic account is free, but serious business users can upgrade to a paid $25/month account to get more search options for people and references. (*www.linkedin.com*)

Twitter

Once thought to be a simple service for the self-involved to announce their whims in 140 typed characters or less, Twitter has evolved into a truly useful tool for breaking news, updates, and even marketing ploys. (But you can still post about what you're having for dinner right now, too.) To get started, sign up for a free account and then choose some people or companies to *follow*—which means you get their Twitter updates displayed on your page along with your own *tweets*. You can often find people's Twitter names advertised on their blogs; news organizations like CNN and NPR shamelessly promote their Twitter feeds; and a search feature helps you see the hot topic of the day and find people or groups to follow. And once you get an account, you can use one of the various desktop or mobile Twitter apps—TweetDeck, Seesmic Desktop, Twitterific, Tweetie, Twitter-Fon, and so on—to keep track of your Twitter traffic wherever you may be. (*www.twitter.com*)

Ning

Want to make your own social network devoted to a topic that interests you? Check out Ning. When you sign up for a free account on the site, you can create your own custom Nings on just about any subject you want. You can also search out and join existing Nings devoted to specific subjects like rave parties in Brazil or England's Manchester United football club. Nings have also been created as public services, like the one that sprung up in 2008 to share information and news from Hurricane Gustav (*www.ning.com*).

 Tip There are even whole web browsers devoted to keeping you in the loop with all your online social life, displaying updates and information from all your favorite sites like Facebook and Flickr. For starters, check out Flock at *www.flock.com*. A Windows version is readily available, and while there is no nicely packaged version for the Linux faithful, the site does have a how-to guide for those do-it-yourself types at *www.flock.com/faq/show/30#q_9069*.

9 Multimedia Fun: Photos, Music, and Video

In addition to serving as your portable office, your netbook can also keep you entertained when the work is done. You can pull in photos from your digital camera, rock out to music files, and enjoy video clips.

True, your netbook's small screen and minimalist video card can't replace your home theater system—or even a desktop PC system with a sizeable monitor and decent external speakers. But hey, neither of those fits in your backpack with room to spare, and a netbook screen is still larger than those in many portable DVD players.

Since most netbooks lack a built-in disc drive, this chapter shows you how to work around that little problem to get music and movies on it. You'll also learn how to import and organize your digital photos, turning the netbook into a really, really big photo album.

Importing Digital Photos

You have a camera full of photos you want to do things with—edit them, organize them, email them to people, upload them to the Web, and so on. The first step is moving them onto your netbook. Your netbook includes simple software to harvest the pictures from the camera, but you can get a dedicated photo-management program like Picasa.

In many cases, you can just connect the camera to the netbook with the camera's USB cable. When you do so, the netbook thinks, "Hey, there's a camera connected to me! I bet there are pictures to import!" Both Windows and Ubuntu automatically detect the presence of the camera and open appropriate software to do the job. Windows opens its Scanner and Camera Wizard, while Ubuntu pops open F-Spot Photo Manager.

If your netbook doesn't automatically detect the camera, you may have to switch the camera to "PC mode" when you connect it to the netbook. You may also have to install the camera's accompanying software onto the netbook. Odds are, the camera's CD includes a driver for Windows XP but not for Linux. Check the camera manufacturer's website for a download version if you don't have an external CD drive.

When netbook and camera come together, it usually goes something like this:

Windows XP

In Windows, if the Scanner and Camera Wizard doesn't automatically open, choose Start →Accessories→Scanner and Camera Wizard. If the Select Device box appears, double-click your camera's name. If the camera and netbook have already taken care of business, click Next. A screen full of tiny thumbnail images appears, representing your camera's pictures. Turn on the checkboxes for the photos you want to download.

Click the Next button and type in a name for this series of imported pictures (*Katie's Graduation* or *Chincoteague Vacation*, for example). Next, tell Windows where to store the photos (turn on the checkbox if you want the netbook to wipe the camera card clean after importing the photos). Click Next to transfer the pictures from camera to netbook. As the software copies the pictures to the netbook, it renames them to something like "Chincoteague Vacation 001," "Chincoteague Vacation 002," and so on. The process takes a few minutes, depending on how many pictures you have.

Once the photos are downloaded, the last box in the Scanner and Camera Wizard asks if you want to publish the pictures to a website, order prints from a Microsoft partner, or move on to something else. If you've installed a photo-management program like Picasa or Photoshop Elements on your netbook, it may jump up and take over the photo-import chores from the trusty Scanner and Camera Wizard.

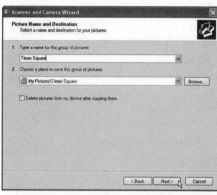

Unless you've changed the storage location, you'll find your new batch of pictures in Start→My Pictures→Chincoteague Vacation (for example).

Ubuntu Linux

The F-Spot Photo Manager recognizes many connected cameras, so all you need to do is click Import to copy the photos over to the netbook's drive. If F-Spot Photo Manager doesn't automatically open when you plug in the camera, choose Applications→Graphics→F-Spot Photo Manager. Once the program is open, choose File→Import. Select your camera as the import source and click Import.

When the thumbnail versions of the photos on the camera appear, you can import all of them (the automatic setting) or choose specific photos by Ctrl-clicking them. At the bottom of the box, you can choose to *tag* (apply a brief descriptive label like *Times Square*) to the incoming pictures and choose a folder on the netbook to put them in. When you're set, click the Copy button to import the images from the camera into F-Spot Photo Manager.

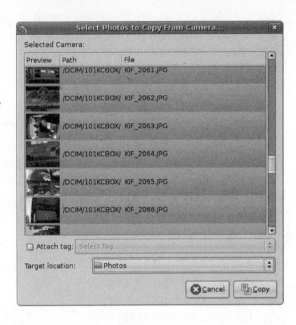

You can see and edit your photos in the F-Spot Photo Manager window. The photo files themselves land in dated folders listed under User→Photos. You can change where F-Spot puts your files, though: choose Edit→Preferences and use the pop-up menu in the box to change the location for incoming images.

 If you don't see your camera listed as an import source, choose Places→Computer. If your camera is hanging out there like a flash drive or other removable memory stick, double-click it to open it and drag the photo files to the netbook's Pictures folder.

Troubleshooting Stubborn Cameras

If the netbook still doesn't recognize your camera, you have a couple of alternative methods for transferring the pictures:

- If your netbook comes with a Secure Digital card slot on the side (many models do) and your camera uses SD cards, pop the memory card out of the camera. Plug the card into the netbook's card slot to copy the pictures onto its hard drive. If the netbook doesn't immediate see the card, you may have use the Windows Scanner and Camera Wizard or the F-Spot Photo Manager's import command to point to it.

- If your camera uses a different type of memory card or your netbook doesn't have an SD card slot, consider an inexpensive memory-card reader. Most cost less than $25, have slots that fit all common types of memory cards, and connect to the netbook's USB port. Pull the card out of the camera, stick it in the card reader, and reel in your pictures.

If you don't want to import the photos through the netbook's built-in picture program, you can also drag the picture files from the memory card to a folder on your netbook's drive. Dragging takes more time and energy, but this way you can put those photo files exactly where you want them.

Organizing Your Photos

Once you get your photos copied from camera to netbook, how you arrange them is up to you. This section offers some basic advice for getting your photos into manageable groups where you can find specific images. If you want to learn how to take red eye out of a shot or crop annoying cousin Leroy out of a family photo, skip ahead to page 225.

Windows XP

Did you import the photos with the Windows Scanner and Camera Wizard and assign each batch of pictures its own labeled folder (page 220)? If so, you'll find your My Pictures folder nicely organized with labeled subfolders and numbered photos. When you want to look at a particular set of photos, just hop to My Pictures and open the appropriate subfolder.

Photo-management programs like Adobe Photoshop Elements or Google Picasa give you even more control over your pictures, both in organizing them into electronic albums and making them look even better. With Photoshop Elements, you can easily tag your photos with descriptive labels that help you find them when searching, say, for all photos you ever took on the *beach*.

You also get a toolbox of photo-editing tools to touch up, enhance, and improve your shots, plus space online to display them. Adobe Photoshop Elements is a powerful program—with a powerful price tag of $100 at *www.adobe.com*. But there's a free trial version you can download to see if you like it before you fork over the cash.

Google's Picasa software is not quite as powerful, but is much more wallet-friendly—it's free. You can download a copy right onto your netbook at *www.google.com/picasa*. When you first run Picasa, it scans your netbook's hard drive for photos and displays them in a big photo browser window so you can see each image.

Picasa doesn't move all your photos to a different location on your netbook. The pictures stay right where you imported them, but you can see and edit them through the Picasa window. There's much more on editing photos in Picasa on page 227.

Ubuntu Linux

Although there's a version of Picasa for Linux on Google's website, your netbook already includes a versatile, free program for organizing your pictures. Yes, it's the same F-Spot Photo Manager software you used to pull the photos off the camera in the first place.

F-Spot displays miniatures of your photos in its main window. If you tagged the pictures when you imported them (page 222), the tag names appear in the list on the left side of the window. Click a tag to see all the photos containing that descriptive label like *Times Square*, *NYC*, or *Chinatown*.

If you forgot to tag incoming photos when you imported them, you can drag thumbnails onto existing tags in the F-Spot window to add them to the set. If you're in the mood to further organize after you've imported a bunch of photos without tagging them, you can add new tags by choosing Tags→Create New Tag and then typing a name. The new tag appears on the left side of the screen, where you can drag photos onto it.

In the same Tags menu, you can also Edit or Delete selected tags (which edits or kills only the tag names, not the pictures associated with them). And when you have a batch of photos selected, you can add or remove tags associated with them by choosing Tags→Attach Tag to Selection or Tags→Remove Tag from Selection.

 Tip If you want to learn more about F-Spot, check out the program's own basic user guide at *http://f-spot.org/User_Guide*.

Editing Photos

Got a photo that's slightly crooked or one that's just a tad too dark? Many good photos can become *great* photos with a bit of help from a photo-editing program. Even better, you don't need a burly industry standard like Adobe's $700 Photoshop to make those pictures perk right up. If you want Photoshop power with fewer frills, the $100 Photoshop Elements for Windows (page 223) fits the bill.

While Photoshop Elements lives on your netbook's drive, there's also a free online version of the program called Adobe Photoshop Express at *www.photoshop.com* that works on any Web-enabled computer. When you sign up for an account, you get 2 GB of online storage. Once you upload your pictures, you can edit, improve, and share them, courtesy of Adobe.

Most free programs can handle commonplace photo fixes—color adjustments, red-eye removal, and cropping. And if you have an Ubuntu Linux netbook, you don't even have to download anything, since your netbook comes with two powerful photo programs: the previously mentioned F-Spot Photo Manager and the GIMP (GNU Image Manipulation Program).

If you have a Windows netbook, Picasa (page 225) is one of your best options. It's easy to use and packs a lot of tools in its free toolbox. (There's a version of Picasa for Linux, as well; you can read more about it at *http://picasa.google.com/linux/faq.html* if you think you might want to give it a spin.)

So what can you do with freebie software? Both Picasa and F-Spot offer the following photo-finessing features:

- **Crop.** Need to trim off parts of a picture, say to cut out an ex-boyfriend or lose a distracting sign in the background? The Crop tool lets you select the part of the picture you really want to see. You can crop without constraints, which may make for an oddly sized photo, or keep the trimming constrained to a normal proportion (which enlarges the main part of the picture to fit the space). In Picasa, click the Crop button on the Basic Fixes tab and then choose your trimming preferences.

In F-Spot, use the pop-up menu in the editing window and choose a proportion to stick with—or no constraint as all—then drag around the desired area with the mouse, and finally, click Crop.

- **Straighten.** If your lovely Gulf of Mexico horizon shot looks like it's tilting downhill, you can level things off with your photo program's Straighten tool. As you nudge the horizontal or vertical axis of the image back into level or plumb, the software discreetly trims the edges of the photo to square everything up.

- **Rotate.** If your vertical shot came in horizontal when you imported it from the camera, you can spin the picture around the right way with the program's Rotate button.

- **Red Eye Removal.** Demonically glowing red eyes is one of the side effects of a bright camera flash in a dark room. Light hitting the blood vessels in the back of a person's eyes causes it, but you can rise above biology with a little digital doctoring. Use the Red-Eye Removal tool on those poor eyes to replace the red with a neutral black. Select the red-eye area of the photo and click the Red Eye button on the program's toolbar to fix it.

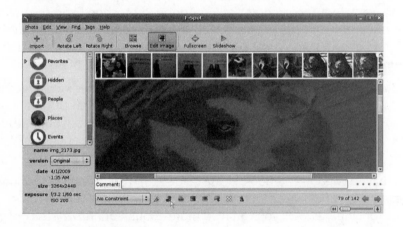

Those are some of the obvious tools. If you want to get a bit more technical, both Picasa and F-Spot let you dig deeper into a picture to make it look better. You can adjust colors, tint, and contrast in your pictures to make them pop. And if you change your mind, you can always undo what you did or go back to the original version of the picture. The next section offers a quick overview of what Picasa and F-Spot can do for you and your pictures.

Tip Want to make slideshows with music and captions, add special effects, and touch-up your photos? Microsoft offers its own Photo Story 3 software as a free download for Windows users at *www.microsoft.com/photostory*.

Photo Editing with Picasa

Double-click any photo in your Picasa browser window to open it for editing. The three-tabbed panel on the left side of the screen offers three sets of mostly one-click fixes that instantly improve the picture. The tabs include:

- **Basic Fixes.** The Crop, Straighten, and Red Eye tools live here, along with buttons that automatically adjust the picture's overall color balance and contrast. Click the Retouch button and drag the onscreen brush over blemishes and other small distractions. Got an outdoor photo where the background is bright but your subject is doused in shadows? Use the Fill Light slider to gently lighten faces. If all of this sounds like too much work, click the I'm Feeling Lucky button to have Picasa itself take a whack at your color and contrast correction. For real fun, use the Text button to give the photo a caption.

- **Tuning.** The Tuning tab mainly consists of sliders that let you do more Fill Light futzing. You can also adjust the Highlights and Shadows sliders to open up and add detail to the light and dark areas of a photo. Moving the color temperature slider lets you change the overall color cast on a photo, making it seem cooler with greenish-blue tints or warmer with more orange-magenta tones. You can also balance the color in the whole image with the Neutral Color Picker button: Select an area of the picture that Picasa should treat as gray or white and it adjusts the rest of the colors in the picture around your chosen neutral area.

- **Effects.** This tab gives you 10 different visual effects to apply to the selected photo with the click of a mouse. You can turn the image sepia or black-and-white, tint it, soften the focus, sharpen it up, give it a glow, and so on. The effects are a lot of fun to play with, so open a photo and give 'em a spin.

If you don't like any of the changes you've made with Picasa's tool tabs, there's always the Undo Tuning button or Picture→Undo All Edits.

 Tip As freebies go, Picasa sports a lot of features, but doesn't include an official PDF or printed manual if you have a question or get stuck on something. Still, you can find plenty of in-depth documentation online. In your quest for Picasa knowledge, Google's own "Getting Started With Picasa" page is a good place to start: *http://snipurl.com/jzl40*.

Photo Editing with F-Spot

F-Spot mixes several of its fine-tuning tools down with the Crop and Red Eye buttons at the bottom of the photo browser window. As you mouse along the bottom row of icons, pop-up tooltips explain their functions: "Adjust the photo colors," for example.

The F-Spot window actually has two buttons for color adjustment. "Adjust the photo colors" brings up a box full of sliders to let you manipulate the look of the picture manually. "Automatically adjust the colors" turns F-Spot loose to analyze your picture and make color and contrast adjustments based on its own programmed judgment.

But back to the manual color adjustment (which incidentally, you can also get to by choosing Edit→Adjust Color). No matter how you get there, you'll find a box with seven slider controls for tweaking your selected image.

At the top of the Adjust Color box is a *histogram*. Although it may look like a little rainbow mountain range, the histogram is actually a dynamic chart displaying, from left to right, all the dark and light tones in the image. Dark shots—midnight on the bayou, for example—have all the mountains pushed to the left side of the histogram, while that bright snapshot of the white-sand beaches of Pensacola will have the histogram mountains bunched up on the left. Photos with a good balance of dark and light areas show the mountain peaks distributed across the histogram.

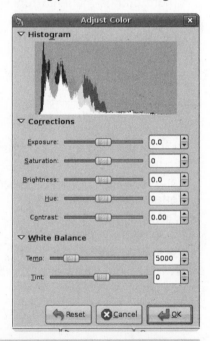

Moving the various sliders shifts the histogram around. This is what each slider does:

- **Exposure.** Move this slider to make your image lighter or darker overall. Shoving the slider too far in either direction leads to a loss of detail, so slide wisely.

- **Saturation.** Increase the intensity of the photo's colors here, say, when that grass you remember being bright green at the ballpark looks a little washed out in your snapshot. You can also go the other way and tone those colors down a bit if they seem garish.

- **Brightness.** Nudge this slider to perk up a slightly dark photo. (Going too far tends to wash out the image, though.)

- **Hue.** If you need to shift all the colors in the image in a particular direction, use Hue.

- **Contrast.** A photo's contrast is the difference between the darkest dark tones and the lightest light parts in the image. Photos with low contrast tend to look muddy. When you add more contrast, the whites get whiter and the darks get darker.

- **Temperature.** If a photo seems too "cool" with a hint of blue cast to it or completely sterile from a powerful camera flash, move the Temperature slide to warm it up with a bit of comforting yellow-orange.

- **Tint.** If the image looks a little too red or a little too green, push the Tint slider in either direction until it looks more balanced.

You can undo all your slider changes by clicking the Reset button at the bottom of the Adjust Color box. If it's too late for that and you want to go back to the way things were, choose Photo→Version→Original. You can also *sharpen* a photo (subtly goosing the contrast between pixels) by choosing Edit→Sharpen.

The editing tools F-Spot provides may be enough for most people. But for Photoshop fans trying out Linux and wishing there was more full-on control for every pixel, there's something more.

Photoshop refugees, meet the GIMP.

Advanced photo editing in Ubuntu

The GNU Image Manipulation Program (whose name has nothing to do with injured legs or *Pulp Fiction* characters) is an open-source answer to Adobe Photoshop's detailed menus and controls. If you need more *oomph* than what F-Spot can offer, right-click the photo in the F-Spot window and choose Open With→GIMP Image Editor. (You can also open it directly from Applications→Graphics→GIMP Image Editor.)

Before you leave F-Spot behind, it prompts you to make a copy of the photo to use in the GIMP. If you're still learning the GIMP, working on a copy is a good idea.

Once the photo opens in the GIMP, your options for photo manipulation explode exponentially. As in Photoshop, you can work in layers, add text, crop, scale, rotate all or parts of the image, and tweak colors until the cows come home.

If you're comfortable with Photoshop or a similarly complex image editor, the GIMP's menu commands and dialog boxes will seem somewhat familiar. If you're new to digital retouching, try starting with the GIMP's own page of free documentation and tutorials at *http://gimp.org/docs*.

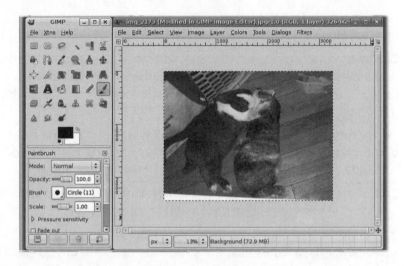

Sharing Photos Online

Now that you've got those pictures looking their best, it's time to share them with the world. With your netbook, you can easily share your snaps by email and on the Web no matter where you (and your Internet connection) are.

Emailing Photos in Windows

Windows makes emailing photos a breeze. It even resizes the images for you to Internet-friendly dimensions for emailing so that your recipients aren't stuck opening giant files. To send a photo file by email, right-click its icon in a folder window and choose Send To→Mail Recipient. A box pops up asking if you'd like to resize the images for email or keep them the original size, which is fine for small, low-resolution pictures. Once you make your choice, Windows cheerfully attaches the selected photo (or photos, if you selected multiple shots) to a new email message for you to address and send.

If you're more task-pane-oriented, you can also select photos and click the "E-mail the selected file(s)" link on the left side of the window.

If you use Picasa for your photo-editing chores, select a photo or photos and click the big Email button at the bottom of the window. Picasa handles the resizing and the slapping of the images onto a new message form. (The first time you try to email photos, Picasa asks which email program you want to use. You can have it remember your choice so you don't get nagged every time you send off pictures.)

Emailing Photos in Ubuntu Linux

As in Windows, Ubuntu also lets you right-click a photo file and choose Send To from the pop-up menu. A box pops so you can choose your email program and fill in your recipient's address. You also get the option to compress the file size to make for faster emailing. This option sends the file at the original size, which can still be kind of big if it's a 12-megapixel photo from a nice camera.

Better yet, have F-Spot handle your emailing chores. Open the program and select pictures to mail, and then choose Photo→Send by Mail. A box pops up that lets you select a mailing size for your images. Click the Create Mail button to stick the pictures in a fresh new email message.

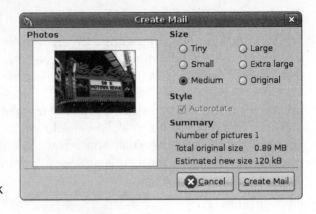

Photo Sharing Websites

Sending just a few photos by email to a few people is easy enough. But what if you want to share 200 family reunion photos with all 50 people that turned up at the event? In cases like this, a photo sharing website can come in quite handy. And as a special bonus, you can even password-protect the collection to keep non-family members from gawking at your online album.

Using a photo-sharing website is a two-step process.

Phase One: Select a Photo Site

First, you have to choose which site to use. Your Internet service provider may offer a few megabytes of server space that you can use for hosting your pictures. If you don't want to wrestle with the technical tasks needed to get the photos online that way, consider a site that's all about photo sharing (like Flickr, Snapfish, or Shutterfly) or even a social-networking site (like MySpace or Facebook) that lets you share photo uploads with your friends and family. And if you already use Picasa and have a free Google account, you can upload your pictures with one click from Picasa to an online Picasa web album.

You met Flickr, Facebook, and MySpace in the previous chapter (page 216), but they're not the only photo-friendly sites in town. Consider also:

• **Shutterfly.** Accounts are free, online storage is unlimited, and you can even get your own personalized web page to show off your stuff. Shutterfly makes money by selling you cards, stationery, mugs, and more adorned with your snaps. (*www.shutterfly.com*)

- **KodakGallery.** You need to purchase something every so often to qualify for free online photo storage and sharing. But the site offers lots of stuff to buy, from prints to knick-knacks festooned with your photographic efforts. (*www.kodakgallery.com*)

- **Snapfish.** Run by Hewlett-Packard, Snapfish also lets you upload photos from your computer or by email and share them online for free. HP is also happy to sell you prints, books, calendars, and key-chains made from your photos. (*www.snapfish.com*)

- **SeeHere.** FujiFilm's answer to Hewlett-Packard and Kodak's photo-sharing efforts also comes with desktop software for Windows that lets you organize and edit your pictures offline. (*www.seehere.com*)

- **Photobucket.** With live slideshows and group albums, Photobucket is sort of a cross between Flickr and MySpace with the ability to check out other people's pictures just as easily as your own. (*photobucket.com*)

- **SmugMug.** Yes, this site charges $40 a year to store and display your pictures, but you get uncluttered, ad-free photo albums, unlimited on-line storage, and plenty of privacy controls. (*smugmug.com*)

Once you've selected your photo-sharing service and signed up for an account, the site gives you your photo page's web address so your friends and family can find them. On most sites, when you upload pictures, you can also specify who can see your photos, either by password-protecting your page or setting up an approved list of people who are allowed to look.

When you've got the particulars worked out, you're ready to move on to the fun part.

Phase Two: Upload Your Pictures

Now that you've got an account with a photo sharing site, all you have to do is put your photos on it. Most sites work much the same way: Look for an Upload link or button on the site's main page, click it, and then choose photos on your netbook's drive.

Depending on which service you're using, you usually get the chance to put captions on your pictures or rename the files, so your viewers will know what they're looking at. You may be given a chance to do this before or after you upload the images. Once you've uploaded your pictures, click the link that says "Share This Album," "Email These Pictures," or something like that.

Ubuntu users can take advantage of an F-Spot feature that lets you upload pictures right from the program to photo-sharing sites like

Flickr, Picasa Web Albums, or SmugMug. With your pictures selected in F-Spot, choose Photo→Export to→ [Flickr or whatever] and type your account name and password in the box that pops up. If you have multiple albums, choose the album you want to add to, choose the picture upload size (smaller is faster), and turn on the checkbox if you want the descriptive tags you've applied to your pictures to ride along up to the Web. Click Export to start the upload.

Using Picasa Web Albums

If you're using Picasa, you get 1 GB of online storage to display your pictures in a Picasa Web Album—your own little corner on one of Google's servers. You sign up for a Web Album by clicking the Upload button on the Picasa toolbar. If you don't already have a Google account from Gmail or one of its other services, you can create one now.

There are a couple of ways to get photos from your netbook to your Picasa Web Album. The most obvious is that big Upload button on the Picasa toolbar. In the Picasa window, select the images you want to put online, and then click the button.

Before you upload, you need to pick the file size for the photos. The smaller 640×480-pixel size uploads faster and looks fine online, but doesn't print very well. Choosing a bigger file size from the pop-up menu means slower uploads but better prints for friends and family who want to download your shots and make their own prints.

In the upload box, you also need to pick the level of privacy, or *visibility*, for your shots:

- **Public.** With this option, anybody who knows your Google account name can probably locate your photos. So can people you even don't know who are searching the Picasa Web Albums site for pictures with specific tags like *lobsters*.

- **Unlisted.** Google gives your pictures and albums incredibly long, complicated URLs that are easy to cut and paste in emails to friends, but nearly impossible to guess. Your photo tags also don't show up in public searches.

- **Sign-In required to view.** This highest level of privacy lets you create a pre-approved list of people who are allowed to look at your pictures. Before viewing your album, people on the list have to sign in with their own Google account name and passwords.

Once you make your size and security decisions, click Upload. Want to tell people about your newly uploaded pictures? Click the Share button at the top of the Picasa window to send email invites.

Alternative ways to upload to Picasa Web Albums

Another way to upload photos to your Picasa Web Album is to visit *http://picasaweb.google.com*. Log in, click Upload, select pictures from your hard drive, and click to upload the batch. This feature is handy for Linux people who use Picasa Web Albums, but don't like the Picasa desktop software.

You can also upload photos by emailing them to your Web Album, but first, you have to set your account to accept the incoming pictures. Log into your account at *http://picasaweb.google.com* and click the Settings button. Click the General tab, jump to the Upload Photos By E-Mail section, and turn on the "Allow me to upload photos by e-mail" checkbox. Type a "secret word" to get a special email address. Copy this address down and click the Save Changes button. Now you just need to email the pictures to this special address to post them in a Web Album.

Picasa Web Albums have their own lengthy user guide online. Check out *http://snipurl.com/k0krw* to explore the finer points of photo sharing, Google-style.

 Tip Need to get nice glossy prints of those pictures to send to your relatives and friends who prefer paper-based photos—but don't own a photo printer? If you're using Picasa, select the pictures you want to use and click the Shop button in the Photo Tray toolbar. Pick your country and then the photo vendor you want to use. If you use Flickr, visit *www.flickr.com/do/more* for info about ordering prints.

Miss dropping off your film rolls at the corner drugstore? Most large chains also let you upload your picture files to their websites, order prints, and pick them up in the store later at your convenience. Check out CVS (*www.cvsphoto.com*), RiteAid (*www.riteaid.com/photos*), or Walgreen's (*http://photo.walgreens.com*) for starters. Walmart (*www.walmart.com*) offers similar services.

Popular MP3 Jukebox Programs

Just as your netbook can be a travel electronic photo album, it can also be a compact music machine, storing and playing your favorite digital audio files. And as discussed back on page 110, it can also load music onto your MP3 player or play music off it.

Both Windows and Ubuntu netbooks come with music-playing software:

- Windows has Windows Media Player, Microsoft's all-purpose program for playing audio and video files. To find it, choose Start→All Programs→ Windows Media Player.

- Ubuntu has the Rhythmbox Music Player. Choose Applications→ Sound & Video→Rhythmbox Music Player.

If you don't yet have any songs on your netbook, the next section tells you how to get some from online music services. If you have a compatible external CD drive to connect to your netbook, you can usually rip tracks from your compact disc collection with your jukebox software, just as you can with a regular computer.

 Tip Don't like Ubuntu's Rhythmbox Music Player? Try Banshee, which can sync music with Google Android phones, many types of iPods, and other music players. Banshee can also stream Last.fm Internet radio and podcasts. Read more about it, as well as install it, at *http://banshee-project.org*.

But say you have a bunch of music files on another computer that you want to put on the netbook for a little travelin' music. You can easily copy those songs onto a USB drive on the first machine and then plug the drive into the netbook and copy them over. You can also ferry music over with an SD memory card if both machines have an SD card slot or if you have a card reader (page 223).

If Windows Media Player is set up to be your go-to audio player, it leaps into action when you double-click one of those song files to play it. You can also have the program monitor certain folders, like My Music, so when you copy audio files into it, Windows Media Player knows about it and displays those tracks in its library, ready to play or add to a *playlist* (a saved set of songs arranged in the order you want to hear them).

To set up folders you want the Media Player to watch, choose Library→Add to Library and pick your locations.

In Rhythmbox Music Player on a Linux netbook, choose Music→Import File or Music→Import Folder to add tracks to the program's database so you can play and playlist them.

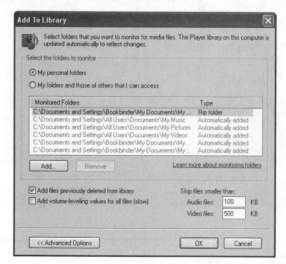

iTunes Tips for Netbooks

Windows netbookers can also download and install Apple's iTunes program, which is a big help if you want to connect an iPod to the netbook (page 110). And even if you don't have an iPod or iPhone to connect, iTunes is a nifty music jukebox program with easy access to Apple's huge digital music store.

If you want to try the software, you can download the Windows version for free at *www.apple.com/itunes*. And while there is no native version of iTunes for Linux, many people been able to run the Windows version of iTunes through Wine—a Linux program that can run some Windows software, as described on page 298.

Transfering music from an iPod

Having iTunes on your netbook is vital if you've purchased music in the past from the iTunes Store on another computer and want to play it on the netbook as well. While songs currently purchased from the iTunes Store don't have integrated copy protection (which means you to have type your iTunes password to play the music), most music purchased before April 2009 usually does.

 Want to copy all your purchased iTunes Store music onto your netbook? Have your iPod do the heavy lifting for you! Just install iTunes on the netbook, choose Store→Authorize Computer, and type your iTunes Store name and password. Next, plug in your iPod. If it's set to autosync (synchronize with only one computer at a time), click the Transfer Purchases button in the alert box that pops up to copy over the tracks you bought with that iTunes account. If your iPod is set to manually manage its content (meaning you can connect it to multiple computers and drag music onto it when you feel like it), choose File→Transfer Purchases From iPod to copy the files to the netbook's copy of iTunes.

Sharing music across a home network

What if your netbook has a teeny, tiny solid-state drive inside and you don't have room to transfer gigabytes of music from your main computer to it? If you have both machines on your home network, you can *stream* the music from Big Burly Computer to Wee Netbook with the iTunes Sharing feature.

You set up sharing in the iTunes Preferences area. On each computer's copy of iTunes, choose Edit→Preferences→Sharing. On the big computer with the music, turn on the "Share my library on my local network" checkbox and choose whether you want to share the whole library or just certain playlists. Click OK. On the netbook, turn on the "Look for shared libraries" checkbox, so the netbook can see the big computer's iTunes library across the home network. Click OK.

Then, look under Sharing in the iTunes Source list on your netbook. You should see the blue icon of the big computer's iTunes library or playlists. Click to select it and then double-click a song to hear it stream across your home network from the big computer's hard drive and out your netbook's speakers.

Playing Digital Music on the Netbook

You don't need a CD player to make music on the netbook. Thanks to the proliferation of legal, online music stores, you can stream or even download millions of songs right to your netbook. All you need is an Internet connection and a credit card.

Apple established the online music store model when it unveiled its iTunes Store in April 2003. The store still works the same way—even on a netbook. In iTunes, click the iTunes Store icon in the Source list to browse its wares. Double-click a song title to hear a 30-second snippet before you buy. When you decide to purchase a song, click the Buy button. A box pops up asking you to log into your iTunes account. If you don't have one yet, click the Create Account button and follow the steps.

While iTunes may be the big fish, there are plenty of other online music stores in the sea. In Windows Media Player, you can check out major online song shops like Napster and Puretracks. Choose Media Guide→Browse All Online Stores to see a window full of shortcuts to online music stores and services.

The Rhythmbox Music Player can also display a few online music stores in its left pane. To show the stores, choose Edit→Plugins and turn on the checkboxes for Jamendo and Magnatune online song shops.

 Note While you can connect your Windows-formatted iPod to a Linux netbook to manage your music, (page 111), Apple doesn't offer any accommodation for Linux. Although the company recently removed copy-protection software from its music files in the iTunes Store, older songs on the iPod that you purchased through your Windows computer's copy of iTunes won't play on the Linux system—nor do audiobooks purchased from Audible.com.

Other Online Music Stores

Amazon.com sells MP3 music tracks that work on just about any computer system, including Linux. To shop, visit *www.amazon.com* and click the MP3 Downloads button. The site asks you to install a bit of software called the MP3 Downloader (choose Windows or Linux) and guides you through installing it. Once you buy MP3 songs (billed to your Amazon account, of course), you can play them in Windows Media Player or Rhythmbox Music Player.

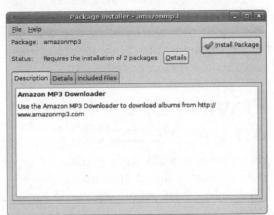

Another site that sells music in the MP3 format is *www.emusic.com*. It has more than five million songs in its catalog. Like Amazon, it also has its own downloading software for Windows and Linux.

Internet Radio

Those crackly AM signals squawking out of a transistor radio brought new music to a lot of people back in the 20th century. Here in the 21st century, though, static and fuzz have given way to smooth streams of sound pouring in over the Internet. Many traditional radio stations now offer a streamed version of their broadcast signal that you can play right on your netbook. And because the stations aren't relying on the broadcast airwaves to push out their broadcasts, you can hear stations from around the world.

 Tip Internet radio has become a personal affair over the past few years, and there are many services out there that let you program your own station with the music you prefer (and fewer mattress commercials). If that sounds appealing, visit Slacker (*www.slacker.com*), Pandora (*www.pandora.com*), or Last.fm (*www.last.fm*).

If you want to get a taste of what's out there, visit radio megasites like Shoutcast (*www.shoutcast.com*) or Live365 Internet Radio (*www. live365.com*). These sites collect radio streams from around the world that you can play right in your netbook's web browser.

Windows Media Player also lists a few streaming radio sites, like Live365.com, which host hundreds of international radio stations. Just click a stream in the neatly categorized list to hear it.

If you're running iTunes, click the Radio icon in the Source list and browse the collection of radio streams that appear in the main window. Double-click a stream to hear it.

Rhythmbox Music Player has a Radio icon on the left side of the window. Click it to see a list of stations you can stream. If you have an account with the Last.fm Internet radio site, you can add a plug-in to Rhythmbox that adds your stations to the program's window. Choose Edit→Plugins and turn on the checkbox for Last.fm. Click the Configure button to type your username and password.

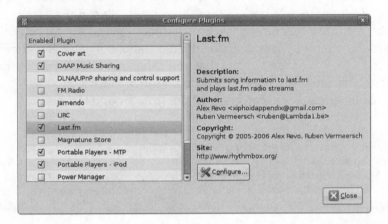

 Radio station and network web pages often have links to their live streams and archived programming for anyone to hear. Want national and world news, for example? Visit National Public Radio (*www.npg.org*) or the esteemed British Broadcasting Corporation (*www.bbc.co.uk/radio*).

Adding your own stations

Windows Media Player, iTunes, and Rhythmbox all let you add your own radio stations as well. All you need is the URL of the station's live stream, which you can find on the station's web page. Most stations have a Listen Now or Listen Live link that lets you stream their current programming from the web page. Right-click this link and choose Copy Link or Copy Link Location from the pop-up menu.

Next, go to your jukebox program and prepare to paste:

- In iTunes, choose Advanced→Open Audio Stream (or press Ctrl+U) and paste the URL into the box. Click OK to add it.

- In Windows Media Player, press Ctrl+U and paste the URL into the box.

- In Rhythmbox Music Player, click Radio in the left pane. Click the New Internet Radio Station button that appears in the toolbar and paste in the URL. Click Add.

Podcasts

Podcasts (those radio-like shows that you can download to listen to on to a portable media player or computer) are also easy to get—and almost all of them are free. With podcasts, you can listen to one episode and move on, or you can subscribe to a podcast's feed and have your netbook automatically download new episodes when they become available.

One easy way to get started with podcasts is to sample and subscribe to them through iTunes. In the Source list, click the iTunes Store icon. When you see the main store page, click Podcasts and start browsing. You can download single episodes of shows with the Get Episode button, or click Subscribe to get them delivered regularly to your computer. When the podcaster releases a new episode, iTunes automatically snags it.

Although iTunes makes the whole podcasts thing incredibly easy, not everyone can (or wants to) use Apple's jukebox juggernaut. If you're new to podcasts, wander into Podcast Alley (*www.podcastalley.com*) for a look around. The site offers links to tons of podcasts on every conceivable topic. It also has links to podcast software and more importantly, the feed URLs to the shows it lists on the site. Click the Subscribe button next to a podcast title you want to add to your collection. The site should reveal the show's URL, which can look something like *http://podhammer.net/?feed= podcast*.

For Linux netbookers, the Rhythmbox Music Player (page 236) can handle your podcast subscription needs. Click the Podcasts icon in the left column and then click the New Podcast Feed button that appears on the toolbar. A box appears for you to paste in the show's URL. Click Add to finish subscribing. To see if new episodes are available, click the Update All Feeds button.

Podcast-grabbing programs like the Juice Receiver for Windows or Linux (*http://juicereceiver.sourceforge.net*) are another way to automatically round up your favorite shows. To add a feed in the Juice Receiver, click the green + button and paste the podcast's URL into the box. The program then goes and looks to see what episodes are available.

Recording and Editing Sound

As long as your netbook has a microphone jack, there's nothing to stop you from hooking up a mic and recording your own sound. You can make your own podcast, record the kids telling a story, email audio greetings, and have all kinds of sound-related run.

Both Windows XP and Ubuntu come with sound-recording software called, appropriately enough, Sound Recorder.

Windows

Choose Start→All Programs→ Accessories→Sound Recorder. Connect the microphone (if the netbook doesn't have one built in). Click the red dot to start recording. Say something. The Recorder goes for 60 seconds. Click the red dot again to con-

tinue recording. Press the black Stop square when you're done. Choose File→Save As to save your recording.

If you need to check the microphone levels, choose Edit→Audio Properties. Your netbook's sound card should be in the Sound Recording area in the middle of the box. Click the Volume button under it to get to sliders that let you adjust the microphone's sound levels. Close the box and click OK.

Ubuntu

Plug in an external microphone (if your netbook doesn't have one built in already) and choose Applications→Sound & Video→Sound Recorder. The Sound Recorder program opens. Pop-up menus in the middle of the screen let you choose the input source for recording (like your microphone) and the file format for the clip. (Choose File→Open Volume Control for sound-level adjustments.)

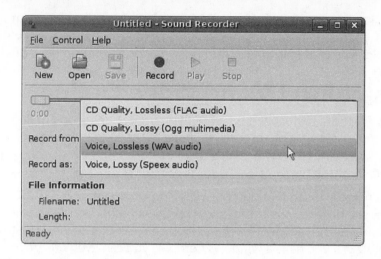

Click the red Record button to start recording. Click Stop when you're finished. Click Play to hear what you recorded; click Save to keep your recording.

Recording and Editing Sound with Audacity

The Sound Recorder programs included with Windows XP and Ubuntu are very basic (and in the case of Ubuntu, somewhat buggy at times). If you want a more full-featured audio program, consider Audacity, free open-source software that can play, record, and edit sound files. Audacity is available for both Windows and Linux.

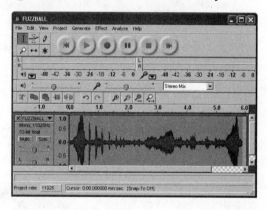

You can download the Windows version at *http://audacity.sourceforge.net*. Once the installer file downloads, double-click the file to install Audacity. If you skip the installer's option to create a desktop shortcut, open it from Start→All Programs→Audacity.

On Ubuntu, choose Applications→Add/Remove, set the Show pop-up menu to "All available applications" and search for *Audacity*. When Audacity shows up in the Add/Remove Applications window, turn on the checkbox to select it, click Apply Changes, and type in your system password. Once the program installation is finished, choose Applications→Sound & Vision→Audacity to start it up.

Audacity can do a lot of things. If you want to learn how to use it to its fullest, check out its user manual, quick reference guide, Frequently Asked Questions page, and tutorials, all at *http://audacity.sourceforge.net/help*.

Watching TV and Video Online

Thanks to those high-speed broadband Internet connections, online video is booming. Moving pictures really *move* when zipping along on broadband. And thanks to advances in encoding and compression, video quality is fantastic these days.

You can watch video by either downloading or streaming it. Downloading means you have to wait a little longer for the actual video clip to arrive, but you're not at the mercy of Internet traffic that may cause your clip to stall and stutter. If you have a Windows netbook, you can even buy downloads of popular TV shows and movies in the iTunes Store (page 240) and Microsoft's Zune Marketplace (*www.zune.net*).

 Tip DVD rental sites like Blockbuster (*www.blockbuster.com*) and Netflix (*www.netflix.com*) offer streaming services that let you watch mainstream Hollywood movies on your Windows computer. CinemaNow (*www.cinemanow.com*) is another digital movie rental site that works with Windows. Amazon also hawks movie downloads in its Video on Demand section at *www.amazon.com*.

Real.com also has video-subscription offerings for both Windows and Linux. You can find the Windows player at *www.real.com/download*. For Linux, go to *www.real.com/linux;* under Advanced Installation Options, click the link for DEB Package. Ubuntu's installation software walks you through the rest of the process.

Windows Media Player can also direct you to online video sources. Choose Media Guide→Browse All Online Stores and click the Video link.

But streaming video is probably the most popular form of video watching, especially in netbooks where space is at a premium. If you're looking for something to watch, consider these sites:

- **YouTube.** The Big Daddy of online video and owned by Google, YouTube is often the first place people look to see that clip of a politician jamming his foot in his mouth or that talked-about TV talent show performance. YouTube members are 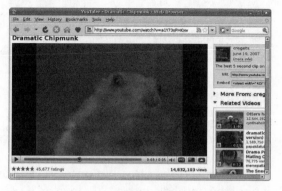 constantly uploading new clips to the site that include everything from homemade songs about hamsters to full-length feature films. (*youtube.com*)

- **Hulu.** Popular TV shows and movies are here for the streaming. The site, which started out as a free service with limited advertising, has been making noise about charging subscription fees in the future. With full episodes of *The Simpsons*, *30 Rock*, *The Office*, and even vintage shows like *Kojak* and *Ironside* to watch online anytime, plenty of people will gladly cough up the cash. (*www.hulu.com*)

- **Vimeo.** A showcase for amateur and indie video, Vimeo is a community-oriented site powered by creative people. It also hosts a large amount of animation and experimental motion graphics. (*vimeo.com*)

- **Veoh.** Combining a lot of user-contributed projects with free streams of commercial TV shows like the original *Star Trek*, *The Twilight Zone*, and *Wonder Woman*, Veoh is also a good site to spend a few hours exploring. (*www.veoh.com*)

- **The Internet Archive.** The site's Moving Images section has more than 182,000 bits of video to stream or download, including Bugs Bunny cartoons from the 1940s and old movies that have fallen into the public domain. But that's not all—not by a long shot. The Archive also has thousands of free audio files to download (Grateful Dead concert recordings, anyone?) and over a million free text files—including e-book versions of popular classics from Jane Austen, William Shakespeare, and other well-known scribes. (*www.archive.org*)

Converting Your DVDs

Just as you can rip the songs from a CD into files to play on the computer, ripping DVD movies to video files is another way to digitize your entertainment for portable viewing. You need a computer with a disc drive and software to convert the discs, but once you create the video file, you can load it onto the netbook with a USB drive or SD card—or copy it from machine to machine over your home network. If space is tight on the netbook drive, you can try *running* the video file from an SD card or USB drive.

Compared to music CDs, DVD movies are more of a legal gray area due to copyright restrictions. Still, many people feel if you bought the DVD, you can do anything you want with it. Plenty of commercial DVD conversion programs for Windows are around, including PQ DVD ($40 at *www.pqdvd. com*) and Apollo DVD Ripper ($40 at *www.dvdtox.com*). Free options include Videora (*www.videora.com*) for Windows.

HandBrake (*http://handbrake.fr*) is an open source program for Windows, Mac, and Linux. It *used* to automatically rip commercial DVDs, until its creators removed that feature from the current version. You can still find tips on the program's home page for decrypting discs anyway, as well as older versions of the program.

Many of these programs were designed to convert movies for iPods, Xboxes, and other gadgets, but you should be able to play them on your netbook, too. And if you're looking for an all-around program that can play video files in just about any format, get VideoLAN's great open source VLC media player for Windows and Linux at *www.videolan.org/vlc*.

Editing Video on a Netbook

With their low-power processors, small screens, and potentially small hard drives, netbooks are not exactly ideal for editing video files. Still, you can see how well (or how badly) your netbook can do the task with the help of a free video-editing program. Windows XP comes with a free program called Windows Movie Maker (Start→All Programs→Movie Maker). If your system didn't come with the program, you can download a copy from Microsoft at *www.microsoft.com/windowsxp/downloads/updates/moviemaker2.mspx*.

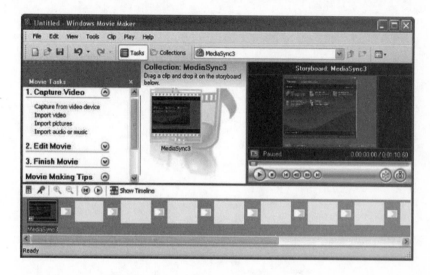

Pinnacle Systems, which makes video-editing software for consumers and professionals, has a free basic Windows program called VideoSpin at *www.videospin.com*.

To give video-editing a spin on Ubuntu, there's an open-source program called PiTiVi. You can find more information and an online user manual at *www.pitivi.org*, and download the program from the Ubuntu software repository by choosing Applications→Add/Remove and searching for *PiTiVi*.

Kino is another Linux video editor you can find in the Ubuntu repository. The program's site at *www.kinodv.org* has more information on using it.

Depending on your netbook's model and configuration, trying to edit video on it can range from excruciatingly slow to passable, so experimenting in a free program means time is the only thing you're burning.

10 Playing Games

Computer games have been around a long time. Accounts dating as far back as 1952 mention a tic-tac-toe program called OXO (or Noughts and Crosses) that was part of Alan S. Douglas's University of Cambridge PhD thesis on human-computer interaction. Other early efforts include William Higinbotham's Pong ancestor, Tennis for Two at New York's Brookhaven National Laboratory in 1958 and Spacewar! (a galactic shoot-'em-up by Stephen Russell at the Massachusetts Institute of Technology in 1962).

While the concepts behind all these games live on well into the 21st century, the hardware to play them on has gotten smaller, faster, and much more powerful. In 1960, the PDP-1 computer that ran Spacewar! was eight feet tall, weighed 1,200 pounds, and cost $120,000. Compare that to a midsize $300 netbook today that weighs 2.5 pounds and can get lost in a tote bag. Not only do you get more bang for your buck in the memory and processing departments, the graphics have gotten *waaaaayyyy* better, too.

Granted, a netbook is not an ideal gaming machine for serious connoisseurs of pristine 3-D graphics with surround sound. But there are plenty of other fantastic games out there—online and off—to challenge your reflexes and wits. This chapter introduces you to some of them.

Games That Come with Your Netbook

Today's computers never let you run out of ways to amuse yourself. If music, video, pictures, and the Internet get boring, you can always play a game. Most of the games included with netbooks tend to be electronic variations on old playing-card standards like Solitaire and Hearts. Windows XP also follows the tradition of many Windows systems before it and comes with that old standby, Minesweeper. (Variations of the mine-flagging game are also available for Ubuntu Linux.)

The number of games included with your netbook may vary by maker, but a few standards usually show up on any system. At any rate, you can find things to play with on a Windows netbook by choosing Start→All Programs→Games. If Ubuntu's your ride, choose Applications→Games to see what's in the toy box.

 Tip Need the rules for the game you want to play? Check under the Help menu on each game's toolbar for instructions.

Windows XP Games

If you like solitaire, Windows XP doesn't disappoint. The system comes with three variations of the classic: Solitaire (the regular classic version with the seven stacks of cards), FreeCell (a variation with eight piles of cards), and Spider Solitaire (*ten* stacks of cards to move around).

If solitaire is not your thing, Windows XP includes the popular card game Hearts, where you pass cards among three computer-generated opponents. The system also comes with a pinball game and Minesweeper, the game where you have to guess the locations of buried mines in a blank grid of squares—guess wrong and an explosion goes off to end the game.

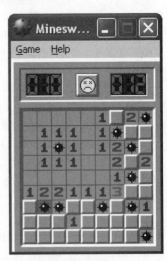

In addition to the standard desktop fare, Windows XP includes several games to play with someone else over an Internet connection. To face off against a faceless online opponent, your choice of battlegrounds includes Checkers, Hearts, Spades, Reversi, and Backgammon.

When you choose an Internet game, Windows sends you to Microsoft's online game server to match you up with someone else looking to play the type of game you selected. If the idea of online gaming appeals to you (it starts to get lonely after that 7,453th game of FreeCell, doesn't it?), skip ahead to page 254 to read more about web-based games.

Ubuntu Linux Games

The games installed on your Linux netbook depend on who you bought it from, but you'll typically find some version of chess, solitaire, and a mine-hunting puzzle game hanging out on the Games menu. You may also get Sudoku, mah-jongg, and Gnometris, (a Tetris-like action game where you fit falling pieces into a rising wall).

Thanks to its lower or nonexistent price tag (compared to Windows, anyway) Linux is big in the education market, which probably explains the abundance of kid-oriented games on some netbooks. For example, Dell's Mini 9 comes with Marbles, miniature golf, and a math game. There's also a full-screen ski adventure called Planet Penguin Racer, which stars Tux, the Linux mascot, sliding downhill while gobbling fish and trying to avoid smacking into trees.

With its online software repository, Ubuntu makes it quite easy to add more games to your arsenal. Just choose Applications→Add/Remove. When the Add/Remove Applications box comes up, click the Games icon on the left side to scroll through the catalog of Ubuntu-friendly games.

Flight simulators, dungeon-crawling games (like Nethack, Rogue, and Angband), war games that let you blow up tanks and planes, billiards, 3-D chess, and a program that lets you smash virtual tomatoes (which are infinitely easier to clean up that the reality-based kind) are among the scores of free games you can add to your Linux netbook.

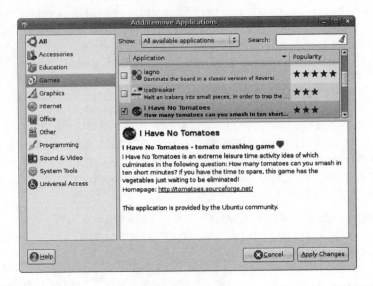

Gaming Websites

Even though your netbook comes with a selection of games to keep you entertained, you might find yourself seeking greater challenges than what Minesweeper and countless games of Solitaire can offer. Your friend, the Web, can help you out here.

Web-based games that you can play in your browser are one way to keep yourself entertained without filling up your netbook's drive. Most of them are free, and you only need a plug-in like Adobe Shockwave to run (the site will politely inform you if you're missing needed software). You may have to look at a browser full of ads as you play, but hey, it's a free game.

If you don't know where to start looking for games, here are a few suggestions.

Game Collections

If you don't know what you want to play, these sites have plenty of different games you can try until you find something you like. Most sites let you play for free, although you may need to sign up for a free account. Some sites may work only with Windows, so check the system requirements if you have trouble getting a site to work on your Ubuntu netbook.

- **PopCap.** Simple, casual games you can learn to play in about five seconds are the focus here at PopCap. The company that came up with the classic Peggle, Bejeweled, and Chuzzle has plenty more to offer— like the inventive Plants vs. Zombies. You can play some games for free online with a special Pop-Cap browser plug-in, while some cost money to download (usually less that $15). (*popcap.com*)

- **MiniClip.** Free is the name of the game here (or the price anyway). MiniClip hosts hundreds of bright, colorful games in several categories, including puzzle games, action games, sports games, and multiplayer games. Tanks, monster trucks, and even real estate acquisitions are among the amusements here. (*www.miniclip.com*)

- **80s Arcade.** Members of Generation X can relive those countless hours at the mall, feeding quarters into a refrigerator-sized machine to get in just one more round of Space Invaders, Centipede, Ms. Pac-Man, Donkey Kong, and more. And unlike in the old days, the mall security guards are not going to hustle you out of the place at 9:00 p.m. (*www.free80sarcade.com*)

- **AOL/Yahoo/MSN.** The Big Three Internet portal sites each have a Games area. You can find everything from classic card games like poker and euchre to word and puzzle games. You can find them at *http://games.aol.com*, *http://games.yahoo.com*, and *http://zone.msn.com*.

> **Tip** Netbook screens tend to be wide and shallow, which can cramp your view of the play area during a game. If you're playing online in a browser, use the browser's View menu to hide as many space-hogging toolbars as possible to give you more room to see. Pressing F11 also pops many browsers into full-screen mode and temporarily gets rid of all the clutter as well.

Chess

Chess players are known for taking their game seriously, and with the Internet in the mix, you can find challenging opponents all over the world—or just brush up your skills at home.

- **The Internet Chess Club.** Billing itself as the longest-running place to play online, the Internet Chess Club hosts an enthusiastic community of dedicated players and around 100,000 online matches a day. Membership in this club has a price, though: $60 a year. (*www.chessclub.com*)

- **World Chess Live.** Designed for novice and intermediate players, this family-friendly chess site hosts software, tutorials, and videos to help players get up to speed. Membership costs $5 a month, plus $1 per additional family member. (*www.worldchesslive.com*)

Fantasy Sports

If managing your own imaginary teams in the world of fantasy baseball, football, or other sports is your thing, the Web has plenty to offer. The megasites Yahoo, AOL, and MSN have their own Fantasy Sports areas, as do ESPN (*http://games.espn.go.com*) and CBS Sports (*www.cbssports.com/fantasy*).

Shooting and Adventure

If you feel the need to shoot things—or just go on quests with players from around the world—here are a few sites to pillage.

- **Shoot the Core.** This site is devoted to *shmups* (short for "shoot 'em ups") and hosts news, forums, and a database of more that 1,200 games to download or play online. (*http://shootthecore.moonpod.com*)

- **Imperia Online.** If you prefer swords to shooters, check out Imperia Online, a browser-based medieval battle strategy game with an international audience. (*www.imperiaonline.org*)

- **Kingdom of Loathing.** A cheeky spoof of role-playing quest games, KoL's graphics—including stick people with swords and martini glasses—won't overload your netbook's video card. (*www.kingdomofloathing.com*)

Downloading Games

Playing games online is fun, but sometimes you need something for those offline moments when Spider Solitaire or slip-sliding penguins have gotten stale. Lucky for you, there are plenty of sites that will give or sell you new casual games. These sites let you download the files from the Web right onto your netbook.

- **Amazon.com.** The ultra-mega-superstore sells just about everything else, so why not game downloads? The Game Downloads area of the site has a large number of Windows titles available for purchase and downloading. Many games are less than $10, and Amazon lets you sample any game on its virtual shelves for free before you buy it. (*www. amazon.com*)

- **Shockwave.** Owned by MTV Networks, Shockwave hosts more than 450 games to play online or download. Categories include puzzle games, action games, strategy, racing, sports, adventure games—plus the old standby digitized card and board games. (*www.shockwave.com*)

- **Download Free Games.** Not every game here is free anymore, but they're all free to try—more than 750 of 'em. This nicely organized site sells many games made by PopCap (page 255), as well as downloadable versions of games previously released on CD, like Risk II and Scrabble. (*www.download-free-games.com*)

But if you find the more casual games too mellow and want to do some serious fragging, read on.

Serious Gaming on a Netbook

Netbooks may not look like they have enough firepower under the hood to run the visually complex, processor-grinding video games that tricked-out PCs, gaming laptops, and console systems churn through with ease. But while Halo 3 may be a bit much for the netbook, the tiny computer is capable of handling a lot more than you think.

Gamers have reported that old and new classics like World of Warcraft, Baldur's Gate, Half-Life, and Quake Live all run fine on the small screen. They're not the latest and greatest, but they're great for a nostalgic gaming experience. You can also experience games you may have missed the first time around—sort of like catching up with a hit show when the DVDs come out.

 Tip If you want to have a decent gaming experience on the netbook, consider maxing out the netbook's RAM. Some come with only 512 MB of RAM but can go up to 2 GB. Slipping another chip inside the machine can make the gaming experience a little faster and smoother. (Page 15 has information on adding RAM.)

Finding Games

Many games still ship on CD and DVD, but you can skip that step and go straight to the download for many of the most recent popular titles. Sites like Steam (*www.steampowered.com*) and FilePlanet (*www.fileplanet.com*) are stuffed with full versions of games you can buy and download like Lineage, Warcraft, Unreal, Delta Force, and more. Prices range from $5 to $50, depending on the game.

While most games are geared towards Windows, you can find a good number of serious Linux games in the ol' software repository (page 71). MAME (the Multiple Arcade Machine Emulator), Warzone 2100, and DooM Legacy may bring back some memories. The Ubuntu community site has more information on games at *https://help.ubuntu.com/community/Games*.

Adding Gaming Hardware to the Netbook

Many games need more controls than what the space bar and arrow keys can provide. If that's your situation, plug a joystick or gamepad into one of your netbook's USB ports. Plenty of hardware makers, including Logitech and Microsoft itself, make USB joysticks that work with Windows XP.

Installing game hardware on a Windows netbook is like installing any USB hardware (Chapter 4 has loads of info on that topic, including speakers and mice). If the system doesn't recognize the device when you plug it into the USB port, you need to install the driver software, either from external disc drive, web download, or installer files copied from the CD (page 89).

Ubuntu Linux can automatically recognize some joysticks and gamepads when plugged into the netbook, but getting certain devices to work properly with Linux can be more difficult than getting them to work with Windows because of driver software issues. If the joystick or gamepad isn't working properly, search the Ubuntu community forums (page 299) for information about Ubuntu and the specific make and model. Someone may have figured out how to make it work and shared the information with the world.

But one reported fix for coaxing a game controller to work goes like this:

1. Choose System→Administration→Terminal.

   It's time to get a command line workout.

2. Type *sudo apt-get update.*

   Press the Enter key.

3. Type *sudo apt-get install joystick.*

   Make sure to set up the joystick to load when you start the netbook. That option saves you from having to kick-start the controller every time you want to play a game.

4. Type *sudo apt-get install jscalibrator.*

   Press the Enter key. This command installs a calibration program on the system.

5. Plug in the USB game hardware. Then type *sudo chmod 666 /dev/input/js0.*

   Press the Enter key and close the Terminal program.

If all goes according to plan, you should be firing away as soon as you start up your game.

11 Protecting You and Your Netbook

The Internet can bring the world to your door—international news, long-distance education, connections with friends around the globe. It lets you discover things you would never see otherwise… like a guy demonstrating how to turn a toaster into a video game console. But where there's good, there's bad, and the dark side of the Internet can be very dark indeed.

You've seen the stories in newspapers and on TV about Internet-enabled identity theft, data theft, fraud, and a thousand and one other scams. Saboteurs turn home computers into zombie slaves and force them to send streams of pornographic junk mail. And there's the old-school stuff: system-crashing viruses, password-stealing programs, and garden-variety hackers swiping bank account numbers right off hard drives.

Sounds scary. Knowing what's out there, there's really no excuse *not* to take precautions for safer computing. This chapter gives you an overview of how to protect yourself (netbook included) from the evils of the Internet. Along with the right software, common sense is your best weapon: *Learn* how to spot the signs of a scam or virus. Knowledge, after all, is power. And a good firewall helps, too.

Ten Online Safety Tips for Netbooks

Top-ten lists are a dime a…er, dozen. The following are general suggestions everyone should know for staying safe online.

1. **Use security software.** Windows computers are a huge target for malicious software. Protection programs may drag down your netbook's speed, but installing the holy trinity—antivirus software, a firewall, and a spyware stomper—is often your first line of technical defense against Internet threats. The next few pages discuss these types of programs in more detail.

2. **Keep your system up to date.** Your system software was probably set up for automatic updates out of the box, but check your security settings to make sure. New threats pop up every day, and you want to make sure both your operating system and security software are up-to-date against *today's* problems, even if you just updated the software *yesterday*.

3. **Don't give out personal information.** Identity theft is rampant and data like your Social Security number and birth date—not to mention credit card and bank account numbers—is what the bad people are after. Be suspicious of any email or web form, no matter how official looking, that asks you for this information. Besides, agencies like the Internal Revenue Service (who scammers often try to disguise themselves as) already have all your personal information on file anyway, taxpayer.

4. **Pick hard passwords.** Using your spouse's name, or worse yet, the word "password" as your password, isn't an effective way to protect your online-banking account. A better password is a complex string of lowercase letters, capital letters, and numbers. After all, *minnesota* is going to be a lot easier for a hacker's password-cracking software to guess than *M1nnes0t@*. Better still, change your passwords regularly.

5. **Stay informed.** Your antivirus company's website can be very informative, with news and alerts about current threats. Visit the site regularly to keep on top of what's going on in the world of malware. Although deeply geeky, the U.S. Computer Emergency Readiness Team (CERT) site is also a great resource, with RSS feeds and mailing lists available to bring the latest news right to you. Sign up at *www.us-cert.gov*.

6. **Keep an eye on your kids.** Netbooks can make great inexpensive laptops for children, who may find the tiny keyboards just the right size. But kids can still get into big trouble on little computers. Just as kids shouldn't talk to strangers in real life, they should avoid them online as well, whether by instant message, email, Facebook, or Skype phone call (page 208). The Wired Safety site is a valuable resource for protective parents: *http://wiredsafety.org*.

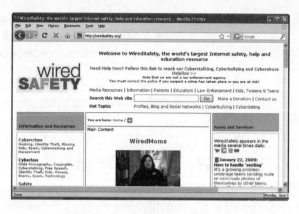

7. **Be wary of public wireless networks.** Sure, free Internet is great, but be wary of doing deeply confidential or personal work while connected to a public or unfamiliar wireless network. When your data is flying back and forth over the radio waves on an unsecure network, evildoers can intercept it. You may not even be connected to a legitimate wireless hotspot: That network called Free Bookstore WiFi may belong to a hacker who's ready to gobble up your personal information. If you're doing official company work on your netbook, ask your tech guru or systems administrator about access through a *virtual private network* (VPN). By using a VPN, you can connect to a private network (like the one in your office) through a public network—but stay more secure.

8. **Email is full of spam and scams.** Yes, it's a great communications tool, but, sadly, most email messages clogging up the Internet's pathways are from people trying to set you up or rip you off. Unwanted junk mail can also carry worms and viruses. Email addresses are easy to fake, so beware of pleas for money even from people you know. And tell your well-meaning pals to stop forwarding virus warnings. Most of those are all fake, too, according to the hoax-stomping site Snopes.com. (*http://snopes.com*)

9. **Back up your files.** Even if a virus wrecks your hard drive or a power surge fries your machine, having a backup of all your important files gives you one less thing to worry about. Page 54 has more on backup options for Windows netbooks, while page 84 discusses the topic for Linux.

10. **Know what to do if the worst happens.** If someone hijacks your netbook, shut it down immediately—or at least sever its Internet access until you can clean the machine. Immediately cancel compromised credit cards. If you think you're a victim of Internet crime like fraud or identity theft, you can turn to a whole page of government resources at *www.usa.gov/Citizen/Topics/Internet_Fraud.shtml*, from another machine, of course.

Keeping Viruses at Bay

Security software—especially if you're using a Windows-based netbook—has become a necessity. Hundreds of thousands of computer viruses, worms, Trojan horses, and other bits of malicious software are cruising the Internet, waiting for vulnerable machines to infest. And they're not just Internet pranks written by malcontented computer-science majors, either. Professional programmers working for international criminal organizations are constantly coming up with new malware with the sole purpose of stealing your personal information.

Fortunately, protection software is easy to find. Since Windows is the malware writer's biggest target, it also has the most security software to choose from. And while Linux has been much less of a target so far, that may change. Using a basic antivirus program can help stop the spread of viruses inadvertently passed on by Windows computers.

 You may see antivirus programs bundled with security suites by many companies. A security suite usually includes antivirus protection, an antispyware program, and firewall software—and often other tools like spam filters and privacy protection. Security suites cost a bit more than a plain antivirus program, but offer more all-around protection.

Windows

A rumor once went around that netbooks were too feeble and underpowered to run security software. While it's true that the Intel Atom or VIA C7 processors aren't quite as robust compared to say, an Intel Core i7 processor revving under the hood of a desktop machine, netbook processors are more than capable of running antivirus and other protective software.

One of the reasons for the netbooks-can't-run-AV rumor was security software's well-earned reputation for hogging up system resources. Some security suites were so bloated, they dragged down the performance of even the most high-powered machines. Recently, though, security software companies got the message and made their programs more compact and efficient.

Your netbook may come with a trial version of an antivirus program like Symantec's Norton Anti-Virus 2009 (*www. symantec.com*). Remember, since new viruses appear every day, it's important to update your antivirus software frequently. If you like the software that came with your netbook, fine. If not, don't hesitate to find one that you like enough to use regularly.

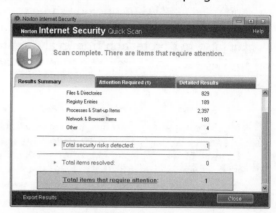

 Commercial programs typically include an automatic update feature, so the program checks back with its maker to snag the new files it needs—often called *virus signatures* or *virus definitions*—to protect the system from fresh evil. When you buy the program (or get it on your netbook), you usually get a free *subscription* for one year's worth of updates. After three months or so, that trial version starts nagging you to pay to "renew your subscription."

Most companies offer free trial versions of their programs by download so you can see how they get along with your netbook. You can also find free antivirus programs that may not update themselves as frequently, but they're still better than nothing.

When shopping for an antivirus product, check to see if it comes in a netbook edition. Suites like Kaspersky Security for Ultra Portables ($40 at *www.kaspersky.com*) were designed especially for small computers.

Other lightweight guard dogs include:

- **Panda Security Cloud Antivirus.** Panda Security claims to be the first to offer *online* virus-scanning and protection. A small local file keeps tabs on your netbook even if you're not online, but the software works mostly from Panda's servers, which frees up your netbook's time and memory. (*www.cloudantivirus.com*)

- **Sunbelt VIPRE Antivirus + Antispyware.** This $30 suite promises to protect your netbook from many kinds of malicious software—while not dragging down the machine's performance. Judge for yourself with the free 15-day-trial version, available to download (along with the full version) on the company's website. (*www.sunbeltsoftware.com*)

- **AVG Anti-Virus Free Edition.** Offering basic protection from viruses and spyware, AVG Technologies' free software also blocks malware on infected web pages. If you pay $35 to upgrade to AVG Anti-Virus Pro, you also get protection from malware invading through an instant-message session, a firewall, a spam filter, and technical support. (*http://free.avg.com*)

 Note Microsoft plans to release its own free security suite by the end of 2009: Microsoft Security Essentials. How well it works compared to the third-party programs remains to be seen. After all, if Microsoft had made Windows more secure to begin with, folks wouldn't need all this antivirus software. Still, if free is the right price for you, keep an eye out for Security Essentials at *www.microsoft.com*.

Linux

Compared to Windows, Linux has relatively few viruses gunning for it. Some gurus pooh-pooh even installing an antivirus program on a Linux system. Others are more cautious and point out that an antivirus program on a Linux computer can at least stop the machine from passing on viruses caught from Windows machines.

If you want to install an antivirus program on your Linux netbook, ClamAV (*http://clamav.org*) is one that's free and available to download from the Ubuntu software repository. Regular ClamAV is a command-line program, though, so if you don't feel like typing a bunch of arcane stuff in the Terminal window, there's the ClamTk program (*http://clamtk.sourceforge.net*) instead—ClamTk is a graphical version of ClamAV and easier for Linux newbies.

Installing and running ClamTk

To install ClamTk, choose Applications→Add/Remove and search for *ClamTk*. When the results come in, turn on the checkbox next to ClamTk and click Apply Changes to install it. (You can also get ClamTk or ClamAV by choosing System→Administration→Synaptic Package Manager and searching for them, although the Add/Remove feature is easier.)

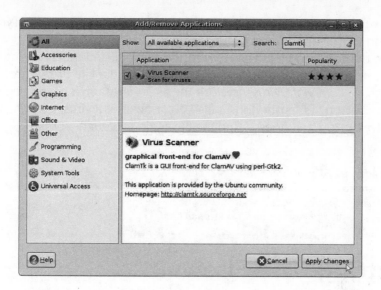

After you install ClamTk, choose Applications→System Tools→Virus Scanner to run it. Just to be on the safe side, you may want to check to make sure the Clam's list of current viruses to spot is up to date; choose Help→Update Signatures.

If you get a snotty message from Ubuntu saying you need to be logged on as root (the all-powerful user described on page 93), before you can update ClamTk's signature files, you need to do a little command-line work to get permission. Choose Accessories→Terminal. Type in *gksu clamtk* and hit Enter; type your Linux system password when prompted. Now, when you go back to ClamTk and choose Help→Update Signatures, you won't get any back talk. To have ClamTk automatically quarantine any viruses it finds, choose Options→Quarantine Infected Files.

To scan the Home directory on your netbook (or just a file or folder), choose an option from ClamTk's File menu. To thoroughly scan a folder and all its subfolders, choose File→Recursive Scan and point ClamTk to the folder in question. Deep scans may take a while, but the program's progress bar keeps you up to date.

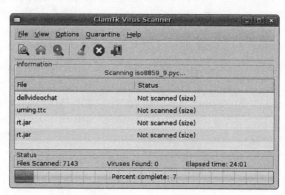

If ClamTk finds a virus, it lets you know about it in the Status column. If you've chosen to quarantine suspicious files, choose Quarantine→Maintenance to see the corralled files. If you're not sure that a file might be a virus, look up its name on the Web or in a virus encyclopedia like *http://threatinfo.trendmicro.com/vinfo/virusencyclo*. If the file in question is a virus, click the Delete button. If ClamTk finds a file you *know* isn't a virus, click the False Positive button so it doesn't find the file again on your next scan.

 Note ClamAv and ClamTk aren't your only Linux options. Panda Security (*www.pandas-ecurity.com*) and F-Prot Antivirus (*www.f-prot.com*) both have commercial software for Linux systems. Avast has a free Linux home edition as well; details are at *http://avast.com/eng/avast-for-linux-workstation.html*.

Putting Up a Firewall

With malicious software blazing across the Internet, your netbook can use even more protection, especially from people trying to connect to your computer to hijack it for their own use or swipe your personal information. "How do intruders get into my computer in the first place?" you may ask.

The answer is through *ports*—little pathways the operating system uses to let connected devices and Internet programs speak to your netbook. Many programs that do business online (web browsers, multiplayer video games, email programs, and so on) use a specific port. But someone who knows how ports work can find an open one and slip in software to take control of your computer.

You can protect your netbook with a security barrier called a *firewall*. A firewall monitors your computer's ports and stops unauthorized programs from getting into your system—or sending information out from it. Firewalls come in two different flavors: hardware firewalls and firewall software programs.

Hardware firewalls are boxes that go between your computer and your Internet connection. You may already be using one and not know it—many network routers also double as hardware firewalls to shield the network from prying eyes. If your home network router uses *network access translation* (NAT), you already have a dandy firewall. NAT technology allows connections *from* your computer but doesn't allow other computers on a different network to connect to yours. (You can read about NAT in detail at *http://computer.howstuffworks.com/nat.htm*.)

Software firewalls, on the other hand, are programs you configure to block unwanted network traf-fic and attention. If you purchase a security suite for your Windows netbook, you may get a personal firewall as part of the package. If you didn't buy a suite, you have a free basic firewall included with Windows. Ubuntu Linux also comes with firewall options.

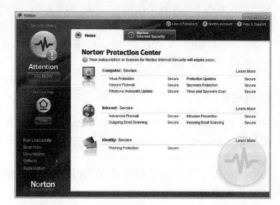

Windows

The original edition of Windows XP had a firewall tucked inside, but it was turned off and many people couldn't even find the darn thing to turn it on. Fortunately, from Windows XP Service Pack 2 onward, the firewall comes turned on, and it's much easier to find. To see it, choose Start→Control Panel→Security Center. (If you're using the Classic view of the Control Panel area, choose Start→Control Panel→Windows Firewall.)

The Security Center control panel has icons to click to open settings for the Windows Firewall, Automatic Updates (page 271), and Internet Options—a collection of settings for your netbook's web browser and network connections.

In the Windows Firewall con-trol panel, you can see which programs have permission to go through the firewall by clicking the Exceptions tab. A list of programs appears. If you need to add an exception or open a port for a particular program (like a multiplayer game that needs a specific port to play through), click the Add Program or Add Port buttons to set things up— check the software's settings guide for any ports that need opening. Microsoft has further instructions for using Win-dows Firewall at *http://support. microsoft.com/kb/875356.*

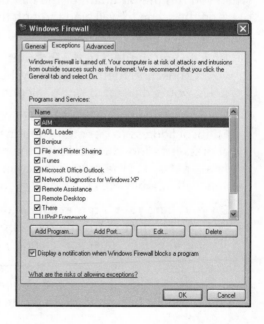

Windows Firewall is not the most intuitive software and it's been criticized for only blocking incoming—but not outgoing—traffic. If you want a more robust gatekeeper, consider a commercial firewall program or at least a more versatile freebie like Check Point's free version of the Zone Alarm firewall at *http://bit.ly/OBr4S*.

Linux

Linux was designed with security in mind and includes a firewall called IPTables tucked away deep in the system. The Ubuntu Community site has a page that explains how it works at *https://help.ubuntu.com/community/IptablesHowTo*, but the program is command-line driven, which may not be your thing.

A graphical-oriented program like Firestarter makes it easier to manage the firewall and its rules. To install it on Ubuntu, choose Applications→Add/Remove, search for *Firestarter*, and install the program as described on page 71.

After you install the software, choose System→Administration→Firestarter. When you run the program for the first time, a Windows-like wizard appears on the scene to walk you through the setup procedure. The wizard will ask a few things, including:

- **How do you connect to the Internet?** Use the pop-up menu to select your connection method, which will probably be an Ethernet device unless you're dialing up with a telephone modem to get online.

- **How do you get your IP address?** Every computer needs an Internet Protocol address to get on the Internet. Turn on the checkbox for "IP address is assigned via DHCP" if the netbook normally jumps onto a home network. (The *eth0* connection is usually your wired Ethernet connection, while *eth1* is probably your wireless connection.)

- **Do you share your Internet connection?** Unless you're letting someone else connect to the Internet through your computer, leave the "Enable Internet connection sharing" checkbox turned off.

When you get to the last screen, make sure the "Start firewall now" checkbox is turned on and click the Save button. Once you start the firewall, it runs quietly in the background in a secure mode.

To see Firestarter in action, choose System→Administration→Firestart er. The three-tabbed box shows you the Status (the network activity), Events (connections the firewall has blocked), and Policy (where you can set up rules for special programs that need to get through the firewall).

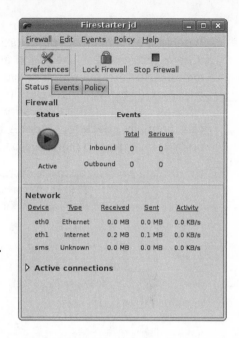

You may not ever need to set up any policies for programs in Firestarter, but if you do, the program has thorough documentation on how to do it at *www.fs-security.com*.

Other Security Software for Netbooks

Keeping your operating system up to date with the latest patches from Microsoft or Canonical (the force behind Ubuntu Linux) is another important security step, since the companies often close up security holes and make other improvements via updates to the system software. You can set each system to automatically check for updates.

- In Windows XP, choose Start→Control Panel→Security Center. In the Security Center control panel, click Automatic Updates. Or, if you use the Classic view of the Control Panel, choose Start→Control Panel→Automatic Updates. In the box, you can make sure the service is turned on and pick a time each day for Windows to check back with the Microsoft mothership for any new updates. (The company tends to push out its big fixes on Patch Tuesday, which is the second Tuesday of each month.) A yellow shield in the taskbar means Windows has new updates either ready to download or currently downloading.

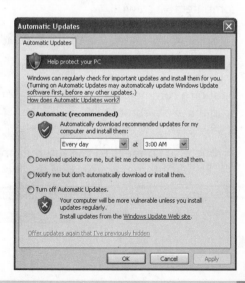

- In Ubuntu Linux, choose System→Administration→Software Sources. Type your administrator password. Click the Updates tab, turn on the "Check for updates" checkbox, and choose Daily from the pop-up menu. Also turn on the "Download all updates in the background" checkbox. (Later versions of Ubuntu may have checkboxes for "Automatic updates," as well as "Install security updates without confirmation.") You can manually check for updates by clicking the yellow exclamation point icon in the top panel toolbar.

Spyware

With Windows XP, you need to be on guard for spyware. These sneaky software chunks can infiltrate your computer by being bundled with a game or program you install—or by more insidious means. Spyware can do everything from compromising your system's security to slowing your computer to a crawl. If you're not using a security suite that includes an antispyware program, you can find help either through a commercial program like Webroot's SpySweeper ($30 at *www.webroot.com*) or through a freeware fix.

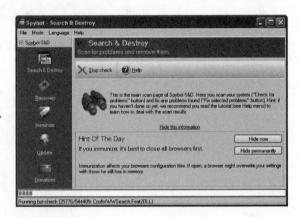

For spy-stomping on a budget, consider Spybot Search & Destroy (*www. safer-networking.org*), LavaSoft's Ad-Aware Free (*lavasoft.com*), or Microsoft's own Windows Defender (*www.microsoft.com/defender*). Once you install an antispyware program, start it and have it hunt down the unwanted software that's invaded your netbook. You're typically presented with a list of intruders after the program sweeps the system, with the option to delete the pests.

Browser Security

Your web browser (probably Internet Explorer or Firefox since you're on a netbook) also has some security settings you can adjust to protect yourself better online. Among other things, you can block pop-up windows, potentially harmful web-page scripts, and unwanted cookies. The CERT site for computer security also has an in-depth list of browser security tips at *www. cert.org/tech_tips/securing_browser*.

Internet Explorer

Choose Tools→Internet Options and click the Security tab. Click the Internet icon and push the slider to High for maximum security. This setting may disable the features of certain websites, but makes for a safer browsing experience.

Click the Trusted Sites icon and then click the Sites button to add the addresses of websites you know and trust—ones you visit regularly, like a newspaper website. (You can set the slider to Medium security for sites you trust.)

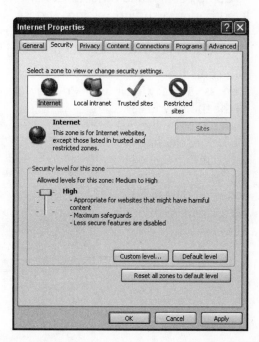

Click the Privacy tab in the Internet options box and then click the Advanced button. This leads to the controls to block *cookies*, those little bits of text a website leaves with your browser. While cookies can be good (they're why Amazon.com welcomes you back by name), they can also let villains track your movements from site

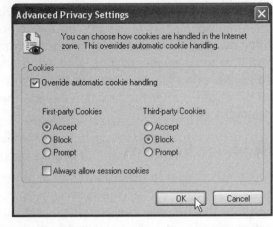

to site. Blocking third-party cookies—ones that comes not from the sites you visit, but from any ad agencies working with them—can help maintain more privacy.

You can also choose to block pop-up ads by turning on the checkbox at the bottom of the Privacy tab. Internet Explorer's Tools menu also has options to block pop-up windows and turn on a phishing filter to warn you against sites trying to *phish*, or dupe you into entering personal information by disguising themselves as legitimate business websites.

Firefox

To dump cookies and other personal information that may have accumulated during a surfing session, choose Tools→Clear Private Data. A box pops up with a list of personal tidbits you can dump out of Firefox's memory, including cookies and your browsing history.

If the box doesn't pop up, choose Tools→Options→Privacy, or Edit→Preferences→Privacy in Linux. In Private Data, click the Settings button to see all the things you can dump. Turn on the "Ask me before clearing private data" checkbox if you want Firefox to ask you what data to flush each time.

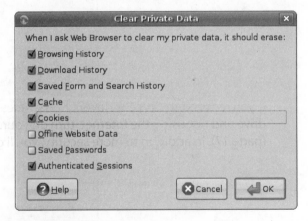

For extra protection from malicious scripts embedded in evildoers' web pages, there's a Firefox add-in called NoScript that shuts down rogue code. You can get it at *http://noscript.net*. Running it may hamper normal scripts on many legitimate websites, so NoScript lets you give your familiar, trusted sites permission to use their scripts with a click.

Out of the box, Firefox has pop-up window blocking turned on. It lets you know when it's blocked a new window by displaying a message just below the browser toolbar. If you want to let the window open, click the Options button in the message bar and choose the option to allow pop-ups from that site.

 Tip If you're entering credit card numbers or other personal information into a website, make sure it's a secure site. Secure sites, which encrypt your data when you send it over the Web, usually have URLs that start with *https://* instead of *http://* and often feature a lock icon at the top or bottom of the window.

Public Wireless Network Security

With the abundance of wireless networks around airports, coffee shops, bookstores, libraries, hotels, and other places where people gather, you and your netbook are never far from the Web. But keep in mind: Not all people are nice. That polite-looking young lady working two benches over from you on the park's free wireless network could actually be rooting around in your netbook's hard drive. Don't leave your security doors ajar.

Unlike your home wireless network, which you can set up with security measures and password-protection (page 123), you don't know who set up the public wireless network—or who else is using it at the moment. With that in mind, take the following precautions when netbooking away from home:

- Make sure you've got a software firewall in place and that it's turned on (page 268).

- Don't type passwords for online accounts linked to credit cards or credit card numbers, and refrain from doing online banking or stock trading in public.

- If you're working on your novel or other files on your netbook's hard drive and not using the Internet, turn off your netbook's wireless radio (page 17). In addition to more security, you'll gain more battery time.

- If your company offers access to its private network through a secure VPN (virtual private network) service, by all means sign up for it. You can still hop onto the Internet over a public wireless network, but you'll be safer when you do.

- If you have a ton of personal files with sensitive information in them, consider encrypting them so even if the files get snagged, opening them will be difficult or impossible. TrueCrypt is a free file scrambler for Windows and Linux at *www.truecrypt.org*. With Ubuntu Linux, you can encrypt files in the OS, but you need to set up encryption keys and other techie stuff first; details at *https://help.ubuntu.com/community/EncryptedFilesystemHowto*. (To be extra safe, make sure you have an unencrypted backup of the files at home.)

Safest of all, leave the files with your personal and financial information back on your home computer and just use the netbook for casual surfing and social networking when you're out and about.

Protecting Yourself: Ergonomic Tips

Ergonomics is technically defined as "the study of people's efficiency in their working environment" but the term is usually used in reference to how you physically work on your computer at your desk. Are you sitting with a healthy posture or are you contorted like a yoga casualty? Can you sit up straight while you work or are your coworkers calling you "Quasimodo" behind your hunched back? Do your fingers get numb after a few minutes of typing?

With their smaller-than-average screens and keyboards, netbooks are not exactly an ergonomic dream machine. They may put less stress on your back and shoulder when toted around town, but that's about it. If your eyes are bleary and your wrists throb after just a few minutes of using the netbook, you're suffering from poor ergonomics. Here are a few things that might ease the pain:

- If you're going to be doing a lot of writing on the netbook, buy one with a keyboard that's close to 100 percent full size, which usually means a screen size of at least 10 inches. Some netbooks with 9-inch screens have to shrink the keyboard down to 85 or 90 percent, which touch typists will definitely feel after a while. Investing in a folding, full-sized USB or Bluetooth keyboard to use with the netbook is another way to type more comfortably when you have a lot of writing to do. You may have to shell out $50 or more, but saving your hands from crippling pain is worth it.

- If your thumb is aching from hitting cheap plastic buttons on the netbook's trackpad, consider doing your navigation with a mouse or trackball (page 88).

- Using the netbook on a table gives you more places to rest your arms. A gel-based wrist-rest may help. Tilt the screen back so you can see it without hunching.

- If you're using the netbook on your lap, prop it up with a book, lap desk, or firm pillow so you're not slouching. (But don't use too fluffy a pillow or you may block the netbook's air vents and cause it to overheat.)

- Take frequent breaks to stretch your arms and rest your eyes.

- For aching arms and fingers, try some exercises designed to help repetitive stress injuries at *www.safecomputingtips.com/rsi-exercises.html*.

But don't kid yourself: If you feel chronic pain when you sit down at any computer, schedule a visit with your doctor.

12 Troubleshooting Your Netbook

No matter how you use it—traveling Facebook updater, portable typewriter, video game console, or all of the above—a netbook is still a computer. And computers have problems now and then.

Figuring out what's wrong with a sick netbook is pretty much like figuring out why a regular laptop or desktop machine is acting up. Is it hardware? Is it software? Could it have something to do with the cappuccino that you just spilled all over the keyboard? (Thanks to the prevalence of wireless Internet access in coffee shops, that last issue is more common than it used to be.)

This chapter takes a look at some tools and principles you can use to figure out what ails your netbook so you can fix it. You'll also learn basic maintenance methods that can keep it running more smoothly and possibly prevent trouble. If worse comes to worst, you'll see what to do if your netbook really needs a major operation—like a full system reinstall.

Whenever this chapter doesn't have all the answers, it tells you where to look for them. This information can make the difference between a happy, functioning netbook—and a flat, three-pound paperweight.

Troubleshooting Common Problems

Netbooks, like their larger laptop cousins, are meant to be portable. Netbooks *go* places. But the more you move the netbook around, quaff chai tea lattes over it, or plop it into the plastic tub for an airport x-ray inspection, the more you increase the odds of something going awry. Here are some quick tips for some of the more common netbook ailments.

- **Power issues.** If the netbook won't turn on, make sure the battery is locked into place and not loose, or that the power cord is firmly plugged into both the wall outlet and the netbook's AC port. If the AC port on the netbook seems loose, there could be problems with the power getting to the netbook; if so, consult a computer repair service. If you've been using the netbook on the road a lot, make sure the battery is charged.

- **Liquid spills.** If you dump coffee, tea, or another beverage all over your netbook, you need to act quickly. Flip it over and remove the battery from the machine to cut the power (if you're running on electrical power, or unplug it and then pop the battery). Keep the netbook upside down to drain the liquid out of the keys. Mop out as much liquid as you can. Let the netbook dry for at least 24 hours, keeping it propped open and upside down. Liquids that contain protein or sugar (milk, soda, orange juice, coffee with milk and sugar) are the most likely to gunk up the keys. Black coffee, tea, and water do less damage. When the netbook has dried, use cotton swabs lightly moistened with distilled water or isopropyl alcohol to clean the keyboard area. When finished, snap the battery back in and see if the netbook works. If not, get thee to a repair shop for a professional evaluation.

- **Wireless connection issues.** If the netbook is on but can't see any wireless networks, check to make sure the WiFi radio is on (page 17). On Linux, also check to make sure you didn't accidentally turn off your wireless card's driver (page 126). Check your wireless settings on your Windows (page 124) or Linux (page 125) system. If you can see networks but can't connect to one, make sure the network you want to use is either an open network (no password required) or that you have the right password.

- **Unexpected shutdowns and crashes.** If the netbook runs fine for awhile but gets hot and shuts down unexpectedly, it may be overheating due to inadequate airflow around it. Make sure nothing is blocking its back and side vents. Consider a laptop cooling pad or lap desk to provide increased airflow.

  If you've added extra memory to it recently, check to make sure the chip is firmly pushed into the slot inside the netbook's RAM compartment. Malicious software can also cause bizarre behavior, so if you don't have security software on your netbook, try installing antivirus and antispyware programs and running them; Chapter 11 tells you where to get various free protection programs.

If you've used Windows, you may have run repair programs to solve registry problems or other common ailments. You can find similar fix-it programs designed just for netbooks. SmithMicro's CheckIt Netbook Utility Suite ($40 at *www.smithmicro.com* or at *www.amazon.com*) is one such collection. It even comes on a USB drive so you can easily install and run it on the netbook.

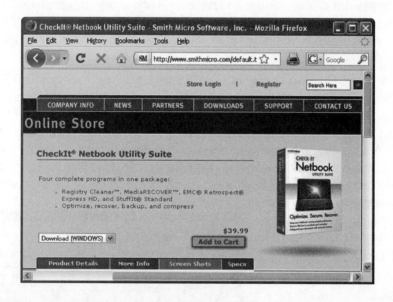

Tip You can often find utility programs grouped together in freeware collections designed to fit on a USB drive. They often include programs that can rescue corrupted files, thoroughly erase files, and scan hard drives. You can usually find a few hits by doing a web search for *USB PC repair kit*. For Ubuntu utilities, check out *http://ubuntu-rescue-remix.org*.

Built-In Windows Help Files

Having trouble getting Bluetooth devices to find each other? Email not downloading? Netbook freezing when you try to shut it down? Your netbook itself may hold the answers (or at least suggestions as to why things aren't working properly). Just choose Start→Help and Support.

When you do, the Help and Support Center appears onscreen, offering links, tips, and troubleshooting guides for a variety of common system snafus. The left side of the window is filled with help links for things like printing, networking, and more. Click the "Fixing a Problem" link at the bottom to visit a page of step-by-step troubleshooting guides for software problems, multimedia issues, email woes, networking hang-ups, printing headaches, and so on.

To get started, click the general category for the problem you're having— "Printing problems," for example. The right side of the window switches to a menu of different dilemmas for printing-related tasks. Click the one that's closest to your situation. If you're trying to solve the mystery of why nothing comes out of the printer, choose the "Fixing a printing problem" link. The next screen takes you to the "Use the Printing Troubleshooter" link. Once you click that, Windows asks you a series of questions designed to help you narrow down the situation and figure out what's wrong.

The Help and Support Center has other useful areas, including a Search box you can use to look up articles by keyword, like *wireless*. If you're new to Windows, you can get a quick tutorial with the Windows Basics section. If the Troubleshooter screens didn't solve your problem, Help and Support's main window has links to online newsgroup discussions where you might be able to get the answer from another Windows jockey. You also get shortcuts to the built-in Windows tools, some of which are described in this chapter, like System Restore (page 286) and Remote Assistance (page 287).

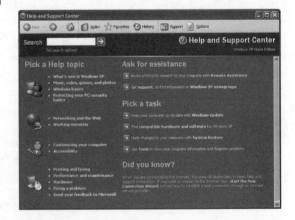

So while it may not have the solution to every problem, the Help and Support Center offers plenty of useful information, and it may just point you in the right direction for the answers you need.

Tuning Up with Windows System Tools

As mentioned back on page 44, the All Programs menu features a collection of System Tools designed to help you use your netbook and keep it running in tip-top shape. Three programs in particular can help.

Disk Cleanup

Created to safely sweep out all the digital clutter you don't need anymore, Disk Cleanup can help you reclaim big chunks of your netbook's drive. The program removes temporary Internet files, old program installers, and other outdated Windows debris. It can also compress old files to make them take up less room, or toss out old Windows components and programs you never use. Disk Cleanup even takes out the trash and empties the Recycle Bin for you.

To use it, choose Start→All Programs→Accessories→System Tools→Disk Cleanup. The program takes a few minutes to analyze the contents of the drive and then presents a list of old files it can safely delete—along with an estimate of how much space you'll save. If you want to see the specific files Disk Cleanup has found in each category, click the category and then click View Files. Once you've decided what you want to delete, click OK to have Disk Cleanup get to work.

To dump more baggage, click the More Options tab in the Disk Cleanup box. In addition to Windows components and unused programs, you can also trim down the number of System Restore points (mini-backups of your system's settings, as page 286 explains) that Windows XP is saving.

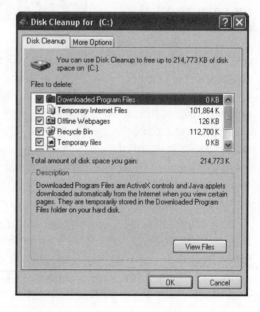

If you decide to remove Windows components, pay attention to the checked boxes to make sure you aren't inadvertently whacking something you use, like programs from the Accessories folder.

Disk Defragmenter

The more you use a computer, the more *fragmented* its files become. Although the word sounds ominous, fragmentation is perfectly normal. It's when the computer stores little pieces of a file around the hard drive wherever it has room for them. You see a complete file when you open it, but the computer is working madly behind the scenes to gather up all the parts. Over time, all this gathering can drag things down and make the netbook seem sluggish.

Time to defragment the drive with Disk Defragmenter. This program carefully analyzes the netbook's drive to find all those scattered file pieces. Then it rearranges them back into contiguous pieces, making it easier and faster for the computer to find them.

To get started, choose Start→All Programs→Accessories→System Tools→Disk Defragmenter. Click Analyze to get a picture of how fragmented your drive is. In the horizontal bar in the top half of the window, the program paints a picture of the drive's state with colored bars, each representing a type of data. If the graphic shows thin scattered colored stripes that resemble a swatch of clown pants instead of bigger, more solid blocks of color, your drive is really fragmented.

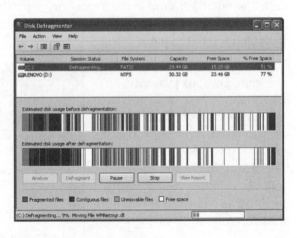

After analysis, Windows announces whether the drive needs to be defragmented. If it does, click the Defragment button and go do something else while Disk Defragmenter gets to work. It may take a while, but when the Defragmenter is done, those colored bars in the bottom bar should look a lot more solid and the netbook should run faster.

Check Disk, the tool formerly known as Scandisk

A formatted hard drive is divided up into tracks, sectors, and clusters, which the operating system uses to keep tabs on where all the stuff is stored on the computer. Over time and with use, though, sectors can go bad, clusters become lost, and the disk may begin to behave slowly or erratically. These problems happen due to system crashes, power glitches, and other file-corrupting incidents.

Windows XP comes with a program that checks for disk errors and tries to repair them. Older versions of Windows called this program Scandisk, but Windows XP calls it Check Disk or the Error-Checking tool. No matter what it's called, running it regularly can help maintain your system.

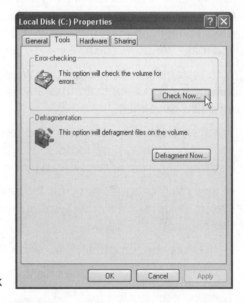

To check your netbook's disk, choose Start→My Computer. In the list of drives, right-click the one you want to scan (usually the C: drive) and choose Properties from the pop-up menu. Click the Tools tab, and then click the Check Now button. The Check Disk Options box pops up. Turn on the checkboxes for both "Automatically fix file system errors" and "Scan for and attempt recovery of bad sectors" before you click Start.

The Check Disk tool wants to have the computer all to itself to work, so it pops up another box giving you the option to run it the next time Windows starts up. Click Yes and then restart the netbook to kick off the scan.

When you restart the netbook, the Check Disk tool takes over with its white text on a two-toned blue background screen. Depending on the size of your drive, Check Disk can take several minutes to an hour to do its thing. (You can skip the scan by tapping any key within a few seconds.)

When it finishes the job, Check Disk reports on whether it found any disk errors, **found and fixed** any errors, or **couldn't fix** the errors it found. If Check Disk starts to find more and more bad sectors during its inspections, your hard drive may be on a downward slope. And it should also serve as a reminder to regularly back up your netbook (page 54).

Using Windows System Restore

A better name for System Restore might be Bacon Saver. System Restore simply takes a series of snapshots or **restore points** of important system files and stores them on your hard drive in case of emergency. These snapshots come in handy later in case you fiddle around with system settings and make Windows crash.

With System Restore, you can take Windows back in time to before the bad thing happened—but not lose any files, email, or other data created or modified since then.

Windows creates its own scheduled restore points, but you can also make your own. A good time to do so is right before you spend an afternoon installing software or tweaking Windows system settings, for example.

In any case, choose Start→All Programs→Accessories→System Tools→ System Restore. When the System Restore window comes up, you have two choices:

- Restore the computer to an earlier time.
- Create a new restore point right this very instant.

If you click the button for the first option, the next screen shows you a little calendar with certain dates in bold, meaning there's a restore point on that day. So if your computer started acting up on Sunday after you stayed up late Saturday night messing around with settings, see if you have a restore point from **before** Saturday.

After you've selected the point in time you want to return to, click Next and let System Restore do its thing. Windows restarts itself afterwards, and when it comes back up, your system should be behaving just like it was before the unfortunate incident.

To create a restore point, click the button next to "Create a restore point" on the main System Restore screen and then click Next. You're asked to type in a name for this point ("Before the shareware games installation," for example), and Windows takes it from there. Later, if you find that Windows is peeved at whatever you did to it after you made the restore point, you can use System Restore to go back in time.

 Note The changes made by System Restore aren't permanent. You can reverse course by going back into the program and picking a different restore point from the calendar.

Using Remote Assistance

Like most people, you may need a little help in life sometimes, especially when a computer is part of your life. Windows comes with a feature that lets people help one another—over the Internet. It's called Remote Assistance, and it lets two people share the same computer screen, with an "expert" controlling the computer of a "novice" to adjust settings and fix problems.

Be careful who you invite to help you with your problems, though, as giving over control of your computer can be dangerous. Still, if you have a computer whiz in the family or a close buddy who knows about this stuff, you can use Remote Assistance to get computer help right in the comfort of your own home.

To get to the Remote Assistance screen, choose Start→Help and Support. Under the "Ask for Assistance" area at right, click "Invite a friend to connect to your computer with Remote Assistance." Windows walks you through the steps from there.

You have three ways of getting your plea for help to your pal. You can ask by instant message if you both use Microsoft's Messenger program (page 200), or you can send an email request. If your email program is messed up and you don't use Windows Live Messenger, you can save the request as a "RAInvitation" file you can copy onto a working computer and mail as an attachment. Unless you directly ask by IM, you need to supply a password that allows your expert to take over the computer.

Once the Expert user accepts the invitation and supplies the password, the Remote Assistance window appears. The Expert clicks the Take Control button onscreen. The Novice (you) gets a dialog box announcing that the Expert would like to take control of the machine. Click Yes if you want the Expert to do the driving. (Hit the Escape key on the keyboard if you want to grab back control of the netbook.)

The Remote Assistance window has a panel of buttons and a chat function that lets you communicate with the other person by voice or instant message. Once the expert assumes control, she can see and move around your computer, fixing problems and so on. When the expert is finished, she clicks the Release Control button to return the reins to you. Click the Disconnect button to end the computer therapy session.

Microsoft has a document on using Remote Assistance at *http://support.microsoft.com/kb/300546*.

Tip If you have another computer that's running Windows XP Professional—say your home-office machine down in the basement—you can connect to it over the Internet from your netbook with a Windows feature called Remote Desktop. The Remote Desktop feature isn't included with the Windows XP Home system installed on most netbooks, so you can't control the netbook from the other PC, but it can be handy to use if you want to get a little work done and need files from your other computer. If this describes your situation, visit *snipurl.com/kzzu7* for instructions on how to set up both the Windows XP Pro computer and the Windows XP netbook.

Reinstalling Windows

If your netbook won't start up properly, or Windows has become hopeless-ly riddled with viruses, or you just want to wipe the netbook's drive, a fresh installation of Windows can fix it all. How you reinstall Windows depends on your netbook, its maker, and the discs (if any) that came with it. Some netbooks keep an image of the Windows system files on a separate hard-drive partition, while some give you a Windows system or recovery disc.

So, because there are so many factors in play and they depend on the hardware you have, the first step is to check the manual or manufacturer's website for instructions on how to reinstall Windows on your netbook's make and model. Microsoft also has its own general step-by-step guide for reinstalling Windows at *http://support.microsoft.com/kb/315341*.

 Note Before you do any sort of repair or recovery procedure, though, back up all your important documents and files (page xx), so they don't get accidentally erased during any emergency procedures.

Having an external disc drive and a copy of a Windows XP installation disc is probably the quickest and most direct way to reinstall the system. Con-nect the drive to the netbook, pop in the Windows disc and follow the onscreen instructions. You may also be able to use the Repair function on the Windows installation disc to fix damaged system components that are tripping up the netbook.

Many of Lenovo's laptops, including its IdeaPad netbooks, include the OneKey Recovery system. By pushing the OneKey button on the key-board, the computer calls up the onboard rescue software. If need be, you can wipe the netbook's drive and reinstall the factory version of Windows that came with it.

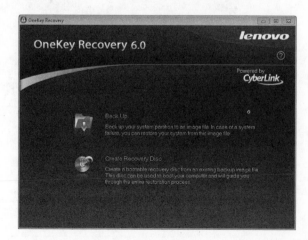

One thing you'll need for pretty much any Windows system reinstallation: your Windows product key. If there wasn't a sticker with a huge string of 25 numbers and letters affixed to your Windows disc, look on the netbook's underside. Lenovo, for example, slaps it on the bottom.

 Tip If you don't have an external disc drive, but have a Windows installation CD and access to another computer with a disc drive, you can also make a bootable USB flash drive, and then install the Windows files onto it and use it to reinstall Windows on the netbook. It's not exactly a simple process, but it can work. Check out *www.missingmanuals.com/cds* for links to demonstration videos and guides from netbook users around the world. You can also use this method to install different versions of Windows (like Windows 7) or even Linux (page 297).

Built-in Linux Help Files

If you're a Linux netbooker, you're part of a growing movement. You may have been attracted by the idea of open-source software, wanted a cheaper machine, or just plain didn't want to deal with Windows. But even without Microsoft's huge corporate Service and Support team to fall back on, help's not hard to find. In fact, it's literally right in front of you—in the top-panel menu bar. Click the blue question mark icon to open up Ubuntu's built-in Help system.

Along the left side of the Ubuntu Help Center window, you see a list of popular topics. "New to Ubuntu?" tops the list, followed by a series of links that take you to pages for adding and removing software, working with files and folders, using the Internet, and so on.

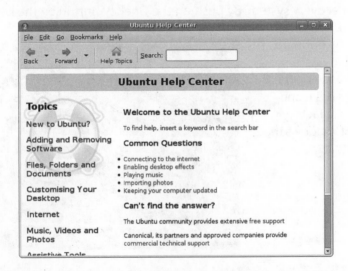

If you have basic questions or just want a simple tutorial for, say, adding codec files so you can listen to music in some of the lesser-known digital audio formats, the Help Center is worth trawling for answers. And if you don't see the topic you're specifically interested in, type it in the Search box at the top of the window.

The Ubuntu Help Center's main page also has a link to the massive web-based help pages written by volunteers for the Ubuntu community. The Community pages cover a huge range of topics, and some volunteers have even created How-To videos and screencasts. You can find it all at *https:// help.ubuntu.com/community*.

Maintaining a Linux Netbook

Compared to Windows, Linux is a fairly self-maintaining operating system. For example, defragmenting your disk (page 284) isn't on your monthly to-do List, since Linux uses a different file system (called *ext3*) that doesn't require the regular defragmentation like Windows' file system.

As for remembering to run a disk-scanning program like Check Disk (page 285) to examine your hard drive for errors, you, O Linux devotee, have it easier as well. Ubuntu automatically does an error-checking scan on its drive after every 30 startups. So if you're coming from a Windows system in your earlier life, that's another thing you cross off your schedule.

Keeping Ubuntu Tidy

Keeping your hard drive from overflowing can be a challenge on any operating system. Be sure to empty your system's Trash regularly: Right-click the orange recycle bin icon in the lower-right corner and choose Empty Trash from the pop-up menu.

Uninstalling programs you don't use frees up disk space as well. You can remove these squatters by choosing Applications→Add/Remove, selecting "Installed applications only" in the Show menu, and then turning off the checkbox next to the programs you wish to remove. Click Apply Changes, and type your system password when requested. Ubuntu then removes the deselected programs.

 Note If you have the Add/Remove Applications window already open and try to open the Synaptic Package Manager, Ubuntu explains that there's already a package manager open and won't open Synaptic until you close the Add/Remove Applications window.

You can also remove programs by choosing System→Administration→ Synaptic Package Manager. Going this route actually gives you more options for removing programs, because you can get rid of *residual configuration packages*. (The files Linux programs need come in *packages;* hence the need for a *package manager* program to get everything installed and uninstalled correctly.)

But sometimes, bits of package residue are left behind after you uninstall a program. That's where the Synaptic Package Manager can help. Open it, and in the left column, click "Not installed (residual config)." If you don't see anything listed, you don't have any residual config bits on your system. If you do see a list of programs in the center of the window, click the ones you want to ditch and choose "Mark for Complete Removal" from the pop-up menu. At the top of the window, click Apply, type your password if asked, and let the Synaptic Package Manager take back a little space on your netbook.

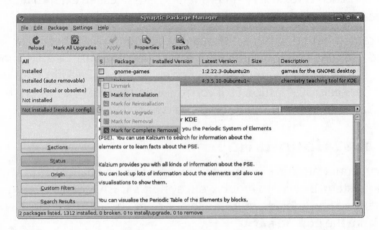

Tip Uninstalling old programs makes room for new ones, so now if you remember seeing something interesting in your netbook's software repositories, you can add it. The Community help file at *https://help.ubuntu.com/community/Repositories/ Ubuntu* has the illustrated details.

Ubuntu Remote Desktop

Thanks to Ubuntu's Remote Desktop feature, you can get help over the network or Internet from your friendly Ubuntu guru. Like the Windows Remote Assistance feature (page 287), Ubuntu's Remote Desktop function lets someone take over your screen to adjust settings or fix problems. But it's a two way street: You can also use Remote Desktop to tap into another Ubuntu computer from your netbook—or even a Windows machine. This setup can be handy if you have files you need to reference back on your home or work computer.

Here's how to set it up:

1. On the machine you want to remotely control, choose System→ Preferences→Remote Desktop.

   In the General tab, go to the Sharing area and turn on the "Allow other users to view your desktop" checkbox. In the Security section, turn on the checkbox requiring the controlling party to ask you for confirmation and the checkbox requiring a password to control your computer. Type the password you want to use (which you'll share with your trusted friend). On the Advanced tab, turn on the "Only allow local connections" checkbox if wish to share access only on your local network. Click Close when finished.

2. On the computer that's going to be doing the controlling, choose Applications→Internet→Remote Desktop Viewer.

   If you're on a local network, you may see the computer that's hosting remote connections listed on the left. If so, select it and then click the Connect button at the top of the window. If you're connecting over the Internet, click the Connect button and type the IP address of the computer you want to control. (If your friend is trying to help you and needs your IP address, you can get it quickly on the Web at *www. whatismyip.com*.) Type the password from the previous step, and you should see the other computer's desktop in your window. Click the Close button when you're ready to end the session.

Connecting to Windows machines

You can also connect to Windows Vista and Windows XP Professional machines, but you first have to set them up to accept remote control. On Vista, click the Start button, right-click Computer, and choose Properties from the pop-up menu. In the left side of the box, click the Remote Settings link. In the box, choose "Allow Connections From Computers Running Any Version of Remote Desktop (Less Secure)" and click Apply. You also need to make sure your Vista account has a password, which you can do by choosing Start→Control Panel→User Accounts and Family Safety→User Accounts, and selecting "Create a password for your account."

On Windows XP Professional, click the Start button, right-click My Computer, and choose Properties from the pop-up menu. In the System Properties box, click the Remote tab and in the Remote Desktop area, turn on the checkbox next to "Allow users to remotely connect to this computer." You also need to make sure your XP machine has a user account password; choose Start→Control Panel→User Accounts to set one up if you don't have one.

You also need to make sure the person's user account on the Windows machine is in the Administrator group or that the user account is on the list of preapproved Remote Users. Click the Select Remote Users button in the System Properties box to add a person to the list.

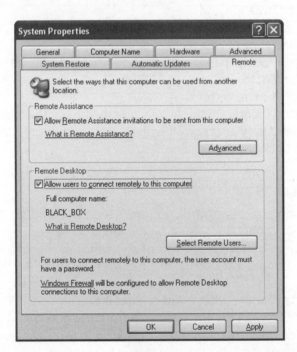

To connect to the Windows machine from your Ubuntu netbook, choose Applications→Internet→Terminal Server Client. In the box next to Computer, type the IP address of the Windows machine, and click the Connect button. (If you can't see the Connect button very well because it's too dark for your netbook screen, hit the Enter key on the keyboard instead.) If all goes according to plan, you next get a box demanding the name and password for the Windows machine. Type these to proceed into your Windows PC to get whatever you need.

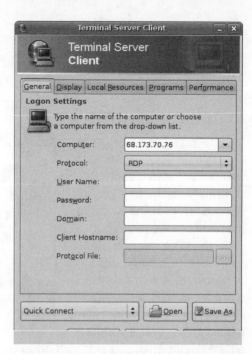

 Note Network security may stymie your remote desktop attempts and you may have to do things like adjust firewalls and security software to allow remote connections. For example, you may need to make a firewall rule that allows traffic on port 3389 or 5900 to get your connections to work. If you're having no luck, check with your network administrator (especially if you are trying to get into an office PC). You can also find tutorials on other remote methods online, like the one at *www.linuxplanet. com/linuxplanet/tutorials/6641/1*.

Installing (or Reinstalling) Ubuntu

There may come a time when you want to (or have to) reinstall Ubuntu Linux on your netbook. Or maybe your netbook came with a different distribution of Linux and you want to switch to Ubuntu, or maybe Windows has finally driven you over the edge with its viruses and spyware. Whatever the case, you have several options for putting Ubuntu on your netbook—including installing the system from a USB drive.

The best part is, you don't have to *buy* the software. It's free. You can download it at *www.ubuntu.com/getubuntu*. Actually, you download the 700-megabyte installer file, which you then can burn to a CD and use as an installation disc. Since your netbook probably doesn't have a CD burner, it's best to do this downloading and disc-making on a more fully equipped computer.

Installing Ubuntu by CD

Now, if you have an external CD drive for your netbook, you can use it to install Ubuntu from the disc you just burned, or from the disc that may have come with your netbook. (The manufacturer may have included a disc of hardware-specific driver software as well, which you'll also need if you're reinstalling Ubuntu.) Make sure you have

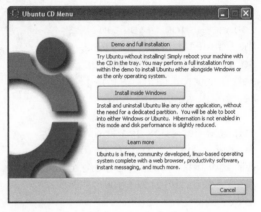

all the documents, pictures, and other files you want to save backed up on a USB stick or other drive.

Once you put the Ubuntu CD in the disc drive and restart the netbook, you should see the Ubuntu LiveCD screen, which includes an Install icon to start walking you through the installation. You work your way through a number of screens, picking a system language, location, keyboard layout, and a username and password. Once you've made your selections, the installer goes about putting Ubuntu on the computer.

 Note If the netbook does not start from the CD, you have to adjust the settings in its BIOS (basic input-output system) to allow booting the computer from the CD drive (or even a USB drive, explained below). Getting to the BIOS varies by computer, but usually it's something like pressing the F2 key, F8 key, or Delete.

If you don't see a key listed onscreen for Setup when the computer starts up, check your manual. Once you get into the BIOS settings, select the Boot area by navigating with the arrow keys and select the CD drive as the first device to boot from. Again, BIOS settings vary, so dig out that manual or look it up on the manufacturer's website.

Installing Ubuntu by USB Drive

Another possibility for installing Ubuntu is putting the contents of the Ubuntu installation disc on a USB drive, booting up from it, and then installing the system on your netbook that way. You can do so in multiple ways, depending on whether you're creating the bootable USB stick on a Windows or Ubuntu machine and which program you want to use to create the USB installer. The Ubuntu community has a page on the various options at *https://help.ubuntu.com/community/Installation/FromUSBStick*.

 Note Not all USB drives work as installation drives for Ubuntu. Kingston DataTravelers, SanDisk Cruzers, Sony Microvaults, and Verbatim Store 'n' Go drives are among those known to work.

One program that works with both Windows and Linux is UNetbootin (*http://unetbootin.sourceforge.net*). To make a bootable USB drive with the Linux installation files, you need a USB drive (one gigabyte or bigger), a copy of the free UNetbootin software, and a fast Internet connection for downloading the Linux installation files.

Making a bootable USB drive with UNetbootin goes something like this:

1. Once you download the UNetbootin program from the website, plug in your USB drive and start it up.

   If you're using the Linux version, you may have to right-click the UNetbootin program icon and choose Properties→Permissions so you can turn on the checkbox next to Execute for "Allow executing file as program."

2. Once the program opens, select the Linux distribution you want from the Distribution pop-up menu.

   Choose Ubuntu from the list. Version 8.0.4 is the current one with long-term support and is often offered on netbooks.

3. Select Disk Image and choose ISO. Then, in the Type pop-up menu (bottom), choose to put all this on the USB drive.

   Click OK. UNetbootin gets busy downloading the Ubuntu installation files and turning your USB drive into a bootable installation stick you can use to install Ubuntu on a netbook without a CD drive.

To install Ubuntu from the USB stick, plug it into the netbook and then restart. The netbook should boot from the USB drive and start walking you through the installation process. If it doesn't start from the USB stick, check your BIOS settings (see the Note on page 296).

Not only can you *install* Ubuntu from a USB drive, you can even *run* Ubuntu from a USB drive. This trick can come in handy if the family netbook runs Windows but you really want to play around with Ubuntu (or you're an Ubuntu loyalist who has to use a Windows machine every once in a while). In fact, there's a whole website full of tutorials devoted to running Linux from USB flash drives at *www.pendrivelinux.com*. Because if that Windows netbook is acting up and you really need to get something done, it never hurts to have a little penguin in your pocket.

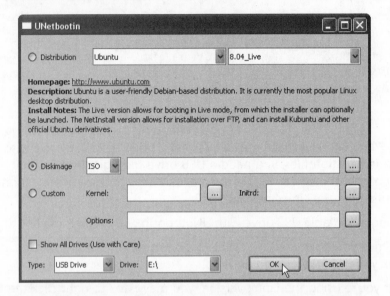

Tip If you generally like your Linux netbook but find there are a few Windows programs that you really miss or need to use, don't whine—try Wine. Wine (a recursive acronym for Wine Is Not an Emulator) is an open-source application for Linux that basically tricks Windows programs into thinking they're running on Windows. If this sort of thing piques your interest, you can read about Wine at *www.winehq. org*. You can install Wine by choosing Applications→Add/Remove and searching for *Wine*. Salut!

Finding Help and Information Online

If you're having a specific problem with your netbook that you still need a solution for, the Web is your friend. Although you may have free technical support by telephone for the first month or two after you buy your netbook, you can see answers in other places when the free phone helpline time runs out.

The Support area of your netbook maker's website is the first stop to make in your search for answers. Page 14 has a list of most major netbook manufacturer's and their web addresses.

For Windows questions, there's *http://support.microsoft.com*.

Ubuntu's searchable help pages are at *https://help.ubuntu.com/community*.

Want to learn more about Linux command lines? You can find free tutorials to please your inner geek at *www.tuxfiles.org/linuxhelp/cli.html*.

 Tip For real-time help with questions, Ubuntu has a number of Internet Relay Chat channels that let you talk to other Ubuntu fans and experts about your system. The Pidgin program (page xx) even works for IRC conversations as well as regular instant messaging. You can find more information on using the Ubuntu IRC channels, along with a lengthy list of discussion topics, at *https://help.ubuntu.com/community/InternetRelayChat*.

Several sites dedicate themselves to all things netbook, and some include how-to videos and user forums:

- **Liliputing.** If it's small and it's a computer, Liliputing has probably written it up. The site has reviews, forums, and plenty of netbook news. (*www.liliputing.com*)

- **Netbook Choice.** A news-heavy site rounding up netbook headlines from all over. (*www.netbookchoice.com*)

- **NetBookMag.** A blogazine featuring videos, product announcements, and news on many kinds of netbooks. (*http://netbookmag.com*)

- **Linux Netbook.** A site dedicated to tiny laptops running Linux. (*www.linux-netbook.com*)

- **Netbook Reviews.** Helpful if you're still in the shopping-research stage—or ready to upgrade already. (*www.netbookreviews.com*)

Some netbooks have even inspired their own fan sites, where owners of a particular brand trade tips and tricks. For example:

- **HP Mini Guide.** Reviews, guides, and gossip on HP's netbook line can be found here. (*www.hp2133guide.com*)

- **UbuntuMini.** A site for Dell Mini 9 owners running Ubuntu Linux, complete with videos and installation guides. (*www.ubuntumini.com*)

By the time you read this book, even more netbook sites and resources will have sprouted up, so don't forget to search the Web. Netbooks may not be for everyone, and they may never become your everyday computer. But the combination of price, portability, and steadily improving hardware and software means netbooks are here to stay. Less *is* more.

Index

Symbols

3-D desktop images, **160**
3G-networks, **129**
37 Signals, **213**
(AOL Instant Messenger), instant
    messaging service, voice
    chats on, **203**

A

Accessibility tools, Windows XP, **44**
Accessories folder
    Linux, **69**
    Windows XP, **43–45**
accessories, netbook, **112–113**
Acer netbooks, **9, 15**
AC port, troubleshooting, **280**
Address bars, browser, **155**
    RSS feeds on, **156**
Address book (Windows XP), **43, 152**
    making new contacts, **179**
    syncing
        to iPhone, **185**
        to personal organizers, **184**
        to smartphones, **184**
        to Web, **185–186**
Administration, System menu (Linux),
    80–82
Adobe Creative Suite, **194**
Adobe Photoshop, **225**
Adobe Photoshop Elements, **223, 225**
Adobe Photoshop Express, **225**
    photos, editing, **227–228**
Adobe Reader
    in Linux, **70**
    in Windows XP, **45**
    viewing PDF files, **191–192**

Adobe Shockwave, **254**
AIM (AOL Instant Messenger), **200**
    transferring files using, **207**
    video chats on, **205**
aircards, **127**
Airplane Mode, Preferences (Linux), **77**
AMD processors, **8**
Android operating system, **3, 9**
antispyware programs, **266**
antivirus programs
    Linux, **266–268**
    security suite bundles, **264**
    using, **262**
    Windows XP, **264–266**
AOL (America Online)
    account, **137**
    calendars, **189**
    contacts in, **180**
AOL Toolbar, **161**
Apollo DVD Ripper, **248**
Apple Safari browser, **151–153**
Application menu
    Linux, **67**
        All Your Programs, **69–70**
    Windows XP
        All Programs, **36, 45**
applications, Windows XP, **43–46**
Ask.com search engine, **154, 161**
Aspire, Acer, **15**
ASUS netbooks, **9, 14**
Atom processors, Intel, **3, 8**
    running antivirus programs, **264**
AT&T netbooks, **129**
Audacity, **245–246**

audio
  Linux
    preferences, **80**
    recorder, **70**
    recording and editing program, **244**
  Windows XP
    recording and editing programs, **44,
      244**
audio in jack, **18**
auto-hide taskbar, **38**
automatic updates, **262**
  Linux, **271, 272**
  Windows XP, **271**
AVG Anti-Virus Free Edition, **266**

B

backing up netbooks
  files, **263**
  in Linux
    external drives, using, **84**
    online, **85**
    USB flash drives, using, **84–85**
  in Windows XP
    built-in, **54–55**
    external drives, using, **54**
    online, **55**
    USB flash drives, using, **54**
Backpack, **213**
Basecamp, **213**
batteries
  buying, **25–26**
  charging, **16, 25**
  life of, **9**
Bing search engine, **154**
BIOS (basic input output system), **296**
Blackberry
  Desktop Manager, downloading, **184**
  networks, **129**
blogging programs, **31**
Bluetooth
  connections
    Internet, **116, 117**
    Linux, **62**
  devices, troubleshooting, **282**

hardware, connecting to
  Linux, **77**
  in Windows XP, **90–92**
    Add Bluetooth Device Wizard, **91**
  keyboard ergonomics, **277**
  linking to phone network, **130**
  mice, adding, **90**
    Linux, **91–93**
bookmarks, web browser, **155**
  adding, **156**
  transferring to other computers,
    157–158
  using on different computers (Firefox),
    160
broadband
  connections, setting up, **119–120**
  home networks, wired, **118**
  mobile, cards, **116, 128**
  mobile service providers, **118**
  service providers, **119, 128**
  wireless connections, **116**
Buddy List (contacts list)
  adding to, **201**
  definition of, **201**
  sending message from, **202**
  status lines, **202**
buffering clips (streaming video), **248**
building netbooks, **14–16**
business programs, **164**
Button bars, browser, **155**
buttons, netbook
  Bluetooth, **62**
  Hibernate, **56**
  Power, **33, 56, 57**
  Restart, **56**
  Stand By, **56**
  wireless radio, **61**
buying online
  accessories, **113**
  batteries, **25–26**
  CD/DVD drives, **104–105**
  games, **257, 258**
  mice, Linux, **89**
  music, **110, 240, 240–241, 246**
  netbooks, **8–12, 14–16**

Powerline neworking kit, **121**
routers, wireless, **123**
television shows, **246**
USB phone data cable, **130**
videos, **246**
webcams, Linux, **109**

C

cable providers, **119**
calculator programs
  Linux, **69**
  Windows XP, **43**
calendars
  online, **187, 189, 189–190**
    adding public calendars, **191**
  programs, **137**
    Linux, **187–189**
    Windows, **186–187**
  sharing, **190–191**
  syncing
    to iPhone, **185**
    to personal organizers, **184**
    to smartphones, **184**
    to Web, **185–186**
cameras, digital
  listing as import source in Linux, **222**
  photos, importing from SD (Secure
    Digital) cards, **222**
Campfire, **213**
Canonical (Linux), **271**
cases (slipcovers), **113**
CD drives, **16**
  external, connecting, **104–105**
CDs
  converting tracks to video files, **237**
  installing Linux from, **296**
  starting netbook from, **296**
cellphones (mobile phones)
  Gmail sites, **136**
  Internet, connecting to, **116, 117, 129**
CERT (U.S. Computer Emergency
    Readiness Team), **262**
changing
  desktop backgrounds, **23, 24**
  search engines, **52**
  size of Start Menu icons, **37**

Character Map, **44**
chats, **202–204**
  video, **205–206**
  voice, **203–205**
Check Disk, Windows utility program,
    285–286
CheckIt Netbook Utility Suite, **281**
choosing
  hard drives, **12–14**
  keyboards, **8, 26–27**
    attributes of, Linux, **78**
    online music stores, **239, 240**
Chrome OS, **3**
Cisco-Linksys router, **123**
ClamTk, **266–267**
Classic Compact add-on, **159**
cleaning up hard drive, **283**
clock preferences, Linux, **68**
closing down
  Linux, **85–86**
  Windows XP, **56**
collaboration websites, **212–215**
Command Prompt program, Windows
    XP, **43**
CompanionLink, **184**
contacts, **178–185, 191**
  making new contacts, **179–181**
  managing Web and netbook, **181**
  syncing
    to iPhone, **185**
    to personal organizers, **184**
    to smartphones, **184**
    to Web, **185–186**
  transferring
    between computers, **181–182**
    from computer to Web, **183–184**
contacts list (Buddy List)
  adding to, **201**
  definition of, **201**
  sending message from, **202**
  status lines, **202**
Control Panel
  Linux, equivalent in, **67**
  views, **42**
  Windows XP, **36**

cookies
  blocking, **273, 274**
  clearing, **274**
Cooliris add-in, **160**
Corel WordPerfect, **164**
cost of Linux vs. Windows XP, **11**
country codes, list of, **202**
craplets, **20**
crashes (unexpected shutdowns), **281**
  due to hard drive errors, **285**
creating
  folders in Windows XP, **49**
  restore points (Windows XP), **286–287**
  shortcuts, folder (Windows XP), **45**
customizing
  desktop
    Linux, **24–25, 63–65**
    Windows XP, **23–24**
  netbooks, **14–16**
  toolbars, Microsoft Office, **168**
CutePDF Writer, **100**

D

data jacks, **18–19**
defragmenting hard drives, **284–285**
deleting email messages, **146, 151**
deleting files, **66**
Dell netbooks
  CD/DVD drives on, **16**
  Desktop Launcher, Linux, **63, 64**
  Inspiron Mini, **8, 15, 60**
  Mini 9, **253**
  online file storage, **85**
desktop
  Linux
    customizing, **25, 63–65**
    Gnome desktop, **64–66**
    Launcher, Dell Desktop, **63–64**
    managing windows, **66–67**
    mode, switching, **80**
  Windows XP
    customizing, **23–24**
desktop, netbooks
  Windows XP
    basics, **37–40**
    calendar programs, **186–187**
    managing, **40–42**

dial-up
  connections, **130–132**
  modems, external, **117**
  service providers, **131**
Dictionary program, Linux, **69**
disk-based hard drives, **12**
Disk Cleanup program, Windows XP, **44**
Disk Defragmenter, Windows XP,
    284–285, 44
disk errors, fixing (Windows XP),
    285–286
Disk Usage Analyzer, Linux, **69, 83**
Display settings shortcut, **24**
distributions, Linux, **60**
Documents folder, **67**
documents, Linux
  pasting date and time to, **68**
Drafts folder, email, **146**
dragging and dropping, files, **148**
DrawPlus, **193**
driver downloads, **89**
DSL (digital subscriber line), **119**
DVD drives, **16**
  external, connecting, **104–105**
DVDs
  converting movies to video files, **248**
  rental websites, **246**

E

Earthlink, **131**
educational games, Linux, **253**
Education folder, Linux, **69**
Eee PC, **14**
Ekiga Softphone, Linux, **70**
  voice chats on, **204**
emails
  deleting messages, **151**
  encrypting, **135**
  file attachments, using, **148–149**
  filters (rules), **147**
  folders, exploring, **146–147**
  forwarding mesaages, **150**
  ISP, setting up, **139–142**
  ISP, using, **136–138**
  message styles, **145**
  offline, working, **145**

printing messages, 150
privacy, 135
programs. *See* specific programs
reading, 143–144
replying to messages, 149
rules (filters), 147
sending, 144–145
  photos, 231
sorting messages, 151
spam and scams, protecting against,
    263
webmail
  accounts, 134–135
  making new contacts, 181
  providers, 135–137
  transferring contacts from computer,
    183
word processing, 137
Empty Trash icon, Linux, 291
Empty Trash pop-up menu, Linux, 291
emulator gaming websites, 259
eMusic, 110
encryption security, Internet, 142–143,
    275
online Linux information, 276
encryption systems, router, 123
ergonomics, keyboard, 276
Error-Checking tool, Windows XP,
    285–286
Ethernet
  cables, 113, 117, 119
    length needed, 121
  network connections, wired, 116
  networks, setting up, 121
  ports (RJ-45), 19
Evolution Calendar, Linux, 187–189
Evolution Mail, Linux, 70, 139
  making new contacts, 179
  setting up, 140
  SSL (Secure Sockets Layer) encryption,
    142–143
ExpressCard slots, 129
extended batteries, buying, 25–26
external speakers. *See* headphones

F

Facebook, 216
fantasy sports, online, 256
favorites (bookmarks), web browser, 155
  adding, 156
  transferring to another computer,
    157–158
fiber optics services (FiOS), 115, 119
files
  email attachments, using, 148–149
  extensions
    .csv (Comma Separated Values), 182
    .doc, Word, 174
    .docx, Word 2007, 174
    .exe, emailing, 149
    .ics, shared calendars format, 191
    .vef (vCard), electronic business cards
      format, 182
  Linux
    browsing for, 73–76
    searching for, 67, 76
  online storage, 85
  transferring via instant messaging,
    207–208
  Windows XP
    finding, 50–51
    organizing, 49
    renaming, 50
    searching for, 51–52
    transferring, 19–23
Files and Settings Transfer Wizard,
    22–23, 44
filters (rules), email, 147
FiOS (fiber optic service), 115, 119
Firefox web browser, 11, 61
  add-ons, 159–160
  anatomy of, 151–153
  antispyware add-on, 275
  bookmarks, 158
    XMarks add-on, 160
  Office Live account, setting up, 170
  pop-up windows, blocking, 274, 275
  shortcuts to, Linux, 67

firewalls
  hardware, 268
  Linux, 270–271
  putting up, 268–269
  Windows XP, 269–270
  wizards, Linux, 270
Flickr, 11, 216
Flock, 218
folders
  email, 146
  Gmail, 148
  Linux, 64
    Application Menu, 69–70
    Home, 73
  Windows XP
    Accessories, 43–44
    Media Player, 237
    organizing files in, 49
    removing programs from, 49
    shortcuts, 39, 45
forwarding emails, 150
Foxit, 192
F-Prot Antivirus, 268
fragmented files, 284
FreeCell, 252
free programs, downloading, 195–196
F-Spot Photo Manager, Linux, 69
  adjusting color histogram, 228–229
  basic user guide, 225
  emailing photos, 231
  importing photos, 221–222
  organizing photos, 224
  photo editing features, 225–227
  uploading photos, 234
full-screen mode, 159

G

games, 251–260
  adding gaming hardware, 259–260
  collections of, 253, 255, 256
  downloading, 257
  emulating, 259
  fantasy sports, 256
  hardware
    Linux, 260
    Windows XP, 259
  Linux, 253–254, 258
  rules, how to find, 252
  setting up browser, 255
  shooting and adventure, 256
  Windows XP, 252, 253, 258
    online games, 253
Games folder, Windows XP, 44
GIMP Image Editor, Linux, 69, 229
  digital photo editing, 225
  working with photos, 194
Gmail
  calendars, 189
  folders, 148
  Labs, 135
  security precautions, 149
  setting up Google Docs, 175
  transferring contacts from computer, 183–184
Gnome desktop, 64–66
GNU Image Manipulation Program, 194, 229
Google Chrome, 151
Google Chrome browser, 151–153
Google Chrome OS, 3
Google Docs & Spreadsheets, 11
  about, 175
  collaborating, 211
  Google Docs Draw, 194
  requirements for, 175
  sharing files with, 211
  tracking revisions, 211–212
  viewers, making, 211
  working offline, 177–178
Google Gears, 136, 177
Google Picasa. *See* Picasa
Google search engine, 154
Graphics folder, Linux, 69
graphics tools, 193–194
GUIs (graphical user interfaces), 38, 63

H

hard drives
  disk-based, 12
  hybrid, 12, 14
  Linux
    error-checking, 291

external, **84**
  adding, **104**
  reformatting, **104**
  space, **82–83**
solid-state, **12**
Windows XP
  cleaning up, **283**
  creating a restore point on, **286–287**
  defragmenting, **284–285**
  external, **54**
    adding, **103**
    backing up to, **54**
    transferring files using, **9, 21**
    USB (Universal Serial Bus), **14**
  fixing errors on, **285–286**
  formatted, structure of, **285**
  internal
    choosing, **12–14**
    space, checking, **53**
  restoring to prior time, **286–287**
hardware compatibility, Windows XP, **10**
Hardware Drivers menu, Linux, **81**
headphones
  adding, **111**
  jacks, **18**
  volume, changing, **112**
Help and Support Center, Windows, **282–283**
Help and Support menu, Windows, **37**
help centers, Linux, **290**
Hewlett-Packard netbooks, **15**
  CD/DVD drives on, **16**
  HP Mini Guide, **300**
  Linux, **60**
  screen size, **8**
hibernate setting
  Linux, **86**
Hibernate setting
  Windows XP, **56**
Highrise, **213**
Home folder, Linux, **73**
home networks
  broadband connections, setting up, **119–120**
  copying purchases into, **238**
  Internet service providers, **117**

phones, using, **118**
sharing iPod music, **239**
wired, setting up, **118, 120–123**
wireless
  problems with, **126–127**
  setting up, **123–126**
Hotmail, **134**
  calendars, **189**
  contacts in, **180**
  log in limits, before closing account, **136**
  Plus accounts, **136**
  transferring contacts from computer, **183–184**
HTML, in emails, **145**
Huddle, **214**
hybrid hard drives, **12, 14**
  advantages of, **14**

I

icons
  Linux
    battery, **68**
    desktop, **65**
    Empty Trash, **43**
    Hibernate, **86**
    Lock Screen, **86**
    Logout netbook, **86**
    network, **68**
    panel adding/removing, **68**
    program update, **68**
    Restart, **86**
    Shut Down, **86**
    sound, **68**
    Suspend (sleep) mode, **85**
    Switch User, **86**
  Windows XP
    Control Panel, **42**
    desktop shortcut, **39**
    Display setting shortcuts, **24**
    Notification Area, **38**
    Recycle Bin, **39**
    Run, **37**
    Start Menu, changing size of, **37**
    System tray, **38**
    views, **41**

IdeaPad, Lenovo
  ExpressCard slots, **129**
  OneKey Recovery system, **289–290**
  screen size, **8**
  S series, **15**
identity theft, preventing, **262**
  government resources, turning to, **264**
images, capturing
  Linux, **106, 108–109**
  Windows XP, **105–106, 108**
IMAP (Internet Message Access
      Protocol), **140, 141, 143**
Import and Export Wizard, **158, 182**
inbox, email, **146**
injuries, preventing ergononmic, **277**
Inkscape, **194**
Inspiron Mini netbooks, Dell, **15**
installing programs
  Linux
    from CDs, **296–297**
    from USB drives, **297–298**
  Windows XP
    from discs, **47, 110**
    from Web, **46**
    precautions, **46**
instant messaging
  programs, **137**
instant messaging (IM)
  Buddy List (contacts list)
    adding to, **201**
    sending message from, **202**
    status lines, **202**
  network services, **200**
  programs, **201**
  transferring files by, **207–208**
  troubleshooting, **206**
  video on, **205**
  voice on, **203–205**
Intel Atom processors
  running antivirus programs, **264**
Intel processors, **3, 8**
Internet
  cellphones (mobile phones),
      connecting to, **116, 117, 129**
  connection kits, **119**
  connections, **116–117**
    broadband

  setting up, **119–120**
  dial-up, **130–132**
encryption security, **142–143**
Ethernet cables, **117, 119**
home networks. *See* home networks
IP address, finding netbook, **295**
navigating, **155–157**
passwords, **117**
powerline networking, **119, 121–122**
public wireless networks, **127–128**
radio, **241–243**
search engines
  Ask.com, **154**
  changing, **52**
  Google, **154**
  keywords, using, **153**
  Microsoft Bing, **154**
  Webcrawler, **154**
  Wolfram Alpha, **154**
  Yahoo, **154**
service providers, **117**
  cost of, **118**
  getting, **118**
  mobile broadband coverage, **118**
  reviews of, **118**
  Web (World Wide Web), **151**
Internet Archive, The, **247**
Internet Connection Wizard, **141**
Internet Explorer, **273–274**
  adding tools, **159, 160**
  anatomy of, **151–153**
  Office Live account, setting up, **170**
  pop-up windows, blocking, **274**
  transferring bookmarks, **158**
Internet folder, Linux, **70**
interoperability, **199**
IP address, finding, **295**
iPhones
  downloading iTunes for, **184**
  freeware websites, **196**
  networks, **129**
  syncing to computer calendars, **185**
  syncing to computer contacts, **185**
iPods
  buying music, **110, 240, 246**
  transferring
    contacts from Outlook Express, **138**

data from Linux, **111**

music from iTunes, **238**

IPTables firewall (Linux), **270**

ISPs

dial-up, finding, **131**

email, setting up account, **139–142**

iTunes, **110**

adding radio stations, **242**

for iPhones, downloading, **184**

Outlook Express contacts on iPod, **138**

Radio icon in, **241**

sharing music on home network, **239**

subscribing to podcasts, **243**

transferring music to iPod, **238**

iTunes Store

about, **240**

copying purchases into network, **238**

Linux and, **240**

subscribing to podcasts, **243**

J

jacks

data, **18–19**

Ethernet, **121**

headphone, **18**

modem, **117**

speaker, **18**

joysticks, USB, installing (Linux), **259**

Juice Receiver, **243**

Jump Lists, **31**

junk mail folder, **147**

K

Kensington slot, **19**

security cable, **113**

keyboards

choosing, **8, 26–27**

ergonomics, **276**

Linux

choosing, **78**

finding symbols on, **69**

shortcuts, **78**

liquid spills, troubleshooting, **280**

size of, **2**

Windows XP

finding symbols on, **44**

shortcuts, Microsoft Office, **167**

keywords, searching for, **153**

L

Language Support system, Linux, **81**

laser printers, protocol, **102**

Lenovo IdeaPad

ExpressCard slots, **129**

OneKey Recovery system, **289–290**

screen size, **8**

S series, **15**

Line Printer Daemon (LPD) protocol, Linux, **102**

LinkedIn, **217**

links, browser, **155**

Linksys, Cisco

Powerline kit, **121**

router, **123**

Linux, **9**

about

background of, **59, 63**

development, **9**

mascot, **253**

origin of name, **61**

overview, **11**

popularity of, **60**

advantages of, **11**

automatic update feature, **262, 271**

CD/DVD drives on, **16**

closing down, **85–86**

distributions, **60–61**

downloading, **12**

finding help online, **299**

Firewall Wizard, **270**

hard drive space, **82–83**

hardware pages, Internet, **89**

Help Center, **290**

installing (reinstalling)

from CDs, **296–297**

from USB drives, **297–298**

online help with, **299**

passwords, setting up, **62**

printers, adding, **100–102**

requirements for, **61**

Linux (*continued*)
  setting up, **61–62**
  sound
    editing, **244**
    recording, **244**
  System menu, **76–82**
  updating, **262**
  user names, setting up, **62**
  websites, **86, 300**
  windows, managing, **66–67**
  Windows programs, running on, **298**
Linux Netbook website, **299**
Linux UVC Driver and Tools, **109**
liquid spills, troubleshooting, **280**
List view, **41**
Littlefox add-on, **159**
Live 365 Internet Radio, **241**
Lock Screen command, Linux, **86**
Login window, Linux, **81**
Log Out command, Linux, **86**
LPD (Line Printer Daemon) protocol,
        Linux, **102**

M

Macbooks
  freeware websites, **196**
  Macbook Air, **2**
magnifier tool, Windows XP, **44**
mail, junk. *See* junk mail
Manage Print Jobs, Linux, **69**
managing
  contacts, Web and netbook, **181**
  Linux desktop windows, **66**
  RSS feeds, **157**
  Windows XP desktop windows, **40–41**
Map Network Drive box, **48**
math computer games, Linux, **253**
maximizing windows, **40**
media card reader, **19**
memory-card readers, cost of, **223**
memory (RAM), **15**
Memory Sticks, **19**
Menu bars
  Linux, **66, 68**
  Windows XP, **40**

menus
  Linux
    All Your Programs, **69–71**
    Places, **67, 73–77**
    System, **67**
    top panel, **67–68**
  Windows XP
    All Programs, **46**
    Help and Support, **37**
    My Documents, **36**
    My Music, **36**
    My Pictures, **36**
    My Recent Documents, **36**
    Run, **37**
    Search, **37**
    Start Menu, **35–37**
    System Properties Box, **37**
mice
  driver download websites, **89**
  Linux
    adding, **89**
    Bluetooth, adding, **91–93**
    settings, **78**
  Windows XP
    adding, **88**
    adjusting, **93**
    Bluetooth, adding, **90–92**
    resizing windows with, **41**
    travel, **113**
microphone jack, **18**
Microsoft
  trial programs, **166, 169**
  webmail
    log in limits, **136**
    making new contacts, **181**
    transferring contacts from computer,
        183
    Windows Live Hotmail Plus accounts,
        136
    Windows Live Mail, **140**
Microsoft Bing search engine, **154**
Microsoft Office
  about, **167**
  Access, **164**
  Excel, **164**
  installing, **165–167**

minimizing ribbon, **167**
OneNote, **164**
PowerPoint, **164**
Publisher, **164**
Quick Access Toolbar, **168**
trial programs, **166**
using, **167–168**
Word, **164**
  drawing tools, **194**
  file extensions, **174**
Microsoft Office Live Workspace
adding documents, **170**
questions and answers page, **171**
setting up, **170–171**
sharing files, **170**
workspaces, creating, **169, 170**
Microsoft Office toolbars, **168**
Microsoft Outlook, **164**
calendars, searching, **187**
making new contacts, **179**
Search Calendars Online link, **191**
transferring contacts, between
  computers, **181–182**
Microsoft Outlook Express, **138**
folders in, exploring, **146–147**
making new contacts, **180**
security warnings, **138, 144, 149**
SSL (Secure Sockets Layer) encryption,
  142–143
Micro-star International netbooks (MSI),
  9, 15
MiFi router, Verizon, **116**
Mini 9, Dell netbook, **300**
minimizing windows, **40**
mobile broadband cards, **116, 128**
MobileMe, syncing contacts to Web, **186**
mobile phones (cellphones)
Gmail sites, **136**
Internet, connecting to, **116, 117, 129**
Moblin operating system, **3, 9**
modems, external
dial-up, **117**
monitors, connecting
Linux, **95–96**
Windows XP, **94–95**
Movie Player, Linux, **70**

movies
rental websites, **246**
streaming, **246**
Mozilla Firefox web browser, **11, 61**
add-ons, **159–160**
anatomy of, **151–153**
antispyware add-on, **275**
bookmarks
  transferring to another computer,
    158
  using on different computer, **160**
Office Live account, setting up, **170**
pop-up windows, blocking ads, **274,
  275**
shortcuts to, Linux, **67**
Mozilla Thunderbird, email program
  (Linux), **136, 139**
setting up, **140**
SSL (Secure Sockets Layer) encryption,
  142–143
Mozy backup service, **55**
MP3 Downloader, **240**
MP3 jukebox programs, **238**
Linux
  Banshee, **237**
  error messages, troubleshooting, **238**
  Rhythmbox Music Player, **236**
Windows Media Player, **236**
setting up folders, **237**
MP3 players
buying music online, **110, 240, 246**
iPods
  Linux and, **111**
  Outlook Express contacts on iPod,
    138
  transferring music from iTunes, **238**
Windows XP, **110–111**
MSI (Micro-star International) netbooks,
  9, 15
Multimedia Cards, **19**
music
buying online, **110, 240, 240–241, 246**
management tools, Linux, **111**
programs, **237**
sharing on home network, **239**
streaming, **239**
transferring to iPod, **238**

Music folder (Linux), **67**
Mute option, Linux, **68**
MySpace, **216**

N

Nano, VIA, **8**
NAT (network access translation),
    firewall, **268**
Nautilus File Browser, **74–76**
Nautilus File Browsers
  adding hard drives, **104**
netbook websites, **299**
networks
  Linux
    adding user accounts, **82**
    add/remove network programs, **82**
    administrative tools, **67**
    connecting to, **75**
    monitoring specifics about, **82**
    power management, **78**
    printers, **81, 101–103**
    proxy configuration, **78**
    settings tools, **67**
    testing connections to, **81**
    time and date, setting, **82**
    wireless connections manager, **81**
  public wireless, **127–128**
  Windows XP
    connections
      programs for, **44**
      transferring files using, **21**
    operating systems, **9**
    ports (RJ-45), **19**
    printers
      setting up, **98–100**
    wired Ethernet connections, **116**
    wireless, **116**
      problems with, **126–127**
      troubleshooting connection to, **280**
New Connection Wizard, **131**
Ning website, **218**
NoScript Firefox add-on, **275**
notebooks, vs. netbooks, **3**
Notepad program, **43**
Notification area, System tray, **38**

notification balloons, **38**

O

OneKey Recovery system, Lenovo,
    289–290
online
  backups, **55**
  file storage, **85**
  games, **44, 253**
  syncing contacts to Web, **185–186**
OpenOffice.org suite, **12, 164**
  add-ons, **173**
  Base, **172**
  Calc, **172**
  downloading, **173**
  Draw, **193**
  Impress, **172**
  Installing, **173**
  Linux, **61, 70**
  Ninja website and, **174**
  opening Word documents, **174**
  support and training, **174**
  Writer, **172**
Opera browser, **151–153**
operating systems. *See* individual
    operating systems
organizing files, **49**
Outbox folder, email, **146**
Outlook, **164**
  calendars, searching, **187**
  making new contacts, **179**
  Search Calendars Online link, **191**
  transferring contacts between
    computers, **181–182**
Outlook Express, **138**
  folders in, **146–147**
  making new contacts, **179**
  security warnings, **138, 144, 149**
  setting up, **140–142**
  SSL (Secure Sockets Layer) encryption,
    142–143

P

package manager program , Linux, **292**
Paint program, Windows XP, **43**

Palm
  Desktop, downloading, **184**
  freeware websites, **196**
  OS Devices, sycing on Linux, **78**
  Pre
    desktop sync solution for, **184**
    syncing, **184**
parental controls, **263**
partition editors, Linux, **104**
Password and Encryption Keys, Linux, **69**
passwords
  Internet, **117**
  Linux, **62**
PDAs, connecting to Linux netbook, **78**,
    184
PDF (Portable Document Format)
    readers
  Adobe, **191–192**
  CutePDF Writer program, **100**
  Foxit program, **192**
  Windows XP, **45**
PGP (Pretty Good Privacy) settings
    (Linux), **78, 135**
phone calls, from netbooks (Skype)
  computer-to-computer, **209, 210**
  computer to regular phone, **210**
  downloading, **208**
  requirements, **209**
  setting up account, **209**
  voice chats on, **204**
phone programs, Linux, **70**
photos, editing
  Linux
    adjusting color histogram, **228–229**
    balancing colors, **229**
    cropping, **225**
    programs, **194, 225, 228–230**
    red eye, removing, **226**
    rotating, **226**
    straightening, **226**
  Windows XP
    balancing colors, **227**
    captions, **227**
    cropping, **225**
    programs, **225, 225–228**
    red eye, removing, **226**
    rotating, **226**

    straightening, **226**
    visual effects, **227**
Photoshop, **225**
Photoshop Elements, **223, 225**
Photoshop Express, **227–228**
photos, importing
  from camera SD (Secure Digital) cards,
      222
  Linux, **221–222**
  Windows XP, **220–221**
photos, organizing, **223–225**
photos, sharing online
  emailing, **231**
  ordering prints, **236**
  websites
    selecting, **232–234**
    uploading, **234–236**
Picasa
  features of, **225–227**
  online help, **228**
  Picasa Web Albums
    guides, online, **236**
    levels of privacy, **235**
Pictures older, Linux, **67**
Pin to Start Menu command, **36**
Places menu, Linux, **67, 73–77, 75**
podcasts, **243–244**
POP (Post Office Protocol) accounts,
      140, 143
pop-up windows, blocking, **273**
  Firefox, **274, 275**
ports
  network, **19**
  operating system, **268**
  USB (Universal Serial Bus), **18**
  video, **17**
power button, **33, 56, 57**
power cords, extra, **113**
powerline networking, **121–122**
printers
  Linux
    adding, **100–102**
    connecting to network, **81**
    default, **77**
  Windows XP
    setting up, **96–100**
printing email messages, **150**

processors, **2**
  AMD, **8**
  Window XP vs. Linux, **11**
programs
  Linux
    Application menu, **67**
    installing, **71–72**
      from discs, **73**
    uninstalling, **73, 291–293**
    updates, automatic, **68**
  Windows XP
    compatibility, **10**
    installing
      from discs, **47, 110**
      from Web, **46**
      precautions about, **46**
    uninstalling, **11, 48**
    updates, automatic, **34**
project management apps, **213–215**
public wireless networks, **127–128**
  security, **263, 275–276**

Q

Quick Access Toolbar, Microsoft Office, **168**

R

radio, Internet, **241–243**
RAM (memory), **15**
  maxing out, **258**
Recent Documents, Linux, **76**
Recycle Bin icons, Windows XP, **39**
registry, repair programs, **281**
reinstalling
  Linux operating system
    from CDs, **296–297**
    from USB drives, **297–298**
  Windows XP, **289–290**
    step-by-step help, Microsoft, **289**
Remote Assistance, Windows XP, **287–289**
Remote Desktop Viewer, Linux, **70, 79, 293–294**
Remote Desktop, Windows, **287**
repetitive stress injuries, preventing, **277**
replying to messages, **149**

residual configuration packages, Linux, **292**
resizing windows, **41**
restore points, Windows XP, **286**
Rhapsody, **110**
Rhythmbox Music Player, Linux, **70, 111**
  adding radio stations, **243**
  choosing online music stores, **240**
  importing music error messages, **238**
  Radio icon, **242**
  subscribing to podcasts, **243**
rich text, in emails, **145**
ripping
  CDs, **237**
  DVDs, **248**
rotating photos, **226**
routers, **118, 120**
  Cisco-Linksys, **123**
  encryption systems, **123**
  MiFi, Verizon, **116**
  wireless, **123**
  WMWiFiRouter, **130**
RSS feeds, **156**
rules (filters) email, **147**
Run menu, **37**

S

Safari browser, **151–152**
safety tips, for netbooks, **262**
Samsung netbooks, **15**
Scandisk (Chkdsk), **285–286**
Scanner and Camera Wizard, **105–106, 221**
scanners, adding
  Linux, **106–108**
  Windows XP, **105–106**
SCIM (Smart Common Input Method),,
  Linux, **79**
screen resolution, Linux, **79**
screensaver preferences, Linux, **79**
screen size, netbook, **2, 8**
scroll bars, **40, 66**
SD (Secure Digital) cards, **14, 19**
  copying music using, **237**
search engines
  Ask.com, **154**
  changing, **52**

Google, **154**
keywords, using, **153**
Microsoft Bing, **154**
Webcrawler, **154**
Wolfram Alpha, **154**
Yahoo, **154**
searching for files, **51–52**
Search menu (Windows), **37**
Search the Internet option, in Search
   Companion, **52**
security
   antivirus programs, Windows XP,
      264–266
   automatic update features, **271–272**
   cables, **113**
   firewalls, putting up, **268–269**
   hardware, **268**
   identity theft
      government resources on, **264**
      preventing, **262**
   Linux, **266–268, 270–271**
   passwords, picking, **262**
   programs, **11, 262**
   public wireless network security, **263,**
      275–276
   slot, **19**
   spam and scams, protecting against,
      263
   tips, **262, 264**
   Windows XP, **269–270**
   wireless network, **123**
Sent Items folder, email, **146**
service providers, **117**
   broadband, **119**
   cost of, **118**
   getting, **118**
   mobile broadband, **118**
   reviews of, **118**
service set identifier (SSID), **123**
settings (Linux), **81**
setting up
   Linux netbooks, **61–62**
   netbooks, **16**
   Windows XP, **33–35**
shareware, **46, 195–196**
sharing calendars, **190**

shortcuts
   definition of, **39**
   Display settings, **24**
   program folder, creating, **45**
shutdowns, unexpected, **281, 285**
shutting down netbook
   Linux, **56, 86**
   Windows XP, **56**
signature files, attaching to emails, **145**
Skype, **208–210**
Smart Common Input Method
      preference (SCIM), Linux, **79**
SmartDraw, **193**
smartphones, **129**
   syncing with Linux netbook, **184**
SMS text messages, **202**
social networking websites
   Facebook, **216**
   Flickr, **216**
   Flock, **218**
   LinkedIn, **217**
   MySpace, **216**
   Ning, **218**
   Twitter, **217**
   Yoono.com, **160**
solid-state hard drives, **12**
   advantages of, **13**
   disadvantages of, **13**
sorting email messages, **151**
SOS Online Backup, **55**
sound
   Linux
      preferences, **80**
      recording and editing program, **70,**
         244–246
   Windows XP
      recording and editing programs, **44,**
         244
spam and scams, protecting against,
      263
speaker jacks, **18**
special-needs tools, **44**
spyware, avoiding, **266, 272–273**
SSID (service set identifier), **123**
SSL (Secure Sockets Layer) encryption,
      142–143

Start menu, 35–37, 42
  Accessories folders, 43–45
  exploring, 51
Startup folder, Windows XP, 45
startup preferences, Linux, 80
surfing the Web, 155–157
Suspend netbook
  Linux, 85
  Windows XP, 56
Switch User, Linux, 86
Sylvania netbooks, 15
SyncIT, 158
system log, Linux, 82
System menu, Linux, 67
  Administration, 80–82
  Preferences, 77–80
System Properties box, Windows XP, 37
System Restore, Windows XP, 44
  using, 286–287
System Tools folder, Linux, 70
System Tools, utility programs
  Windows XP, 44
    tuning up with, 283–286
System tray notification area, Windows
    XP, 38

T

tablets, stylus-based, 88
Taskbar, Windows XP, 38
Task panes, Windows XP, 40
telephone calls, from netbooks (Skype)
  computer-to-computer, 209, 210
  computer to regular phone, 210
  downloading, 208
  requirements for using, 209
  setting up account, 209
  voice chats on, 204
telephone programs, Linux, 70
Terminal, command line program
    (Linux), 69
tethering procedures, 129
Text Editor, Linux, 69
ThinkFree, 215
Three-D desktop images, 160
Three G (3G) networks, 129
thumb drives (USB pocket flash), moving
    files with, 20

Thunderbird (Mozilla)
  Linux, 136, 139
  setting up, 140
  SSL (Secure Sockets Layer) encryption,
    142–143
Time Menu, Date and (Linux), 68, 82
Title bars, , 40
toolbars
  Microsoft Office
    customizing, 168
  web browser
    AOL (America Online), 161
    Ask.com, 161
    Google, 161
    Microsoft Live Search, 161
    StumbleUpon, 161
tools, adding browser, 159–162
top panel (Gnome desktop)
  menus, 67–68
trackballs, 88
transferring
  bookmarks to other computer,
    157–158
  files, 19–23
    by instant messaging, 207–208
    using external hard drives, Windows
      XP, 9, 21
    using Windows XP networks
      connections, 21
  Hotmail contacts from computer,
    183–184
  webmail contacts, 183
Transfer Wizard, Files and Settings,
    22–23, 44
trial software, uninstalling, 35
troubleshooting
  Linux
    connecting to Windows netbook,
      294–295
    emptying system Trash, 291
    error-checking hard drive, 291
    finding help online, 299
    help files, 290–291
    Remote Desktop, 293–294
    starting netbook from CDs, 296
    uninstalling programs, 291–293

Windows XP
  finding help online, **299**
  hard drive errors, **285–286**
  liquid spills, **280**
  power issues, **280**
  reinstalling Windows, **289–290**
    step-by-step help, Microsoft, **289**
  restoring hard drive, **286–287**
  shutdowns, unexpected, **281**
  using Remote Assistance, **287–289**
  webcams, Linux, **109**
  Windows problems, **282–283**
  wireless network connections, **280**
Turn Off Computer box, Widows XP, **56**
TV shows, buying, **246**
Twitter, **217**

U

Ubuntu Linux. *See* Linux
Update Manager, checking for updates
    (Linux), **82**
USB (Universal Serial Bus)
  dongle, Internet connections, **116**
  flash drives, **54**
  hard drives, **14, 21**
  hubs, **113**
  joysticks, **259**
  keyboard ergonomics, **277**
  keyboards, **8**
  Linux devices
    backups using, **84–85**
    device overview pages, Internet, **89**
    drives, **297–298**
    printers, adding, **100–101**
  memory sticks, **14**
  PC repair kit, **281**
  phone data cable, **130**
  phone modems, **117**
  pocket flash, **20**
  ports, **18**
  printers, Windows, **96–100**
U.S. Computer Emergency Readiness
    Team (CERT), **262**
user account, Linux, **82**
  setting up, **62**
utility programs, **44**
  CheckIt Netbook Utility Suite, **281**

Disk Cleanup, Windows, **283**
Disk Defragmenter, Windows, **284–285**
removing Windows components, **284**
searching for, **281**

V

vCards (electronic business cards), **182**
Verbatim Notebook Essentials kit, **113**
Verizon
  DSL (digital subscriber line), **119**
  FiOS (fiber optice service), **115, 119**
  netbooks, **129**
Verizon MiFi router, **116**
VGA connector, **18**
Via C7 processors, **264**
videos
  buying online, **246**
  conferencing programs, Linux, **70**
  editing, **249**
  folders, Linux, **70**
  online, **246–248**
  ports, **17**
views, window
  Detail, **41**
  Filmstrip, **42**
  Icon, **41**
  List, **41**
  Thumbnail, **41**
  Tille, **41**
virus definitions, **265**
viruses and Windows XP, **11**
virus signatures, **265**
VPNs (virtual private networks), **263**
  setting up (Linux), **81**

W

Web. *See* Internet
web browsers
  adding tools, **159–162**
  anatomy of
    Address bars, **152, 155**
    bookmarks, adding, **156**
    Buttom bars, **152, 155**
    History list, **155**
    Links bars, **152, 155**
    Main window, **152**

web browsers (*continued*)
    Menu bars, **152**
    scroll bars, **152**
    Search boxes, **152**
    Status bars, **153**
    Tabs, **152**
    title bars, **152**
  changing start-up page, **157**
  Firefox. *See* Firefox web browsers
  Google Chrome, **151**
  in full-screen mode, **159**
  Internet Explorer. *See* Internet Explorer
  Nautilus File Browsers, **74–76**
    adding hard drives, **104**
  navigating Internet, **155–156**
  Opera, **151**
  Safari, **151**
  security, Internet Explorer, **273–274**
  text, adjusting, **153**
  toolbars, add-on, **160**
  Windows Live Mail, Microsoft, **140**
webcams
  adding, **108–109**
  cost of, **205**
Webcrawler search engine, **154**
webmail
  accounts, **134–135**
  providers, **135–137**
  sites, **134**
  transferring contacts from computer, **183**
WEP (Wired Equivalent Privacy), **123**
WiFi
  connections, **62**
    mobile broadband cards, **116, 128**
    troubleshooting, **280**
  hotspots, **127**
  networks, range of, **127**
  Protected Access (WPA), **123**
Wind netbooks (MSI), **15**
windows
  Linux
    managing, **66–67**
    settings for, **80**

Windows XP
  maximizing windows, **40**
  Menu bars, **40**
  minimizing windows, **40**
  resizing, **41**
  views, changing, **41**
Windows 7 operating system, **3, 31**
Windows Address book, **43**
  making new contacts, **179**
  syncing
    to iPhone, **185**
    to personal organizers, **184**
    to smartphones, **184**
    to Web, **185–186**
Windows Explorer, **44**
  finding files with, **50–51**
  Map Network Drive box, using, **48**
Windows Firewall control panel, **269**
Windows Help and Support Center
  Fixing a Problem link, **282–283**
Windows Live Calendar, **189**
Windows Live Essentials, **31**
Windows Live ID, **170**
Windows Live Mail, **140**
Windows Live Messenger, **200**
  transferring files using, **207**
  using with Remote Assistance, **287**
  video chats on, **206**
  voice chats on, **204**
Windows Media Player, **44**
  adding radio stations, **243**
  choosing online music stores, **239, 240**
  online video sources, **246**
  setting up folders, **237**
  streaming radio from, **241**
Windows product key, **290**
Windows System Restore, **286–287**
Windows Vista, **10**
  connecting to Linux netbook, **294–295**
Windows XP
  about
    overview, **10–11**
    updating system, **262**

utility programs, 283–286
wizards
    Add Bluetooth Device, 91
    Add Printer, 99
    Import/Export Wizard, 158, 182
    Internet Connection Wizard, 141
    New Connection Wizard, 131
    Scanner and Camera Wizard,
        105–106, 221
advantages of, 10
automatic update feature, 262, 271
backup program, 55
Bluetooth devices, 90–91
CD/DVD drives on, 16
closing down, 56
connecting to Linux netbook,
    294–295
Control Panel, 42
desktop. *See* desktop, Windows XP
disadvantages of, 11
files
    finding, 50–51
    organizing, 49
    searching for, 51–52
Files and Settings Transfer Wizard,
    22–23, 44
freeware websites, 196
hardware compatibility with, 10
help files, 282–283
Home Edition, 30
    about, 30
    Backup program, 55
installing programs
    from discs, 47
    from Web, 46
    precautions about, 46
monitors, connecting, 94–95
Paint program, 43
printers, setting up, 96–100
Professional, 30
reinstalling, 289–290
    step-by-step help, 289
Remote Desktop feature, 288
restrictions on computer makers, 31
setting up, 33–35

sound
    editing, 244
    recording, 244
Start Menu, 35–37
System Restore, 286–287
uninstalling programs, 48
WordPad, 44
Windows XP Search Companion, 52
Wine (Wine Is Not an Emulator), 298
Wired Equivalent Privacy (WEP), 123
wired Ethernet network connections,
    116
wireless connections, 116
    manager, Linux, 81
    secured, 117
wireless networks
    problems with, 126–127
    troubleshooting connection to, 280
wireless radio, 126
wireless-radio button, 61
WMWiFiRouter, 130
Wolfram Alpha search engine, 154
WordPad, 44
WordPerfect, 164
word processing, email, 137
working online, collaboration websites
    for, 212–215
world daylight/darkness graphic, Linux,
    68
World Wide Web. *See* Internet
WPA (WiFi Protected Access), 123

X

Xbox Live account, 170
XMarks add-on, 160

Y

Yahoo, 134
    log in limits, 136
    search engine, 154
    Toolbar, 161
Yahoo Calendar, 189

Yahoo Mail
  contacts in, **180**
  transferring contacts from computer,
      183–184
Yahoo Mail Plus Accounts, **136**
Yahoo Messenger, **200**
  transferring files using, **208**
  video chats on, **206**
  voice chats on, **204**

Yahoo, website
  Fantasy Sports, online games, **256**
  games area, **255**
Yoono.com, **160**

Z

Zoho, **213**